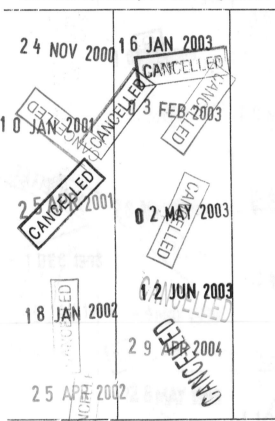

The Strategic Decision
Challenge

THE WILEY SERIES IN CONTEMPORARY STRATEGIC CONCERNS

Editor DAVID HUSSEY

The Implementation Challenge
The Innovation Challenge

The Strategic Decision Challenge

Edited by

David Hussey

Visiting Professor of
Strategic Management,
Nottingham Business School,
Nottingham Trent University

JOHN WILEY & SONS

Chichester · New York · Weinheim · Brisbane · Singapore · Toronto

Other Wiley Editorial Offices

John Wiley & Sons, Inc., 605 Third Avenue,
New York, NY 10158-0012, USA

WILEY-VCH Verlag GmbH, Pappelallee 3,
D-69469 Weinheim, Germany

Jacaranda Wiley Ltd, 33 Park Road, Milton,
Queensland 4064, Australia

John Wiley & Sons (Asia) Pte Ltd, 2 Clementi Loop #02-01,
Jin Xing Distripark, Singapore 129809

John Wiley & Sons (Canada) Ltd, 22 Worcester Road,
Rexdale, Ontario M9W 1L1, Canada

Coventry University

Library of Congress Cataloging-in-Publication Data

The strategic decision challenge / edited by David Hussey.
    p.   cm. — (Wiley series in contemporary strategic concerns)
    Includes bibliographical references and index.
    ISBN 0-471-97480-3 (cloth)
    1. Decision-making.   2. Strategic planning.   I. Hussey, D. E. (David E.)
    II. Series.
    HD30.23.S767   1997
    658.4'012—dc21   97–25694
                                                        CIP

British Library Cataloguing in Publication Data

A catalogue record for this book is available from the British Library

ISBN 0-471-97480-3

Typeset in 10/12pt Times by Dobbie Typesetting, Tavistock, Devon.
Printed and bound in Great Britain by Bookcraft (Bath) Ltd, Midsomer Norton, Somerset.
This book is printed on acid-free paper responsibly manufactured from sustainable forestry, in
which at least two trees are planted for each one used for paper production.

CONTENTS

ORIGINAL PUBLICATION REFERENCE

Unless otherwise indicated the first publication was in the journal *Strategic Change*, volume, issue and year shown. New material was written especially for the book.

INTRODUCTION

Successful business strategies rest on three pillars: flair and creative thinking; sound understanding of the situation, which normally requires analysis and method; and the ability to implement. If the flair and creativity are lacking, the best analysis will result only in "me too" or mechanical strategies. If the analysis is missing or ignores sound principles, strategies may be misconceived and brilliance may be overwhelmed by lack of relevance. If implementation is defective, even superb strategies may fail because the right actions are not taken, or not taken at the appropriate time.

In the first three of these collections which, with some exceptions, are drawn from the journal *Strategic Change*, I have tried to address each of these pillars. *The Implementation Challenge* (Hussey 1996) was followed by *Innovation Challenge*, and this current book goes some way to providing the third pillar. Each book has at least one specially written chapter, to help co-ordinate the other chapters and to insert some ideas that are important to the subject but which have not been covered in papers in the journal in quite the way that is needed.

It would be wrong to suggest that a book of this size contains everything that could be written about strategy and strategic decision making. It is a vast subject. What this book can do is to offer some insights into things which are important, show that this is an area which shtsaventsavenould receive more attention, and build bridges to other sources of information. The last chapter, which provides a glossary of techniques for strategic analysis, in particular gives a brief description of numerous techniques of analysis, with references to articles or books that provide more detail.

Before the glossary is reached, there is much in the book which should be helpful. That it covers an issue which requires attention is revealed in the first chapter, which was written for the book, although I had the opportunity on the way to try out the thinking in closely related papers presented in Japan and the UK. With the benefit of hindsight it is possible to see that for decades many organizations have not achieved the degree of success which they sought in their strategic moves. This does not mean that they all fail, although it has weakened many organizations so that they have been taken over by others, or become the inferior partner in a merger. Lack of understanding of the business environment is revealed in the continuation of strategic actions which are already past their sell by date, lack of creative thinking is shown by the number of copycat strategies where most of the competitors in an industry follow each other first into and then out of an area of diversification (Emily Boyle in chapter 2 calls these Pied Piper strategies). Failure to implement is clear from the low success rate of acquisitions, and major change initiatives like total quality management, downsizing, and business process re-engineering (some figures are given in chapter 1). So many organizations could be a lot better than they are. Sometimes the historical study reveals that a strategic action may have brought short term gains, but been wrong for the longer term.

Chapter 2 shows what can be learned by studying an industry, financial services, which is facing major upheaval in its business environment, and illuminates issues around the lack of original creative thinking in the strategies of some of the firms.

In chapter 3, Samuel Ho takes inspiration from the writings on strategy of Sun Tze, and has developed a modern model for developing strategy which relates to these ancient principles. This is not the first time that the relevance of the principles to modern business has been discussed, but Ho's approach is a useful way of beginning to think about strategic decisions.

Another model for strategic decision making is offered by Gordon Greenley in chapter 4. This provides a simpler, but no less relevant, framework than Ho's and relates to the market place.

All the chapters described so far are about some of the basic ideas behind strategic decisions. With Sylvia Handler's chapter 5 we move into a particular approach to determining strategy, based on how each decision increases shareholder value. Her chapter is drawn from her own research into how some of the leading British organizations who are proponents of this principle actually apply it.

Organizations have always been concerned about their competitors, and many of the principles are long established. However everything received a new focus in the landmark work Porter, 1980, and few organizations would now make strategic decisions without some consideration of competitors. The next three chapters look at various aspects of building competitive advantage and analysing the competitive situation. The contribution from Frank Winfrey, Michael Michalisin and William Acar (chapter 6) deals with some of the issues in obtaining sustained competitive advantage. Per Jenster and Peter Birklin follow this in chapter 7, dealing with competitor and industry analysis, which has to be one of the most important elements to be considered in any strategy. Usually this sort of discussion can deal only in principles, so we are fortunate in being able to include chapter 8 by Sebastian Crawshaw on the results he obtained from undertaking industry analysis in his organization. This chapter is also of value because it shows how industries merge, and that what is relevant comes from looking at the subject from a customer's viewpoint.

The next principle of strategy which is examined is in chapter 9, by Hans Hinterhuber and his colleagues from Innsbruck University. This suggests how core competences might be identified and used. Core competences can be seen as an evolution of the thinking about critical success factors, and are one of the most useful contributions to strategic thinking to emerge in recent years.

In chapter 10 Seiichiro Yahagi argues that a rational approach should be used to develop strategies for the improvement of managerial efficiency, and offers a technique for doing this.

Outsourcing as a strategic option has come to the fore during the 1990s, although as a concept its origins are much earlier. In chapter 11, David Jennings gives practical guidelines for outsourcing decisions, illustrated with a number of examples.

In one sense outsourcing is a form of alliance, although not what is usually meant by the term strategic alliance. In chapter 12, Wendy Hall and Jan Eppink give an industry study, in this case airlines, of strategic alliance strategies, and look at what has been happening and some of the implications.

We know from numerous research projects over more than twenty years (references are given in my opening chapter) that around half of all mergers and acquisitions fail. Unfortunately the book is not long enough to offer a guide to merger strategies and their implementation, but chapter 13, by Sue Cartwright, Cary Cooper, and Joseph Jordan, is interesting because it sheds light on the nationalities favoured for companies chosen as merger and acqusition targets by companies of another nationality. Drawn from original research, it also shows how easy it is for managers to define the business world in terms of what they are comfortable with, rather than what is really there.

The book is more about ideas than techniques, but often analysis is facilitated by a structured methodology. As already mentioned, my last chapter gives a basic glossary of techniques and shows where more information may be obtained about each of them.

The book will not define your organization's strategy for you, but the expertise of its contributors will set you on a path which will help you to improve the decisions you make.

David Hussey

STRATEGIC MANAGEMENT: PAST EXPERIENCES AND FUTURE DIRECTIONS

David Hussey

David Hussey & Associates

My involvement in strategic management began in mid 1964, when I returned to the UK after working on industrial development planning in government service in a developing country. I took a job as a project analyst in the UK local headquarters of a US multinational, and about a week later my boss said that we were now the corporate planning department. When I asked what that was, he said that he did not know, but we were lucky because no one else in the organization knew either. At that time the total bibliography on the subject, world-wide, would probably have filled no more than two sides of a piece of paper. Our main source of information was a subscription service from Stanford Research Institute, which issued regular pamphlets on aspects of the subject. The first comprehensive book on corporate strategy was Ansoff, 1965. Sheer chance positioned me as one of the first practitioners of corporate planning in the UK, at a time when there were not all that many in the world.

I have begun here in order to illustrate three points.

- I have been an observer and student of strategic management for long enough to develop both an appreciation of what it can do and a regret that so often it is misapplied, and so cannot deliver all the potential benefits.
- My own initiation to the subject was a good example of the "muddle through" approach which I believe is one of the reasons for the planning

The Strategic Decision Challenge, Edited by David Hussey
© 1998 John Wiley & Sons Ltd

dilemma which has exercised my mind for the past 15 years, which I will come to in a moment.

- The role of chance in my own career illustrates two points which are true of corporate strategy: first, the organization has to position itself so that it can take advantage of the things it cannot forecast and secondly, it has to be able to recognize an opportunity when it occurs.

Much has happened in strategic management since those early days. The volume of books and articles has reached a point where it is impossible to read them all, and the subject itself has gone through several changes of name: long range planning to corporate planning to strategic planning to strategic management. One hopes that there has been an evolution of concept to match the changes in name.

GRAPPLING WITH A DILEMMA

This dilemma is why so many companies and sometimes whole industries have suffered strategic failure, despite the fact that many employed a process of strategic management of one style or another, while at the same time the research tells us that companies that plan outperform those who do not. The evidence for this will be examined shortly; my observations on failure are largely confined to the UK and it may not be the same in other parts of the world. However the conclusions have, I believe, a wider validity and indicate some of the ways in which strategic management might evolve as we move into the new century.

There are many strands that twist into the rope on which I hang my conclusions; the first of these which I will examine is the evidence for the success or failure of the formal approach to strategic planning.

STRATEGIC PLANNING: SUCCESS OR FAILURE

Most organizations which have followed the strategic planning path have been seeking better strategic decisions through improved analysis, a more future-oriented approach, more effective co-ordination of different functions and activities and wider management involvement in the planning process. In the early days of planning, at least, involvement was seen as one of the keys to success, in that it could unlock more brain power to think of solutions, would bring into the process both those at the coal face and those in the ivory tower, and motivate all managers so that plans were implemented. In fact it is debatable whether this is enough to ensure either sound strategies or their implementation, and it will be necessary to return to the premise later in this paper.

The classic planning process has postulated a blend of top-down and bottom-up thinking that in theory enables the final plan to be a rational amalgam of all viewpoints, argued out in a constructive manner. In fact observations by Hussey, 1979, and research by Gluck et al, 1980 showed that many different approaches to strategic planning/management evolved, and newer approaches co-existed with the older ones. A defect of much of the early research on planning benefits is that it made no distinction between the various possible approaches to planning. Goold and Campbell, 1987 identified a number of different styles of planning in diversified organizations and argued that the most effective style depended on the business situation of the organization. Goold, Campbell and Alexander, 1994, later extended this work to examine how different parenting styles could add value to an organization. The work by Ansoff and his colleagues demonstrates that the most effective approaches to planning are situational: the findings relate the optimum approach to strategy and planning to the degree of turbulence faced by the organization, and demonstrate that a poor fit of the two will result in an adverse impact on profitability. Sample references are Ansoff and McDonnell, 1990, Ansoff, 1991, and Ansoff et al, 1993.

With hindsight, it is possible to argue that the early research did not explore the many nuances that have been observed since. The serious questioning of whether the formal approach to planning contributed to profits began towards the end of the 1960s. Initially replies to the question of value were either on the lines of "it must be good because so many people do it", or examples of the rather rare situations where an obvious benefit had occurred within seconds of the arrival of a corporate planner.

Human ingenuity soon found a way of measuring the impact of planning, and a series of studies were carried out in the USA proving that planning did pay. Most were based on some form of matched pairs analysis, for example comparing performance of each planning company with its non planning pair. Some studies also looked at the performance of planning companies before and after they commenced to plan. Examples of research are Thune and House, 1970, Vancil, 1970, Ansoff et al, 1970, Herold, 1972, Schoeffler et al, 1974, and Malik and Karger, 1975. Although individual firms were found that did well without planning, on average those that planned tended to do better than those that did not plan.

The case seems to have been made, at least in the USA, that strategic planning is beneficial and does improve the economic results of those companies that practise it.

It seems to me that the research proves beyond doubt that strategic planning can be beneficial, but common sense tells us that it will not be beneficial in every situation. If it is applied badly it is unlikely to succeed. There are also degrees of success: not all organizations set a high enough level of expectation from their planning work and are therefore too easily satisfied.

The real issue is that strategic decisions have to be made and implemented whether or not the company has a formal approach to planning; these decisions can be good or bad and implementation can be excellent or poor.

LONG TERM SURVIVAL AND SUCCESS

Every generation of managers believes that the changes it is facing in the business environment are more severe and more frequent than ever before. Even allowing for the human factor, that any change an individual is having to cope with is felt to be more challenging than the change someone else is experiencing. I believe that fitting the organization to the environment has always been difficult, has become even more difficult over the past 35 years, and will become even harder as we move into the next century. Strategic management is to a large extent about setting corporate strategy in relation to the opportunities and threats of the market place and the business environment. What I have often found puzzling is the fact that so many large organizations in Europe and the USA, most if not all of which would claim to be practising strategic management, seem to produce similar strategic moves. Is it that all the analysts in an industry look at the same facts and reach the same conclusions? This might be true, but seems unlikely because many of the strategies have been reversed by the entire industry only a few years later. In the mid 1970s it was fashionable for airlines to move into the hotel business: a decade later most had moved out of hotels to concentrate on the core airline business.

British retail banks began a rush in the 1970s to buy US banks, most of which could operate at the retail level in only one state. High prices were paid, and in some cases the loss over many years dragged down performance. The Midland Bank, for example, was acquired recently by Hong Kong and Shanghai Banking Corporation, and it is possible to argue that one causal factor was the large losses, reputed to have reached £1 billion, made as a result of their acquisition of Crocker Bank in the USA in 1980: Crocker was sold to Wells Fargo in 1986. A second legacy of the acquisition was an over exposure in loans to Latin America (Beaver and Jennings, 1996).

Another strategic hare which the financial services industries followed like a pack of hounds was the acquisition of estate agents (what the Americans call realtors). The chase began in the mid 1980s, in the belief that the firms who acted as agents for the sale of houses, would also be a vehicle for the sale of mortgages and house insurance. Banks, building societies and insurance companies paid vast premiums to acquire businesses, which for the most part plunged into loss and by the early 1990s were being sold, sometimes back to the original owners, for a fraction of their purchase price. For example, Prudential Insurance is reported to have paid £230 million for its chain of estate agents. In 1989 alone it lost £49 million on them, and in 1991 sold the chain at a capital loss.

These examples are not all British. What I should like to do now is to focus on the UK, to look at the general trends in the business environment over successive decades, and the responses that organizations have made to these.

> One contributory factor to the relative economic decline of the UK has been continued strategic failure by British business in general. Whole industries have declined and disappeared and although in some cases this has been because of a "natural" change in economic advantage, in others it has been because foreign competition has had a superior strategy to the British firms. There is no natural reason why Japan should have been able to destroy the British motor cycle industry, or become world leaders in the car industry: superior strategic thinking features highly as a reason. (Hussey, 1984)

TRENDS AND STRATEGIC RESPONSES TO 1970

Channon, 1973, identified four major trends in the environment of British firms in the 25 years to 1970.

1. After the second world war the major industrial problems were those of reconstruction and the relief of shortages. During the 1960s the change was from a sellers' to a buyers' market.
2. The removal of the restrictive practices which have protected the inefficient, and the changed relationships with the countries of the former Empire which began to demolish the tariff advantages given to British companies.
3. "Consumer aspirations rose with growing affluence, and government undertook to fulfil these aspirations by seeking economic growth." (Channon, 1973)
4. Rapid changes in technology brought new products and processes, and an increase in the scale of development costs in industries such as aircraft and computers.

To the issues listed above we should add that the power of trade unions grew over the period, with many restrictive labour practices, and industrial relations tended to be adversarial.

Channon's research showed that the strategic responses to the changes he had observed were not always adequate. The following analysis is based on his work, supplemented with other sources.

One major response to the trends was the wholesale adoption of diversification strategies. Channon, 1973, showed that only 24% of the top

100 companies were diversified in 1950, compared with 60% by 1970. Channon noted the failure of many British acquisitions. Few British companies attempted to rationalize their acquisitions.

> Frequently, acquired concerns were allowed to continue along much as before without real influence from the parent. The acquisition was in name only but not in managerial action. (Channon, 1973, p. 240)

Buckner, 1974, found that, in the period 1960–70, over half of diversification moves were failures, and that the failure rate was higher when diversification was by acquisition rather than internal development. Similar findings on the failure of acquisitions have been found consistently in surveys in Europe, the UK and the USA right up to the present decade, suggesting that the issue is not unique to the UK, and that there is a constant failure of either the strategy, its implementation, or both. All but the first of the following studies found a failure rate of around 50%: Kitching, 1967, 1973, British Institute of Management, 1986, Porter 1987, Hunt 1988, and Coopers & Lybrand, 1993.

A second, almost universal, action was the adoption of the multi-divisional structure by the vast majority of major companies. However, although many of the features of the US pattern of multi-divisional management were adopted, many traditional elements of the British system remained, which were often enough to prevent many of the benefits of the divisional structure from being gained.

Channon, 1973, noted many deficiencies of British industry in marketing and strategic thinking, and in a failure to innovate. British concerns were production or quality oriented, without due regard to the needs of the market place.

Just as there seem to be no lessons learned about acquisition, so it seems that deficiencies of marketing continue. A decade after the period researched by Channon, 1973, the *Finniston Report*, a Government sponsored committee of enquiry into the engineering professions stated:

> Sectorial studies, from shipbuilding to electronic components, have cited opportunities missed and markets lost due to non-price factors. These range from failure of British producers to innovate or to match changed requirements, through specific short-comings in the design or performance of products, to a general reputation of British goods for inferior quality, late delivery and unreliability in service (for example, the provision of spares). (HMSO, 1980, p. 18)

TRENDS AND STRATEGIC RESPONSES, 1971 TO 1980

Luffman and Reed, 1984, studied the performance of British industry through the 1970s. In this decade change became discontinuous, occurring in sudden jumps rather than as smooth transition. Most of the factors behind the changes were not unique to the UK, and were shared to a greater or lesser extent by many other nations. They identified a number of critical economic factors, but gave only one of the major causal triggers for change, the oil crisis of 1973. It is necessary look more broadly before returning to some of the other findings of the Luffman and Reed research.

The decade saw an increase in global competition, although this was not always fully recognized for what it was. The motor cycle industry moved into its death throes; the main domestic car producer, British Leyland, would have gone into liquidation had it not been rescued by the government of the day, and it was one of many companies rescued in this way. Many traditional industries declined. The National Enterprise Board, which had been set up by the socialist government to take shareholdings in companies to stimulate their development, used its available funds in taking over the shares of the lame duck companies which would otherwise have closed. International competition was intensified when the UK joined the EEC in the mid 1970s.

For most of the decade much management attention was given to industrial relations. White collar unions grew in strength and there were many strikes. By the end of the period a change of government, which came to power on the slogan "put Britain back to work" had begun to curb the power of the unions.

Luffman and Reed, 1984, found from their study that acquisition was a favoured strategy, and

> By 1980 only 496 of the 835 companies remained in independent operation with 315 companies having been subject to takeover or merger (p. 4).

Sixty-three per cent of the takeovers were by firms in the sample. The survey concluded that companies which further diversified during the period

> ...have performed considerably better than non-diversifiers with respect to shareholders' return, sales growth, and increases in ROCE (p. 174).

While there is no reason to doubt the findings of this research, it raises a question over whether the results were only short term, and if the strategies truly considered the need to think in terms of global competition in many industries. Knowledge of what happened in the 1980s makes it clear that not all the strategic moves were well founded.

I should like to insert a personal anecdote here to demonstrate my point. In late 1980 Vickers, one of the most respected firms in British engineering, merged with Rolls Royce Motors. I was invited to help the executive directors develop a strategy for the overall group. Vickers had followed a process of planning previously, but it was a bottom up process that developed lengthy documents but never produced a defined over-arching corporate strategy. The new entity had 33 business units. Discussions with a number of the business unit managing directors revealed that many were focused only on the UK market, despite the fact that their businesses were subject to global competition. The study of the Vickers portfolio, which had been built up by acquisition, much of it during the 1970s, revealed that although they had many businesses which were capable of growth and development, they did not have the resources to develop all to be world class competitors. The strategy developed after the merger was to concentrate on a small number of core businesses, and to divest most of the remainder to provide the capital to enable the organization to operate as a world class performer. The point of the story is that all the acquisitions made during the 1970s had been based on past earnings and were assessed on a UK rather than a world canvas. The move back to core business became a key feature of many British companies in the early half of the 1980s, demonstrating that much of the merger mania of the late 1960s and the 1970s was not based on sound appreciation of the competitive arena.

During this decade inadequate attention was being given by British companies to becoming competitive with suppliers from other countries. From 1973 to 1980, the average annual productivity growth in UK manufacturing was 0.2%, much lower than that of competitor nations (Norse, 1982).

TRENDS AND STRATEGIC RESPONSES: 1981 TO 1997

One major difference in the UK environment since 1981 has been a much improved industrial relations environment, as changes in legislation reduced the power of trade unions, and two recessions changed attitudes to employment. Many of the most critical environmental pressures which UK businesses have faced, and are facing still, are world wide. They know no geographical boundaries; few countries and few organizations are immune to them, and the broad strategic responses of businesses to these trends are not unique to any one country.

Strong forces continue to shape the environment in which we operate, and old concepts of management have to be re-examined against the challenge of the world we live in today, and the world we believe we will live in tomorrow. While there will always be many new issues in the external business environment which will affect the organization from time to time, and which will impact on the corporate strategy, we can also see some long running trends which have been with us through the whole period and which will continue into the future.

The forces described here are unlikely to surprise and will fit the observations of most managers. However, they were not derived by guesswork, but from a number of studies undertaken in Europe and the USA, such as Sullivan (1989), Barham and Bassam (1989), and Barham, Fraser and Heath (1988).

Competition

Competition has increased, and for most industries it is no longer possible to define competition within the boundaries of a particular country. More and more organizations are compelled to think of their business in global terms, and most others are subject to more intense competition. The European Union has been one of many factors which has increased competition in member countries, even when the markets themselves are not global.

Customers are More Demanding

In the developed world, life styles have changed and the expectations of the whole population have steadily increased and continue to rise. Many people in the developed countries see poverty as relative rather than absolute deprivation. With higher expectations and more choice, it is not surprising that the individual consumer is less tolerant of poor products and service, and more vocal in expressing dissatisfaction. The industrial customer is more demanding, and has to be in order to attain the cost levels and to supply the quality and timeliness of delivery that enable him/her to compete. While the new requirements bring opportunities for the whole supply chain to work in a more co-operative manner than may have been traditional, there is much less willingness by individual customers to condone failures. Few can afford to do so, if they are to succeed in their own markets.

Accelerating Pace of Technological Obsolescence

Product life cycles are shortening. This has a positive advantage in that it keeps markets growing: these days we are unlikely to run in to the old problem of Singer Sewing Machines who made products that would last for many years, but without the technological advances that would make people want to upgrade to the next level. It also means that the time to exploit a new product or innovation is much shorter than in the past, and if too long is spent in development, the product may be nearly obsolete before it is launched.

Plant and office equipment become obsolete more quickly. Businesses which cannot afford to update, or which take too long in launching new innovations, have a great competitive disadvantage.

Pressure to Deliver Shareholder Value

Top managements of public companies have always had to balance the needs of shareholders for dividends and share price growth against the needs of the business. What became apparent through the 1980s was that many strategic actions taken by organizations reduced shareholder value. Conglomerate organizations fell out of fashion with the stock market. Evidence of their failure to be worth as much as the sum of their individual parts was provided by high profile acquisitions which led to the sell-off of most of the parts, leaving the acquirer with either a handsome profit or retaining the plum business while recovering the full investment from the sale of the other businesses. An example is Hanson Trust's acquisition of Imperial Group, where the prices realised by divesting some of the companies in the group meant that they retained the cash generating tobacco business for a net cost well below its true value. Hanson's shrewdness helped focus the minds of shareholders and managers on issues of shareholder value.

COMMON RESPONSES TO THE FORCES FOR CHANGE

The response to these trends has led to a number of remarkably similar actions across many organizations and industries. The past ten years have been called a decade of restructuring. Common actions taken by many organizations have included the following.

- Seeking a reduction of costs, with more attention being given to competitive positioning.
- Attention to time as a strategic issue, and attempts to reduce cycle times throughout the organization.
- Changing structures to achieve a closer relationship with customers.
- More emphasis, in Europe and the USA, on quality. Japan already had this emphasis.
- Attempts to change the culture of organizations to enable them to react faster and more effectively to market requirements.

Cost Emphasis

Businesses have always been concerned about their costs. The new emphasis has been on costs compared to those of competitors, and much of the new thinking has been about ways of achieving comparative advantage. One of the manifestations of this was the emphasis on becoming a world class manufacturer. The concept embraces more than costs: it covers also quality and innovation. Hayes, Wheelwright and Clark (1988) define world class:

> Basically, this means being better than almost any company in your industry in at least one important aspect of manufacturing (p. 21).

For most organizations it was no longer enough to gain an improvement over their own previous year's activities. Long term success is only possible if organizations in some way do better than their competitors.

The most important thing was the recognition that the criteria for success lay outside the business, and that meeting internally generated targets was irrelevant unless they happened to be as good as or better than the performance of competitors.

Another feature in the 1980s was the rise in popularity of benchmarking. Many organizations misunderstand benchmarking and see it as just a comparison of ratios. In fact it should be a comparison of the processes that caused the ratios. There are many success stories of successful benchmarking projects, including companies such as Ford and Xerox. Lessons can be learned from organizations that are not competitors: for example, Motorola was reputed to benchmark against motor racing pit stops, to gain insight into ways of improving change over time on assembly lines.

Benchmarking does not itself cause change, but it is a means to deciding where changes are needed. Karlöf and Östblom, 1993, argue that benchmarking should be part of an approach to the learning organization.

Even more fashionable, and much more widely applied, are the sweeping "downsizing and de-layering" actions which have swept through most organizations on both sides of the Atlantic. A more recent attempt at a politically correct description is "rightsizing". The aims are usually to reduce costs, to push decision making further down the organization to the closest possible point to the customer, and to change culture. Kinnie, Hutchinson and Purcell, 1996, reviewed the published research studies.

> There is increasing evidence, however, to suggest that the majority of downsizings are unsuccessful — the anticipated economic and organizational benefits fail to materialise. In the USA between two thirds to three quarters of all downsizings are unsuccessful from the start (Howard, 1996). A study in the USA by the Wyatt Co (1994) found that few downsizings meet their desired goals in terms of increased competitiveness and profitability. The majority of organizations meet their immediate cost reducing objectives but this improvement is not sustained in other areas, especially in the long range goals of improved service and increased competitive advantage. The findings of another study by Kenneth de Meuse et al. (1994), show that for the three year period after the downsizing announcements firms making redundancies had ended up with lower profit margins and poorer returns on assets and equity than equivalent firms who do not downsize.

The latest concept to hit the headlines is business process re-engineering (BPR). Again, not all organizations that claim to undertake BPR are truly doing so: many have followed the common habit of renaming existing activities without properly taking on board the changes required by the new concept. Coulson-Thomas, 1996, researched the use of BPR across Europe:

> Almost as many definitions of BPR were encountered as the number of cases examined. An increasingly wide range of activities from "change programmes" to "de-layering" are now commonly referred to as "BPR". In some instances, the label or description has been retrospective, i.e. applied *ex* post or "after the event."

BPR is about the complete rethinking of how processes are undertaken, and the result of a successful BPR exercise is fundamental change. Johansson, McHugh, Pendlebury, and Wheeler, 1993, describe BPR as

> ...the means by which an organization can achieve radical change in performance as measured by cost, cycle time, service and quality... (p. 15).

The change in emphasis is the focus on the business

> ...as a set of related customer oriented core business processes rather than a set of organizational functions (p. 16).

The most serious findings by Coulson-Thomas, 1996 were that most BPR exercises examined were really process simplification rather than re-engineering, and were being undertaken for medium term cost and time savings and not for longer term strategic benefits

> What is clear is that many of the BPR solutions being adopted are yielding cost benefits today at the price of inflexibility tomorrow. Thus paths and options are being limited and prescribed in order to 'speed things up' in ways that can reduce the scope for creative thinking and innovation.

This leaves us uncertain over whether the 59% of UK organizations which reported BPR activity in 1995 (Grint and Willcocks, 1995) were really applying BPR. Surveys in the US show that a very high percentage of BPR initiatives are unsuccessful (Hammer and Champney, 1993 — 50–70% failure). The success rate in the UK is unlikely to be any higher.

Time as a Strategic Issue

Time has always been seen to have business significance. In modern business, when the development of new products or improvements takes longer than for competitors, there is a multiple impact. The opportunity to gain revenue from the product may be considerably reduced by the competitor who can respond quicker, costs are likely to be higher than when the product was conceived, and customers may feel let down because expectations are not met.

The pressure is not just to improve, but to improve enough to get ahead of competitors. Typical steps taken by organizations to achieve this include new approaches to project management, closer working relationships between internal functions, the involvement of suppliers and customers in the development and simultaneous engineering.

Closeness to the Customer

The more exacting demands of customers have led to a new industry: consulting and writing about customer focus. For many, this has been no more than using a few words of the new jargon or making some other cosmetic change.

Carlzon, 1987, triggered a revolution in thinking with the "moment of truth" concepts. This was each moment when a customer came into contact with an employee. In fact the concept was not invented by Carlzon, and had previously been published in Normann, 1978, and in other articles by this author. What Carlzon had done was to apply it very successfully through a mix of restructuring and training so that the front line people were seen as the most important, with the rest of the organization there to support them. In order to give the front line greater ability to maximize the value of these moments of truth, levels of bureaucracy were removed, the rule book which had previously required matters to be passed upwards for decision was scrapped and decision making power was delegated to the front line people to enable them to act in the interest of the customers.

Many organizations have followed this lead of seeing the organization as an upside down pyramid, with the people who face the customers at the top and everyone else, including the chief executive, being there to enable them to work effectively. A natural result was to remove blockages to communication and decision making, blockages frequently identified as layers of middle management which were removed because, in theory, the role they played was now being undertaken by the people who shared the moments of truth with the customers.

There is another trend in responses which applies to industrial organizations. This is the tendency for suppliers and buyers to work closer together, partly because of the ways in which this can reduce overall costs in the chain, and partly to take time out of development projects. Moving from an antagonistic relationship to one of co-operation is also one of the ways in which overall quality can be improved. There has as a result been a trend to preferred suppliers, who understand each other, which gives both sides the opportunity to plan production more effectively, schedule investment and work on quality and value.

Emphasis on Quality

Another approach taken up by numerous organizations has been total quality management (TQM). Although many have walked this road, and spent vast sums on TQM to try to achieve the necessary changes, not every organization has travelled the full journey. Many have underestimated the length of time that such major changes take, and many have not given the amount of management time needed to make them work (partly because managers underestimated the time they should spend on the initiative in the first place).

Unfortunately, despite its success in Japan, and the fact that over two thirds of the UK's top 500 companies have introduced TQM (Abram Hawkes, 1993), it appears that only 8% of British managers believe that it has been successful in their companies (Wilkinson et al., 1993): note the samples are not directly comparable.

The other universal approach to quality has been BS5750 (ISO9000), which is an endorsement that the organization has the procedures in place to produce quality but does not by itself create a quality culture or ensure a quality product.

My expectation is that increasingly organizations will find that TQM can not deliver when it is applied in an organizational vacuum, which asks people to behave differently on quality matters than they do on any other aspect of the business.

Culture Change, Flexibility and Fast Reaction

We looked earlier at one aspect of the strategic importance of time. There is another, which is the ability of the organization to respond quickly to events which could not be foreseen. Although some of the delayering initiatives have also been intended to serve this purpose, there are also accompanying trends. One which has come to the fore in the last decade is the announced intention to change culture. The reasoning seems to be that a chief executive recognizes a mismatch between the existing culture, which reflects the behaviours needed for the success patterns of the past, and the business situation the organization now faces. One of the pioneers of this route was General Electric in the USA, where Jack Welch took action to make the whole organization "lean and agile". Leanness might come from delayering, but agility is a cultural attribute.

The search for flexibility and fast response has taken other forms. Flexible working has become more than a minority activity, giving the employer the ability to turn costs on and off like a tap. There are many consequences of this, and it has become a subject in its own right. Similarly one of the reasons for outsourcing activities may be cost, although for many organizations it is to give greater flexibility, as it leaves someone else with the problem of adjusting capacity to a decline in work.

SUCCESS CAN BE TRANSIENT

During the 1980s a number of companies were regularly identified by government and the financial press as a good example to British industry. The chief executives were praised for their vision as they re-shaped their businesses by acquisition, and the growth and profitability achieved were seen as the results of a sound strategy. By the early 1990s, many of these organizations were in trouble, resulting in some cases in their breakup, and in others in a change of chief executive and complete change in strategy. Can a strategy be considered to be good when it leads to cash flow problems in the organization, and has to be reversed after only a few years?

Success can also be long lasting, and in focusing on widespread problem areas I should not like to leave the impression that all organizations are misdirected in their strategy. There are many examples in the UK of organizations that have had clarity of vision over many years, with strategies to support this, and have also achieved consistent success in their results: Marks and Spencer, the retailers, and British Airways are examples of the older organizations and the Virgin organization is an example of one of the golden companies of the 1980s that continues to be successful.

The fact that an organization has been mentioned as making a strategic mistake, does not necessarily imply that all its decisions are wrong. Midland Bank, for example, which I criticized for its US acquisition, was very successful with its launch of First Direct, a new retail bank which had no branches but gave a 24 hour service over the telephone, and was able to target and choose the type of clients it wanted. This was adventurous and innovative, and great care was taken to understand the market needs and in the way the new bank was implemented.

EXPLORING THE DILEMMA

I should like to return to the dilemma with which I began this paper: why an apparently beneficial approach to preparing for the future seems unable to stop so many organizations from making major strategic mistakes.

It is easy to see that a process which achieved better co-ordination between different parts of the organization, achieved a measure of motivation through a shared vision and stimulated some thought about strategic options and improvements, could bring short term benefits while failing to deal with deep seated issues or develop strategies that made long term sense. Under these circumstances planning could bring improvement, while failing to move the organization from the path that would eventually take it to relative or absolute failure. What is certain is that those planning the futures of organizations over the periods studied could not have intended many of the outcomes, yet for the most part those responsible for determining strategy would have been people of intelligence and experience. If we accept that my diagnosis is correct, it is worth spending some time trying to explore what might be done to improve matters.

I would suggest four areas which could account for the failure of so many organizations to achieve the quality of strategic thinking that has been needed in the past, and which will be even more critical as we move into the next century. The areas are:

- failure to analyse the situation before strategic decisions are made
- failure to implement strategic decisions
- problems with the process of planning itself
- incomplete understanding of many of the concepts by those claiming to apply them.

Failure to Analyse Effectively

In theory, analysis is an objective, rational process divorced from behavioural influences. In practice this is not true, and even the choice of what to analyse and the selection of information for analysis are coloured by beliefs and attitude, and sometimes by wishful thinking. Analysis can be used to stimulate a creative process and to test the ideas that emerge (Ohmae, 1983, p. 4). It can also be used to imprison and to constrain thinking so that it follows preconceived notions.

Some years ago (Hussey, 1984), I coined the phrase "perceptual boundaries" to explain how managers saw the world in which they operated. The boundaries are not what is true, but what is believed to be true. It is a natural and human trait to simplify the world by shutting out certain possibilities.

> Most of us recognize that the world-as-we-see-it is not necessarily the same as the world-as-it-really-is. Our answer depends on what we heard, not what was really said. The consumer buys what he likes best, not what is best. Whether we feel hot or cold depends on us, not on the thermometer. The same job may look like a good job to one of us and a sloppy job to another. (Leavitt, 1978, p. 25)

In Europe generations of medieval men had an absolute certainty that the world was flat, like a large plate. Because of this they made logical decisions, like not sailing too close to the edge in case they fell off. But in reality these decisions were not good ones, because the perception on which they were based was faulty.

I believe that perceptual boundaries are one of the major influences on strategic decision making. The managers of the motorcycle companies made decisions which would have been logical had their perception of the world been accurate. They *knew* that their motor cycles were the best, that their engineering talent was superior, that the market would always want a British motor cycle, and that factories should be run on the basis of satisfying the UK demand, and having a surplus to export. But the world was not really like that, and even when the attack by Honda on the world market followed a totally different appreciation of reality, British companies did not change their perception. They *knew* that no one could make motor cycles at those prices and so cried foul and dumping, rather than undertaking the change in thinking which would have made them realize that their perceptions were wrong.

The motor cycle industry was only one example of many that began to feel intensified competition in the 1960s and 1970s. As we have already seen, Vickers was one of many companies that followed a strategy of diversification through the 1970s, but based on a perception that they were a British manufacturing company operating mainly in a British market and not seeing the need to compete globally.

The perceptual boundaries are often common across whole companies and industries, which means that no one challenges the foundation on which the strategies are built and there is little investment of resources in the collection and analysis of information which does not fit the perception.

When companies are profitable, few organizations take steps to think about a challenge that can be vaguely foreseen over the horizon, and do not allow themselves to think seriously about how this might change their perceptions of the strategic arena.

Unless strategy making succeeds in challenging the perceptual boundaries, organizations will continue to produce what are effectively logical solutions to the wrong problem. As we have seen, the experience with BPR, which is an approach which is intended to challenge all the boundaries, is that it rarely succeeds in producing radical solutions because of the way it is applied. However, this is to anticipate one of my other problem headings which I will come to later.

The second difficulty I see is that many organizations either fail to use appropriate methods of analysis, or in some cases do not apply properly those methods they do use. The fault is usually due to both lack of knowledge of the technique and inadequate information. Managers may chat glibly about the value chain, industry and competitor analysis, or draw a portfolio chart where SBUs have been placed by instinct rather than objective analysis. Lists of strengths and weaknesses are displayed: often I have seen only two strengths in a plan (a strong chief executive and an effective management team) and several pages of weaknesses, few of which have strategic significance.

Even what is used can be corrupted by the perceptual boundaries. The best analysis of an industry, or of the corporate portfolio will only be as good as the definitions used. If the analysis is undertaken only on an inappropriate segment of the market or too restrictive a geographical area wrong readings will be given which may help keep the organization within the invisible walls of its perceptual boundaries.

Failure to Implement Strategic Decisions

Strategic success in the first instance requires an appropriate strategy, but this by itself is not enough. It also requires that the strategy be implemented successfully. For many years many of the planning books seemed to assume that if strategic planning involved line managers, implementation would inevitably follow. There are good arguments for widespread participation in certain circumstances, but only when it fits both the culture of the organization and its strategic situation. Although participation may improve motivation and increase the "buy in" to a strategy, there is much more to implementation than this.

There are both behavioural and analytical dimensions to the process of strategic decision making and the subsequent implementation of strategy. In many cases what appear to be the hard, analytical processes are affected by hidden behavioural or soft considerations. The selection of information for rational analysis would appear to be a totally rational activity. In fact, because a choice has to be made of what information to analyse, it may be overlaid by behavioural issues. The manager's perceptual boundaries will exclude information as irrelevant, when it reality it may be critical. Once an analysis has been completed, it has to be interpreted and the interpretation, however objective the analysts and managers try to be, will be affected by behavioural considerations. It is not unknown for managers to suppress findings which are at variance with what they would like to do.

There are also soft and hard elements which need to fit together if the strategy is to be implemented. These are elements such as the culture of the organization and the way the structure works. If there is a natural fit there may be no problem. This is often the case with an incremental strategy, which effectively requires the organization to do more of the same. Where the strategy requires fundamental change, there may be a clash, in which case either the strategy or the behavioural element has to change. The 1990s have seen a spate of organizations engaged in culture change, to improve the ability of the organization to implement the strategies considered essential for the decade. British Petroleum's Project 1990 is one example of change on a massive scale, but there are also examples in the privatized businesses of gas, water, and telecommunications, and in what is going on in the National Health Service. In fact it now seems to be almost as fashionable to have a culture change, as it was to follow competitors down the same strategic path. But I am being cynical.

The repeated failure of acquisition suggests that implementation considerations are cut off too soon. An acquisition strategy is not implemented when the shares have changed hands: that is only step one. It is only implemented when the strategy behind the acquisition is fulfilled. The bulk of the implementation task occurs after the completion of the ownership transactions.

Kaplan, 1995, found that many organizations have a

> ...fundamental disconnect between the development and formulation of their strategy and the implementation of that strategy into useful action.

Four major barriers to effective implementation were identified.

- Vision that could not be actioned, because it was not translated into operational terms.
- Strategy that is not linked to departmental and individual goals (incentives are tied to annual financial performance instead of to long range strategy: only 21% of executive management and 6% of middle management have objectives that are tied to the strategy).
- Resource allocation that is based on short term budgets and not on the strategy (only just over a third of organizations have a direct link between the strategy and the budgeting process).
- Control that is directed at short term performance and rarely evaluates progress against long term objectives.

In theory, Human Resource Management should pay a large part in helping to implement strategies. The Europe-wide Price Waterhouse Cranfield survey, 1991, shows that no more than 50% of organizations have HRM policies that might be directly linked to corporate strategy, and this is an optimistic interpretation of the figures. In the UK Tovey, 1991, and Mason, 1993, found that a large number of organizations took a superficial view of where HRM could contribute in the implementation of strategies such as acquisition or downsizing. Downsizing can only be said to have been implemented when the new organization is functioning effectively, and the hardest part is after the changes have been announced. Some of the downsizing failures reported earlier might have been avoided had more attention been paid to the HR issues.

Problems with the Process of Planning

There has been an almost continuous stream of research into what is the best process for planning strategy, and why some organizations seem to be better at it than others. It is not hard to see how a poor process can either fail to lead to effective strategies, despite good intention failing to stimulate any creative strategic thinking and thus reinforcing the perceptual boundaries, or can give the delusion that there is a strategy when in fact there is none. Early researchers tended to relate one common concept of planning to all firms (see, for example, Warren 1966, Ringbakk, 1971, Steiner, 1972, Grinyer and Norburn, 1974, Steiner and Schollhammer, 1975, and Martin, 1979), but nevertheless contributed to an understanding of many of the factors that contribute to the successful or unsuccessful design and operation of a planning process.

The sad thing is that many organizations still slip into pitfalls which were identified over a decade ago. The more recent research often underlines the conclusions of the earlier studies. Common management faults include: treating planning as something different from the management process; lack of understanding of planning; failure to involve the right people in the process; lack of interest in the process by top management; failure to obtain the necessary information to enable strategies to be developed; political issues around the power structure of the organization and the calibre of the people involved.

From observation of many UK planning processes I would say that too many are bottom up systems with little top down influences, which is a recipe for ensuring that real strategic thinking is disconnected from the planning process.

There is one school of thinking which is pursued by many organizations, which is an incremental approach to strategy formulation, and which argues that strategy is developed through a sequence of steps and probes, rather than as a big jump as the result of detailed analysis. This has been associated with Quinn's concept of "logical incrementalism", 1980, and Mintzberg, 1994, "emergent and deliberate strategies". Although labelled in some books as postmodernist, to distinguish it from what has been called the modernist approach begun by Ansoff, 1965, in fact these views have similarities with a concept discussed well before Ansoff's landmark book was published. Lindblom, 1959, compared what he called the *rational-comprehensive* approach to strategy formulation with the *successive limited comparison* approach and argued that some strategic situations were so complex that not only was the successive limited comparison approach actually used by many, but that sometimes it was the only practical approach. In a sense, the strategies emerged from the knowledge obtained from the results of the actions taken. These ideas are sometimes misused, in may be comforting to claim to be following the fashionable emergent route. However, they can also be interpreted as part of a situational view of what is an appropriate planning process for a given organization.

Two other situational views have already been discussed; the environmental turbulence approach of Ansoff, and the role of head office approach of Goold and Campbell. There are other situational factors which perhaps should receive more attention than I have found in the literature, such as the culture of the organization, the style of its management, cultural differences between the organization's main countries of operation, and the size of the organization, although it is also possible to argue that some at least of these factors may sometimes need to be changed to enable the optimum fit of the planning process with the external environment.

My leaning is to a more situational approach, which means that I do not have to get into an argument about which approach to strategy is best, as there is no one best for every organization. However, there are many second bests for all organizations, many of which appear to be chosen regularly. Certainly, many planning processes reinforce the existing boundaries of perception on a regular basis, which is only good when reality and the perceptions are the same.

I offer some broad principles for effective planning processes.

There are some fundamental principles which are important for effective corporate planning. First, *management must have the will to make plans work.* No outsider can create this, although he may be able to help management understand the actions that must be taken and their implications. Second, *contrary to normal architectural practice, building must start from the top down.* The foundations must be in the boardroom . . .

Third, *the emphasis of the planning process must be on strategy.* A common approach is for goals and assumptions to go down the organization and detailed plans to go up . . . In most organizations this is not a good mechanism for identifying and dealing with the strategic issues. What we find appropriate is a strategic review concept, which ensures that the right type of analysis is carried out; that there is participative and objective discussion between corporate top management and the heads of business units; and that strategic issues are identified from both corporate and divisional perspectives . . .

Fourth, *the breath of life must be put into the process by the company.* No ready made blue print for corporate planning can be handed on a plate to an organization . . .

Fifth, *if the planning process allows for the involvement of lower level managers, this must be genuine involvement.* While very organization has to decide on the appropriate involvement for its own situation, implementation must be more than lip service . . .

Finally, *planning must give attention to objective analysis and human behaviour.* Good planning must be well rooted in objective analysis. But this is only part of the equation. Human organizations are not logical machines, and to be effective plans need more than a sound analytical base. The process must also give weight to human behavioural issues, such as motivation, power structures, fear, creativity, and the like. The way planning is approached for a particular organization must achieve the correct balance between the two. Processes which consist solely of cold analysis will lead to plans that do not get implemented: those which are all participation and no analysis lead to misdirected plans which quite probably will be implemented to the detriment of the organization. (Hussey, 1978, slightly shortened)

Incomplete Understanding of the Concepts by Those Claiming to Apply Them

One of the problems of the period studied is that too many organizations took the job titles and buzz words of a new concept and claimed to be applying it, but carried on in much the same way as before. The new concept was corrupted and not properly applied. Thus we saw that in the 1960s the divisionalization concept used by British companies was not the American concept that they purported to emulate: sales directors became marketing directors through their 1960s, yet we have already seen that as late as 1978, many organizations had not changed from a sales oriented approach; from personal experience I would argue that in many organizations there is little difference even today. We also saw how benchmarking has been confused with ratio comparisons, and how BPR has been attached as a label to all sorts of activities which are not BPR. In much the same way, the title Director of Strategic Management does not necessarily mean that the organization practices strategic management.

Words are not the same as actions and the sort of corporate self delusion that goes on in many organizations, where top managers believe that they are following the latest theories when in fact they are not, is harmful. Using the new jargon is not the same as using the new concept.

Towards the Next Century

Where does all this take us, as we move towards the next century and the challenges that this will bring? It is a realistic assumption that the near future will be at least as turbulent as the near past and may be even more turbulent. Discontinuous change will be the norm. There will be a continuation of the global competitive pressures discussed earlier.

In my analysis I avoided mentioning the major changes within the former communist world, the upheaval that these countries are still facing, and the many trouble spots throughout the world.

Population forecasts as we consider the next century give rise to concern about the way the world is developing. Taylor, 1992, in a study for the US army, suggests that world population will move from 5.384 million in 1991 to 8,647 million by 2025. In 1991, 77% were living in the less developed countries, but this is forecast to reach 83.7% by 2025.

These figures suggest that the early years of the next century will bring many more external issues that will impact on businesses, and that more attention must be paid to the environmental interface than the norm implied by our study of the past.

We have no lack of concepts to draw on in the area of strategy formulation and analysis, and although I am sure that the new century will see the birth of new approaches, as well as the re-invention of many old ones that have been forgotten, I think we have enough to take strategic thinking into the future. But this does not mean that nothing needs to be done, and I see four areas which must be dealt with if organizations are to enjoy success in the future: a focus on implementation, challenging the perceptual boundaries; detailed exploration of the impact of strategies; and applying new concepts properly.

1.   *More attention should be given to implementation* — those making strategy should not assume that complex plans will be implemented successfully: they must ensure that they are implemented.

It is difficult for an organization to learn from its mistakes unless it knows whether a failure is due to a poor strategy, or bad implementation. In reality strategy will be much better if the implementation issues are thought through, as far as is possible, when the decisions are made: it is at this point that some of the big issues will emerge.

This issue is beyond the scope of this book, but interested readers will find an extensive treatment of implementation in a companion volume, Hussey 1996a. A related issue, strategic human resource management, is explored in Hussey 1996b.

2. *Continuous challenging of the perceptual boundaries* — no long lasting vision and supporting strategies can be built on a false premise. Much more emphasis needs to be placed by top management, strategic planners, and those involved in management education on finding ways to challenge the perceptual boundaries. The needs include the following:

- More attention to obtaining and using information about what is going on in the external business environment, in markets and among competitors. It is not that such information is ignored at present, but it is often focused too much on things close to home and does not always take a global approach. It is also difficult for the human mind to cope with too many strands of information, which means that more care must be given to analysis and presentation.
- Analysis must be used to expand the basis of thinking, and not to restrict it. To me, this means using several methods to analyse a situation, each of which may illuminate a different aspect of the situation. In mentioning analysis I am not advocating any particular process of planning, but I believe that wherever a strategic idea comes from, it requires analysis to establish where it fits in the context of the organization's situation and what the implications are likely to be if it is accepted.
- As I stated earlier, I believe that the process of planning that is right for a particular organization is contingent on the situation of that organization: there is no one universal answer, although there are many wrong ones for the particular organization. However, whatever the process it must be strategic, must ensure that strategic considerations cover all aspects of operations and not just marketing and acquisition, and should not become a straitjacket for the organization. Somehow it must free the corporate mind, so that what is believed about the strategic arena is constantly probed and checked. It should challenge prejudice, not reinforce it.
- Strategy should be creative and entrepreneurial, and it should not be forgotten that an individual firm can often change the battleground on which competitive wars are fought. Today's perceptual boundaries may have a close fit with reality, but the firm or its competitors can often change that reality.

3. *The need for detailed exploration of the impact of strategies* — the need for analysis does not end with the strategic decision. It is, of course, commonplace

for organizations to examine the expected financial results of a course of action, using techniques such as discounted cash flow, and this is to be encouraged. However something more needs to be done.

The first requirement is to think through the whole strategy and not just the initial action. Acquisition failure can be because of any one or more of three failures of analysis: a misconceived action, failure to think through and implement the actions that will enable the acquisition to deliver the intended benefits, or over-extension financially, which means that the resources to support the financing of the acquisition are inadequate. It is clearly not possible to identify everything that will arise when a strategic move is started, but it is possible to do much better than many organizations do at present.

Strategy should drive the organization. The research (Kaplan, 1995) mentioned earlier showed that in many organizations this did not happen, and what drove the organization was short term profit issues and an annual budget which was not derived from the strategy. The desirable relationship of strategy to the organizational variables is expressed in Figure 1.1, which is my variant of an approach which has a long pedigree (see, for example, Leavitt, 1964, and the Mckinsey 7S model, described in Peters and Waterman, 1982, page 10).

The model I use (Figure 1.1) shows the strategic change as the driver of the organization, and the results has the desired benefit flowing out of the organization. Eight variables are given for the organization, and the idea is that these should be examined each time there is a change in strategy, since the results, or implementation of the strategy, will be less likely to occur if the machine of the organization is not appropriate for the fuel of the strategy.

I suggest this model as a first step to thinking through every aspect of a strategy, and believe that such an approach would increase the success rate for many organizations. A little thought around Figure 1.1 will lead to the conclusion that many of the issues that need consideration will be in the area of human resource management.

By itself this additional analytical step is not enough. There is a need to make the analysis more dynamic, by thinking through the responses of competitors and others who may influence success, and the counter measures that may result. Van der Heiden, 1996, demonstrates the scenario approach, and of course the concepts of Ansoff, 1990, are also based on a dynamic view of the business environment. What goes on in the market place is not static but much of our analysis is, and one of the best ways to challenge the perceptual boundaries may be to explore the "what if?" questions in greater depth.

4. *Doing Things Properly* — If all organizations used analysis to challenge as well as to explain and explore, and if they gave much more consideration to the implementation aspects of strategy, I have little doubt that many of the strategic failings identified in this chapter, with the advantages of hindsight,

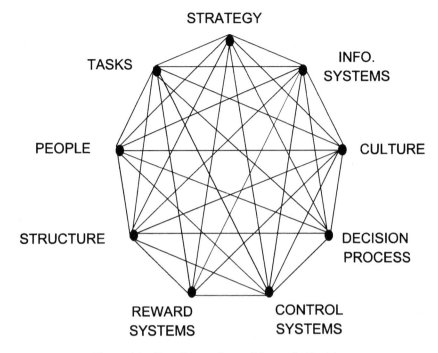

Figure 1.1   Two Dimensions of Strategic Decisions

could have been avoided. It still leaves one other caution, which may be more relevant for those who do not read this book than for those who do.

It is to beware of chasing the rainbows that are the latest fads of analysis, and to apply only those new concepts of management which are appropriate for the organization, and which are properly understood and used. This would banish fashions and fads, and slow down the failure rate of some of the approaches (see, for example, what was said earlier about BPR and TQM). The only problem I have with this essential requirement is that I do not know how to change human nature in order to achieve it!

REFERENCES

Abram Hawkes Plc and Kingston University, 1993, *A report on TQM within the UK's 500 largest companies.*

Ansoff, H. I., 1965, *Corporate Strategy*, McGraw-Hill, New York.

Ansoff, H. I., 1991, Strategic Management in a Historical Perspective, in Hussey, D. E., editor, *International Review of Strategic Management*, Volume 2.1, Wiley, Chichester.

Ansoff, H. I. and McDonnell, E., 1990, *Implanting Strategic Management*, 2nd edition, Prentice Hall, London.

Ansoff, H. I. et al, 1970, Does planning pay? The effect of planning on success of acquisition in American firms, *Long Range Planning*, Vol. 3, No. 2.

Ansoff, H. I. et al, 1993, Empirical Support for a Paradigmic Theory of Strategic Success Behaviours of Environment Serving Organizations, in Hussey, D. E., editor, *International Review of Strategic Management*, volume 4, Wiley, Chichester.

Barham, K. A. and Bassam, C., 1989, *Shaping the Corporate Future*, Unwyn Hyman, London.

Barham, K. A., Fraser, J. and Heath, L., 1988, *Management for the Future*, Ashbridge Management College and the Foundation for Management Development, UK.

Beaver, G., and Jennings, P. L., Midland Bank Plc, *Strategic Change*, Vol. 5, No. 4.

British Institute of Management, 1986, *The management of acquisitions and mergers*, Discussion paper number 8, Economics Department, September.

Buckner, H, 1974, Seeking new sources of earnings, in Hussey, D. E., editor, *The Corporate Planners' Yearbook, 1974–5*, Pergamon, Oxford.

Carlzon, J., 1987, *Moments of Truth*, Ballinger, New York.

Channon, D. F., 1973, *The Strategy and Structure of British Enterprise*, Macmillan, London.

Coopers & Lybrand, 1993, reference unavailable.

Coulson-Thomas, C. J., 1996, Business Process Re-engineering and strategic change, *Strategic Change*, Vol. 5, No. 3.

De Meuse, K., Vanderheiden, P. and Bergamann, T., 1994, Announcing layoffs: their effect on corporate financial performance, *Human Resource Management*, Vol. 33, No. 4.

Gluck, F. W., Kaufman, S. P. and Walleck, A. S., 1980, Strategic Management of Competitive Advantage, *Harvard Business Review*, July/August.

Goold, M. and Campbell, A., 1987, *Strategies and Styles*, Blackwell, Oxford.

Goold, M., Campbell, A. and Alexander, M., 1994, *Corporate Level Strategy*, Wiley, New York.

Grint, K. and Willcocks, L., 1995, Business Process Re-engineering in theory and practice: business paradise regains?, *New Technology, Work and Employment*, Vol. 10, No. 2.

Grinyer, P. H. and Norburn, D., Strategic Planning in 21 UK Companies, *Long Range Planning*, Vol. 7, No. 4.

Hammer, M. and Champney, J., 1993, *Re-engineering the Corporation: A Manifesto for Business Revolution*, Nicholas Brealey, London.

Hayes, R. H., Wheelwright, S. C., and Clark, K. B., 1988, *Dynamic Manufacturing: Creating the Learning Organization*, Free Press, New York.

Herold, D. M., 1972, Long range planning and organizational performance, *Academy of Management Journal*, March.

HMSO, 1980, *Engineering our Future: Report of the Committee of Enquiry into the Engineering Profession*, HMSO, London.

Howard, C., 1996, The stress on managers caused by downsizing, *The Globe and Mail*, January 30.

Hunt, J., 1988, Managing the successful acquisition: A people question, *London Business School Journal*, Summer, 2–15.

Hussey, D. E., 1978, How to plan success, *Management Today*, November.

Hussey, D. E., 1979, The Challenge of Corporate Planning, *Professional Administration*, 9.4 April.

Hussey, D. E., 1984, Strategic management: lessons from success and failure, *Long Range Planning*, Vol. 17, No. 1.

Hussey, D. E., editor, 1996a, *The Implementation Challenge*, Wiley, Chichester.

Hussey, D. E., 1996b, *Business Driven Human Resource Management*, Wiley, Chichester.

Johansson, H. J., McHugh, P., Pendlebury, A. J., and Wheeler, W. A., 1993, *Business Process Re-engineering*, John Wiley, Chichester.

Kaplan, R., 1995, *Building a Management System to Implement Your Strategy: Strategic Management Survey: Summary of Findings and Conclusions*, Renaissance Solutions, London.

Karlöf, B. and Östblom, S., 1993, *Benchmarking*, John Wiley & Sons, Chichester.

Kinnie, N., Hutchinson, S. and Purcell, J., 1996, Report by the University of Bath. The People Management Implications of Leaner Ways of Working, *Issues in People Management* No. 15, Institute of Personnel and Development, London.

Kitching, J., 1967, Why do Mergers Miscarry?, *Harvard Business Review*, November/December.

Kitching, J., 1973, *Acquisitions in Europe*, Business International, Geneva.

Kitching, J., 1974, Winning and Losing with European Acquisitions, *Harvard Business Review*, March/April.

Leavitt, H. J., 1964, Applied Organizational Change in Industry: Structural, Technical and Human Approaches in Cooper, W. W., Leavitt, H. J. and Shelly, M. W., editors, *New Perspectives in Organizational Research*, Wiley, New York. (An abridged version appears in Vroom, V. R., and Deci, E. L., 1970, Management and Motivation, Penguin, London.

Leavitt, H. J., 1978, *Managerial Psychology*, University of Chicago Press, Chicago.

Lindblom, C. E., The science of 'muddling through', *Public Administration Review*, Vol. 19, Spring, pp. 79–88. Reprinted in Ansoff, H. I, editor, 1969, *Business Strategy*, Penguin, London.

Luffman, G. A. and Reed, R., 1984, *The Strategy and Performance of British Industry, 1960–1980*, Macmillan, London.

Malik, Z. A. and Karger, D. W., 1975, Does long range planning improve company performance?, Management Review, September.

Martin, J., 1979, Business planning: the gap between theory and practice, *Long Range Planning*, Vol. 12, No. 6.

Mason, A., 1993, *Management Training in Medium-sized UK Business Organizations*, Harbridge Consulting Group, London.

✦Mintzberg, H., 1994, The Rise and Fall of Strategic Planning, *Harvard Business Review*, Jan–Feb.

Normann, R. et al, 1978, *Utvecklingsstrategier for svenskt servicekunnande*, SIAR, Stockholm.

Norse, D., 1982, The UK and its OECD Competitors, *Long Range Planning*, Vol. 15, No. 5.

Ohmae, K., 1983, *The Mind of the Strategist*, Penguin, London.

Peters, T. J. and Waterman, R. H., *In Search of Excellence*, Harper and Row, New York.

Porter, M. E., 1987, From Competitive Advantage to Corporate Strategy, *Harvard Business Review*, May/June.

Price Waterhouse/Cranfield, 1991, *The Price Waterhouse Project on International Strategic Human Resource Management*, Centre for Human Resource Management, Cranfield University School of Management, Bedford.

Quinn, J. B., 1980, *Strategies for Change*, Irwin, Homewood, Illinois.

Ringbakk, K. A., 1971, Why planning fails, *European Business*, Spring.

✦ Schoeffler, S., Buzzell, R. and Heany, D., 1974, Impact of strategic planning on profit performance, *Harvard Business Review*, 52, 137–145.

Strategic Management, Volume 4, Wiley, Chichester.

Steiner, G. A., 1972, *Pitfalls in Comprehensive Long Range Planning*, Planning Executive's Institute, Oxford, Ohio.

Steiner, G. A. and Schollhammer, H., 1975, Pitfalls in Multinational Long Range Planning, *Long Range Planning*, Vol. 8, No. 2.

Sullivan, P., 1989, *Managing in the 1990s*, unpublished research, Harbridge House Inc, Boston, MA.

Taylor, C. W., 1992, *A World 2010: A New order of Nations*, Strategic Studies Institute, U.S. Army War College, Carlisle Barracks, Pennsylvania.

Tichy, N. M. and Devanna, M. A., 1990, *The Transformational Leader*, reprint of 1986 edition with additional preface, Wiley, New York.

Thune, S. S., and House, R. J., 1970, Where long range planning pays off: findings of a survey of formal and informal planners, *Business Horizons*, August.

Tovey, L., 1991, *Management Training and Development in Large UK Business Organizations*, Harbridge Consulting Group, London.

Vancil, R. F., 1970, The accuracy of long range planning, *Harvard Business Review*, September/October.

Van de Heijden, 1996, *Scenarios: The Art of Strategic Conversation*, Wiley, Chichester.

Warren, E. K., 1966, *Long-Range Planning: The Executive Viewpoint*, Prentice-Hall, Englewood Cliffs.

Wilkinson, A., Allen, S. and Snape, E., 1993, Quality and the manager, *Institute of Management Report*, Institute of Management, London.

Wyatt Company, 1994, *Best Practices in Corporate Re-structuring*, Toronto, Ontario.

2

DEREGULATION AND THE PIED PIPER APPROACH TO DIVERSIFICATION

Emily Boyle

School of Management, University of Ulster at Jordanstown

- Deregulation of the financial services sector over the past quarter of a century has caused radical change in both the structure of the industry and the strategies of its institutions.
- Between 1980 and 1986 the deregulation of the mortgage market intensified the competitive rivalry between different types of financial institutions.
- In response to this, Lloyds Bank took the lead and diversified into estate agency in 1982.
- Between then and now, many other financial institutions, particularly insurance companies and building societies, followed Lloyds example.
- In the 1980s this diversification was further encouraged by the boom in the housing market.
- In 1989 the boom collapsed. Some financial institutions — the Prudential Insurance Co., Abbey National and the Nationwide Building Society pulled out of estate agency altogether. Others reduced the size of the operations.
- Despite this, in 1993 90 per cent of the UK estate agents were still in the hands of financial institutions.

INTRODUCTION

Over the past quarter of a century the increasingly turbulent business environment in the West has stimulated the deregulation of a wide range of

The Strategic Decision Challenge, Edited by D. E. Hussey
© 1998 John Wiley & Sons Ltd

industries. This process has often affected not only the structure but also the very nature of the industries involved. Industries affected by deregulation tend to exhibit a common pattern of development. The stages in this pattern of development are as follows: firstly, prior to deregulation, there is regulated strategic torpor. Then, when deregulation is mooted pre-deregulation jockeying takes place. This is followed by the advent of deregulation, shakeout and finally by relative competitive stability (O'Reilly, 1995, p. 124). During the advent of deregulation stage industries normally experience

> many new entrants, severe competition throughout the industry, strategy variety as players seek distinctive strategies to follow and niches to exploit and severe profit erosion as price becomes the premier axis of rivalry. (O'Reilly, 1995, p. 124)

Sometimes, however, when one firm in the newly deregulated industry adopts a very successful new strategy its example is followed by a swarm of imitators from the industry. These firms expect to gain the same competitive advantages from the move as the strategy's initiator, irrespective of the impact that their adoption of the strategy may have on the situation. Where the strategy adopted is one of diversification it has been termed the Pied Piper approach to diversification. The firm that originally diversifies may be likened to the Pied Piper of Hamlyn, whose strategy is so attractive to its competitors that just like the children in the story they follow it irrespective of its implications and possible consequences.

The mass diversification of UK financial institutions into estate agency after Lloyds Bank entered the industry in 1982 provides a prime example of the phenomenon. In this article both the reasons for the institutions' copying Lloyds Bank and the consequences of the strategy are considered. Particular emphasis is paid to the impact of changing levels of government and industry regulation and deregulation among the various constituents of the financial services industry at the time, especially as they related to the mortgage market.

DIVERSIFICATION AND DEREGULATION

Diversification has long been recognized as one strategy available to managers wishing to elaborate or alter their organization's definition of its core business (Ansoff, 1965, p. 109; Mintzberg, 1991, p. 76). It can be achieved either organically by the firm developing a new activity from scratch, usually based on its own R and D efforts or, more commonly nowadays, through mergers and acquisitions (Mintzberg, 1991, p. 79). A diversification strategy can be either explicit or implicit (Porter, 1980, p. 3). It can also be either deliberate or emergent, developing and altering over time as unanticipated opportunities present themselves to the firm (Mintzberg, 1989, p. 29). Theoretically, the primary reason for a firm adopting any kind of strategy is to gain competitive advantage over its rivals and thus maximize shareholder value. The problem for managers is knowing just what strategy to adopt. Diversification by acquisition offers one option. As Reed and Luffman (1986, p. 30) point out

> The point of adopting a strategy of diversification has always been and always will be, to derive the particular benefits offered by having a broader product-market base.

Generally, the benefits of diversification to the organization are seen as being fourfold — first, that it encourages the efficient allocation of capital; secondly, that it helps to train general managers; thirdly, that it spreads the firm's risks across different markets; and finally, that it makes the whole organization more strategically responsive (Mintzberg, 1991, p. 72). Diversification is obviously a costly business but, Abell and Hammond (1991, p. 656) argue, once a firm has diversified, the greater its involvement in the new activity, the quicker its costs will fall and its benefits will accrue due to the impact of the "experience effect".

Unfortunately, despite these arguments in favour of diversification, evidence suggests that, in the past, diversified firms have performed poorly, particularly if they have moved into unrelated businesses (Porter, 1987, pp. 43–45; Schliefer and Vishny, 1991, pp. 51–57). According to Porter (1987, p. 51) who carried out a long-term study of the diversification strategies of 33 leading US corporations their track record "has been dismal". He therefore suggested that before a firm diversifies it should consider three issues. These are, firstly, the attractiveness, either actual or potential, of the industry into which the firm intends to diversify and secondly, the cost of entry into the industry. If it is too high it may capitalize all future profits from the move. There is a close relationship between these two issues in that the more attractive an industry appears to be the higher the entry barriers into it will be. The third issue to be considered is the extent to which the firm will gain competitive advantage overall from the acquisition.

The extent to which firms consider these issues before acquiring a new business is unknown. Certainly, despite the damning evidence on the effectiveness of diversification through acquisition, many businesses still find it a very attractive proposition, particularly where there is intense competitive rivalry within the industry and there are clear advantages to be gained from having a distinctive strategy. According to Porter (1980, p. 90) the intensity of competitive rivalry within an industry is determined by the number of competitors, the distribution of power among them, the amount of differentiation between their products, the level of their fixed costs and the rate of industry growth.

The level of competitive rivalry in an industry generally intensifies dramatically during the advent of deregulation as it becomes increasingly destabilized with the influx of new firms into it. Thus the formulation and implementation of distinctive strategies is particularly significant for the firms affected at this time. Unfortunately, however, those firms which had previously been members of the industry have no real experience of this process due to the lack of competitive rivalry experienced in industries during the period of "regulated strategic torpor", when entry barriers to the industry are generally prohibitively high and industry stability and cooperation among competitors are the norm (Porter, 1980, p. 90). For these firms copying the successful innovative strategies of their new competitors may make good sense. Mintzberg (1991, p. 76) points out that "there can be a place for copycats" where there is "enough room in a market and a management without the skill or will to differentiate". Again Olins, (1989, p. 134) argues "Peer pressure ... is rarely cited as a basis by which corporate growth is determined. But in real life it often is". He cites (1989, p. 134) the following example:

> A few years ago some of the major British banks raced each other into the US. They were so busy copying each other they didn't notice what they were buying. It wasn't long, just a few years after, that they were racing each other out again, a few billion dollars lighter.

As well as a lack of 'will and skill' to develop their own distinctive strategies firms in newly deregulated industries many adopt a copycat strategy if they see it as a way of retaliating to what they interpret as an aggressive move on the part of the innovating firm. Porter (1950, p. 95) argues that if this retaliation is rapid and effective then the original move "may leave the mover no better off and even worse off".

Diversification through acquisition is one of the most accessible strategies available to firms in newly deregulated industries as it provides the diversifying firm with the opportunity to differentiate itself from the other members of the industry. However, given the nature of newly deregulated industries it is almost inevitable that any successful diversification through acquisition by one player should lead to a swarm of imitators. Perhaps the most surprising aspects of the mass diversification of the UK financial institutions into estate agency during the 1980s were its extent—almost all the major building societies and a large number of insurance companies and banks were involved, on the one hand, and its duration—the institutions' acquisition spree spanned eight years—on the other hand.

THE MORTGAGE MARKET BEFORE DEREGULATION

Prior to 1980 the mortgage market was dominated by building societies whose business accounted for approximately 80% of it. Often these mortgages were linked to endowment policies provided by insurance companies. This proved very lucrative for the insurance companies (Thomson, 1993). In the 20 years preceding 1980 the number of building societies in the UK had declined significantly from more than 700 in 1960 to less than 160 in 1980. At the same time the market share of the top five had steadily increased from 37% of total building society business in 1950 to nearly 60%. (Wright, 1987). The two largest societies were the Halifax with total assets of nearly £25,000 million and the Abbey National, which has subsequently become a bank, with assets of nearly £20,000 million. The next largest society was the Nationwide. Its assets were just over half those of the Abbey National.

Banks were also players in the mortgage market. However, until 1980 their participation was restricted by a number of

> direct controls, the most notable, perhaps, being the 'corset', the supplementary special deposit scheme, which was introduced at various times between 1974 and 1980. (Howcroft and Lavis, 1986, p. 57)

The share of the UK mortgage business in the hands of the banks at this time was approximately 20% (Wright, 1987). Most of this business was in the hands of the four London Clearing Banks. Non-retail banks, such as merchant and investment banks, which do not deal directly with personal business, were generally not involved (Howcroft and Lavis, 1986, p. 13). This situation changed significantly as a result of deregulation.

THE DEREGULATION OF THE MORTGAGE MARKET

The British financial services industry, along with those elsewhere in the Western world, had, since the early 1970s, been coming to terms with the destabilizing impact of the combined forces of "such factors as new technology, international banking, saturated markets and new entrants" on the industry (Taylor, 1989, p. 285). Increasingly, these forces rendered legal and other restrictions relating to the industry irrelevant and precipitated its gradual deregulation. Given the diversity of activities carried out under the umbrella term of "financial services" it was inevitable that different sectors of the industry should go through the stages of the deregulation process at different times as the restrictions pertaining to each were whittled away. By the 1980s the mortgage sector of the industry was ripe for deregulation.

The deregulation of the mortgage market occurred first in the banking sector. In 1980 controls such as the "corset" were finally abandoned. This not only allowed the banks to compete more directly with building societies for mortgage business but also gave them a considerable competitive advantage over building societies because of the other financial services they could offer. In these circumstances non-retail banks, for example, investment and merchant banks, which had previously not lent mortgages, became involved. Overall, the banks' share of the mortgage market rose from 20 to 50% (Thomson, 1993). Where the new entrants into the mortgage market did not deal with personal customers their mortgages were often linked to endowment policies and offered to the public by the insurance companies instead. For example, the Prudential Insurance Co.— Britain's largest insurance company — linked up with Citibank to enter the mortgage market (Roberts, 1986; Thomson, 1993). Under these circumstances building societies came to regard the insurance companies involved as direct competitors in the mortgage market.

Aware of the increasing pressure that they were facing from these new competitors; the Abbey National Building Society withdrew from the Building Societies Association's interest rate fixing cartel in 1983 (Balmer and Wilkinson, 1991, p. 23). This was followed in 1987 by the implementation of the Building Societies Act which introduced "powers for societies to make unsecured loans and to provide a range of financial services as well as services relating to land" (Gartland, 1987). One of the benefits of the Act noted by commentators was the potential it offered larger building societies "for getting into the estate agency business", into which both a number of banks and insurance companies had already diversified (Gartland, 1987).

These deregulating measures allowed the building societies, retail banks and insurance companies (backed by investment and merchant banks) to compete directly with each other in the mortgage market. They therefore needed to pursue differentiation strategies in order to gain competitive advantage. However, the very nature of mortgages and other financial service products causes enormous problems for firms trying to pursue a distinctive strategy. It has been well established that the public find it much more difficult to differentiate between a variety of services than a variety of products (Olins, 1989, p. 34). With financial services the problem is heightened by the ease with which both new services and new pricing strategies can be copied. The Chief Executive of the Halifax Building Society is cited as commenting. "The only lead time with a product is programming time", whilst a manager of the National Westminster Bank argued that it just took 15 minutes to respond to a change in a competitor's prices (cited in Balmer and Wilkinson, 1991, p. 26).

Given the problems of product and price differentiation combined with the fact that the majority of players in the newly deregulated mortgage sector had previously been members of highly regulated industries, it was almost inevitable that many of those involved should concentrate their strategic efforts on copying their competitors' successful moves rather than on seeking new or alternative strategies for themselves.

DIVERSIFICATION BY THE FINANCIAL INSTITUTIONS INTO ESTATE AGENCY

At the beginning of the 1980s estate agency in the UK was a very fragmented industry. Most players "were small businesses with local reputations" (Olins,

1993). Firms required little fixed capital to operate. As one commentator put it "The only requirements (to open an estate agency) are the price of some shopfitting, some advertisements in the local paper, a photocopy machine and a desire to succeed" (Brewerton, 1990). Furthermore, the housing market which had been very buoyant at the end of the 1970s had begun to slow down. Whereas the annual average rise in house prices was 29% in 1979, it fell to 6% in 1980 and 1% in 1981 (*The Times*, 9 January 1980, 5 January 1981 and 2 January 1982). In these circumstances, the industry did not appear particularly attractive. Entry barriers were low and effective retaliation to new participants by existing players was unlikely.

It was against this background that Lloyds Bank decided to diversify into estate agency. Newly liberated from the "corset" it was able to participate more freely in the mortgage market than previously. In its efforts to extend its range of facilities it embarked upon a strategy of offering "womb to tomb" financial services to the public. The ability to capture a share of the mortgage market was pivotal to this strategy. It believed that if it owned a country-wide chain of estate agents it could sell not only its mortgages but also its other financial services to home buyers through its agency branches (Philips, 1982).

Thus, early in May 1982 it acquired the Norfolk-based estate agency, Charles Hawkins and Son. A fortnight later it took over Geering and Collier, an estate agency operating in the Kent and Sussex region. These two acquisitions gave the bank control over 16 estate agents' offices. The bank renamed the estate agencies the Black Horse Estate Agencies to identify them with its logo (Philips, 1982). Commentators applauded the move by Lloyds as making "sound commercial sense" as it gave the bank "an excellent market place for its mortgage schemes". (Philips, 1982) Because of the fragmented nature of the industry its participants were not in a position to offer any effective retaliation. However, one representative of the industry expressed concern that "if other banks join in the race to buy up estate agents around the country' the estate agents" code of conduct "could be thrown out of the window". (Cited in Philips, 1982)

Lloyds might have expected retaliation from other financial institutions. However, initially they preferred to wait and see. It was not until 1985, by which time the housing market was recovering dramatically and the verdict on Lloyds strategy was that it was 'both logical and pragmatic with the result that it has proved profitable and entirely satisfactory' (Howcroft and Lavis, 1986, p. 164) that other firms involved in selling mortgages followed it into estate agency. In that year, the Prudential Insurance Co., Royal Assurance Co. and Hambros, the merchant bank and parent of the insurance firm, Allied Dunbar, all began buying up estate agency chains with a vengeance.

However, these companies were only partially motivated by the success of Lloyds Bank. They were also motivated by the imminent introduction of the Financial Services Act of 1986 which would oblige them to sell their products through either tied agents or independent brokers. They felt that estate agents could easily be "converted into instant chains of tied agents". (Thomson 1993) The newly acquired estate agencies were renamed Prudential Property Services, Royal Life and Hambro Countrywide, respectively. By August 1986 Hambro Countrywide had become the largest chain in Britain with 385 branches. In that year General Accident Insurance Co. also joined the fray (Olins, 1993).

However, it was the implementation of the Building Societies' Act in January 1987 that turned the trickle of Lloyds Bank imitators into a swarm. Building societies, which had previously been legally prevented from diversifying and had no experience of real strategic rivalry, felt particularly threatened by the developments. Since the withdrawal of the "corset" the building societies' share of the UK mortgage market had fallen significantly. John Spalding of the Halifax Building Society argued that with the other financial institutions running estate agencies there was

> a very real danger that societies could be pushed away from the customer. His first port of call in the house buying process is the estate agent and we could find our mortgage business going elsewhere. (Cited in Wright, 1987)

The situation was exacerbated for them by the continuing boom in house sales. Since 1982 house prices had risen by approximately 10% per annum. The large building societies therefore retaliated to the banks and insurance companies' moves by following their example. Both the Nationwide and the Halifax moved into estate agency almost immediately.

Meanwhile, the buoyancy of the housing market encouraged those financial institutions already in estate agency to expand their operations. By the end of 1987 Royal Life controlled 639 offices and had overtaken Hambro Country-wide as Britain's leading estate agency. Prudential Property Services and Hambro Countrywide had 618 and 465 offices, respectively, whilst BHA controlled 450 branches, Nationwide 435, General Accident 421 and the Halifax 271 (Eadie, 1987). Further acquisitions by Prudential Property Services three months later caused it to leapfrog over Royal Life to become the largest estate agency business in the country with 651 offices (CW, 1988). A year later it still held this position and had increased its number of offices to 805 (Park, 1989)

More and more financial services firms diversified into estate agency, building up increasingly widespread networks. In 1987 it was reported,

> Hardly a week goes by without one of the new nation-wide estate agency networks announcing it has scooped up yet another small local firm in some part of the British Isles. (Eadie, 1987)

As one commentator put it, "Hardly any insurer or building society could bear to stand on the sidelines". (Olins, 1993.) Even those financial institutions which were initially sceptical about the strategy found themselves being sucked into it. For example, in January 1987 a representative of the Abbey National had argued that the whole thing was nothing more than a fashion, that there was no "return in it" and that there were "some bad colds to be caught there", and yet by the end of that year it had established its Cornerstone chain (Wright, 1987). Later, Charles Toner, managing director of new business at Abbey National, admitted, "Frankly we went into it because others were doing it". (Thomson, 1993).

Most of the financial institutions simply bought up existing independent estate agencies, making the industry appear increasingly attractive and pushing up the entry barriers to the business. One ex-estate agent claimed that he was "approached by six major players". He eventually sold the firm to Prudential Property Services for £24 million (Thomson, 1993). Prices spiralled upwards, far outpacing the true value of the actual businesses involved. In one instance the seller estimated he had been paid 12 times as much as the business was really worth. In 1987 and 1988 financial institutions were paying up to £400,000 per office. Late in 1988 the Royal Insurance Co. bought the 250 branch William H. Brown chain, which was making annual profits of £6 million, for £90 million (Thomson, 1993). A number of the financial institutions further increased the cost of diversification by refurbishing all the newly acquired branches and introducing computer systems to them. Prudential Property Services was known to have spent up to £60,000 per branch on refurbishment alone (Thomson, 1993).

Some financial institutions, including the Woolwich Building Society, realized the folly of this approach and either set up their own estate agency businesses from scratch, or stayed on the sidelines till demand abated. (Olins, 1993). For example, Legal and General 'decided not to go in until prices fell' in 1989 and Scottish Widows only became involved in 1990 (Olins, 1993; Bond, 1991).

THE COLLAPSE OF THE HOUSING MARKET

During the 1980s the majority of financial institutions were willing to absorb the soaring costs of diversification in the belief that they would be recouped through the operation of the experience effect. Such a strategy was feasible so long as the housing market remained buoyant. However, in 1989 it collapsed. The number of home purchases fell from 2.1 million a year in 1988 to 1.5 million in 1989. Average house prices fell by nearly 1%. The estate agency businesses of the financial institutions faced "multi million pound losses". (Smith and Park, 1989) A number of them, including the Nationwide Anglia and Leeds Permanent Building Societies, began to cut back on their estate agency operations. Prudential Property Services closed 120 branches and shed 1000 jobs.

In the following year with the continued collapse in the housing market the Prudential decided to pull out of the business completely and began to divest almost immediately. The chain was sold in four lots, the final sale being made in May 1991. Over the six years between 1985 and 1991 the Prudential had spent £330 million buying up estate agencies (Thomson, 1993; Miller, 1994). The sale of its whole chain realized only £30 million (Olins, 1993). However, two of the lots were bought up by other financial institutions. The Woolwich purchased one consisting of 191 branches, and Connell, the estate agency subsidiary of Scottish Widows acquired the other consisting of 99 branches. (Bennett, 1991; Bond, 1991). Thus, in early 1993 Britain's "top nine estate agency chains" were still owned by insurance companies, banks and building societies (Olins, 1993). However, some, including the Cheltenham and Gloucester and the Bristol and West building societies and General Accident Insurance Company, were cutting back their activity drastically (Tehan, 1993). In March of that year the Abbey National decided to sell its Cornerstone chain of estate agents. It was sold in August for a mere £8 million. Between 1987 and 1993 the Abbey National had accumulated losses of £240 million on the business (Thomson, 1993). By the time the Abbey National had managed to dispose of its Cornerstone chain other financial institutions, including the TSB, Cheltenham and Gloucester, Northern Rock and Bristol and West building societies, had also intimated their intention of complete withdrawal from estate agency (Miller, 1993). The housing market continued to be sluggish in 1994 and in October the Nationwide Building Society sold its entire estate agency chain for a single pound to Hambro Countrywide (Miller, 1994).

Despite these failures the estate agency business in the UK continues to be dominated by subsidiaries of the financial institutions. Hambro Countrywide, the subsidiary of Hambros merchant bank, is the largest chain, controlling about 6% of the UK market. In the ten-year period between when it entered the market and August 1995 it amassed trading losses of almost £100 million. In the half year up to August 1995 it sold 18,000 houses fewer than in the same period of the previous year. Its pre-tax losses for the six-month period were £5.82 million (Tempus, 1995). It and the other financial institutions still involved in the estate agency business claim that they remain fully committed to it. However, the champion of the estate agency business at Hambros bank since its original diversification is no longer directly involved in the bank's management (Tehan, 1995). Thus, it may well be that rather than the financial institutions being committed to their estate agencies the exit barriers from the business are just too high at present to contemplate the move.

CONCLUSION

The mass diversification of the UK financial institutions with Lloyds Bank acting as the Pied Piper was the industry's response to the staggered deregulation of the mortgage sector. The early deregulation of the banks provided Lloyds with the opportunity to take the initiative and to diversify into estate agency in an attempt to set up a chain of 'womb to tomb' one stop financial services shops throughout the country. It also provided insurance companies with the opportunity to become more actively involved in the mortgage market using funds provided by non-retail banks. This direct involvement in offering mortgages to the public coupled with the need to implement the impending Financial Services Act prompted a number of foresighted insurances companies to follow Lloyds example and move into estate agency. The building societies, whose activities were still circumscribed by government restrictions and whose share of the mortgage market had been significantly eroded by the deregulation of the banks were only awaiting their chance to retaliate in kind when the deregulating Building Societies Act became operational. Furthermore, the continuing buoyancy of the housing market on the one hand, and the need to accrue the benefits of the "experience effect" on the other hand encouraged those financial institutions which had entered estate agency to buy up and to set up more and more estate agents offices throughout the country. The prices at which estate agency businesses changed hands soared, pushing up the entry barriers to the industry. Inevitably, there came a time when the demand for housing began to fall. Suddenly, there was a surplus of estate agencies. Their value began to fall rapidly. A few of the financial institutions were able to divest of their chains before too much damage was done. However, the increasing deterioration of the housing market pushed up the exit barriers for those financial institutions remaining in the industry making withdrawal virtually impossible. Thus, for many of the financial institutions which rushed headlong after their competitors into estate agency in the late 1980s the businesses they bought are now nothing but very heavy millstones round their necks.

Despite this, the notion of one-stop shopping for financial service products which first motivated Lloyds Bank to move into estate agency has resurfaced with the acquisition of the life insurer Clerical Medical by the Halifax, which has itself subsequently become a bank. However, the mortgage market is no longer seen as a major vehicle for this one-stop shopping. As one industry member said "mortgages are now a dog eat dog market. The demand has shrunk and the capacity has grown." (Lynn, 1996) In the future it is believed that one-stop financial services shopping will be driven by the sale of "savings rather than debt products". Nevertheless, it remains to be seen whether other banks and building societies will follow the Halifax into life insurance in the 1990s in the way that they followed Lloyds Bank into estate agency in the 1980s. Perhaps they will be more circumspect this time round.

REFERENCES

Abell, D. F. and Hammond, J. S. (1991). Cost dynamics: scale and experience effects. In: Henry Mintzberg and James Brian Quinn (eds), *The Strategy Process*, 2nd ed., Englewood Cliffs, Prentice Hall, pp. 643–656.

Ansoff, H. I. (1965). *Corporate Strategy: An analytic approach to Business Policy for Growth and Expansion*, McGraw Hill, New York.

Balmer, J. M. T. and Wilkinson, A. (1991). Building Societies: Change, Strategy and Corporate Identity, *Journal of General Management*, **17**,(2), pp. 20–33.

Bennett, N. (1991). Pru sells estate agents, *The Times*, 24 January.

Bond, M. (1991). Pru sells estate agencies for £4.5 m, *The Times*, 15 February.

Brewerton, David (1990). Prudential shuts the stable door, *The Times*, 1 July.

CW, (1988). New Respectability cuts no ice, *The Times*, 2 March.

Eadie, A. (1987). What Home Movers can expect from the new professionals, *The Times*, 19 December.

Gartland, P. (1987). New Freedom for Building Societies, *The Times*, 1 January.

Howcroft, J. J. and Lavis, J. (1986). *Retail Banking: The New Revolution in Structure and Strategy*, Oxford, Basil Blackwell

Lynn, M. (1996). Welcome to the one stop shop, *The Sunday Times*, 31 March.

Miller, R. (1993). Kicking a costly habit, *Observer*, 22 August.

Miller, R. (1994). Big players continue to bale out of Britain's estate agency market, *The Times*, 12 October.

Mintzberg, H. (1989). *Mintzberg on Management*, London, Free Press.

Mintzberg, H. (1991). Generic strategies. In: Henry Mintzberg and James Brian Quinn (eds) *The Strategy Process*, 2nd ed. pp. 70–81, Prentice Hall, Englewood Cliffs.

Olins, Rufus, (1993). Estate agency story has no Abbey ending, *Sunday Times*, 7 March.

Olins, Wally, (1989). *Corporate Identity*, London, Thames and Hudson.

O'Reilly, D. (1995). Classical competitive strategy in newly deregulated industries— Does it apply? In: D. E. Hussey (ed.), *Rethinking Strategic Management*, Chichester, Wiley, pp. 123–145.

Park, M. (1989). Estate agents fear shake out, *The Sunday Times*, 29 January.

Philips, B. (1982). Blackhorse leads: more will follow, *The Times*, 2 June.

Porter, M. E. (1980). *Competitive Strategy: Techniques for analysing Industries and competitors*, New York, Free Press.

Porter, M. E. (1987). From competitive advantage to corporate strategy, *Harvard Business Review*, May–June, pp. 43–59.

Reed, R. and Luffman, G. A. (1986). Diversification: the growing confusion, *Strategic Management Journal*, 7, pp. 29–35.

Roberts, J. (1986). On the trail of the yuppies, *The Times*, 15 November.

Schliefer A. and Vishny, R. W. (1991). Take-overs in the 60s and 80s: evidence and implications, *Strategic Management Journal*, Special Winter Supplement.

Smith, D. and Park, M. (1989). Financial institutions sell estate agencies, *The Sunday Times*, 19 November

Taylor, Glen (1989). The changing structure of financial services. In: Morgan, G. (ed.), *Creative Organization Theory*, Sage, Newbury Park, pp. 285–289.

Tehan, Patricia, (1993). Abbey National's estate agency division up for sale, *The Times*, 3 March.

Tehan, P. (1995). Hambros returns to merchant banking, *The Times*, 16 November.

Tempus, (1995). Haunted Housing, *The Times*, 23 August.

Thomson, R. (1993). The lenders fold their cards, *Independent on Sunday*, 22 August.

Wright, D. (1987). Societies build up to the brave new world, *The Sunday Times*, 4 January.

3

COMPETITIVE STRATEGIES THROUGH SUN TZE'S *ART OF WARFARE*

Samuel K. Ho

Luton Business School, University of Luton

- This chapter: explores the extent to which the Sun Tze's *Art of Warfare*, a set of 2300-year-old Chinese military strategies, is analogous to some contemporary business strategies on competition;
- identifies that there are few comprehensive guidelines for management to apply the ideas in competitive strategy, particularly in the Western world;
- uses a systematic approach to develop a model through Sun Tze's *Art of Warfare* for businesses to achieve success against competition;
- develops a winning model which provides a structured framework for the successful deployment of Sun Tze's idea in businesses;
- uses some mini-cases to illustrate applications of the model and a hypothetical case entering into a new market to demonstrate how to formulate winning strategies step-by-step by using the model.

INTRODUCTION

Sun Tze was a great military leader and warfare genius in China. He was born during the Warring States period (473–211BC). Different State Commanders (seven of them in total) were battling among themselves for the kingship of China. Sun Tze wrote an extraordinary military treatise, *The Art of Warfare*, which consisted of 13 chapters and used only 5600 words to exhibit the secrets of success on the battlefield (Table 3.1). His book was widely used in China by

The Strategic Decision Challenge, Edited by D. E. Hussey
© 1998 John Wiley & Sons Ltd

strategists and emperors ever since and numerous warfare successes have been achieved by those who followed his strategies.

CONTEMPORARY LITERATURE ON SUN TZE

The literature available on Sun Tze's teaching is still very limited. Various piecemeal examples have been used to illustrate the potential of *Art of Warfare* in business. Broadly speaking, the existing literature can be classified into three main categories.

Direct translation

Those researchers who directly translate the 13 chapters of Sun Tze from Chinese to English. Some of them are in cartoon form and others are in simple English (Lip, 1989; Chung, 1991). They are easy to understand but lack the full exploration of the spirit of the *Art of Warfare* on business applications.

Interpretation with examples

Most of this literature has reorganized the 13 chapters under different headings which include strategic management, human resources management, finance management and information management (Cheung, 1990). Some of them are divided into different processes such as decision-making process, production management process and sales process (Lee *et al.*, 1995). Chow (1994) has elaborated on Sun Tze's underlying use of military concepts and strategies — the

Table 3.1 Sun Tze's 13 Chapters of the *Art of Warfare*

Chapter	Title
I	Laying a Plan
II	Waging a War
III	Offensive Strategy
IV	Power of Defence
V	Energy
VI	Opportunism
VII	Manoeuvring
VIII	The Tactical Variation
IX	Marches
X	Terrain
XI	The Nine Situation
XII	Attack by Fire
XIII	Use of Spies

Table 3.2   Similarities Between Hugh Davidson and Sun Tze's Ideas

Hugh Davidson — Offensive Marketing (POISE)	Sun Tze — *Art of Warfare*
*P*rofitable • proper balance between firm's needs for profit and consumer's needs for value	Offensive strategy • aim of warfare is not only for winning, but also for profit
*O*ffensive • must lead the market and make competitors followers	Opportunism • those who arrive early at the battlefield will be in a position to take the initiative
*I*ntegrated • marketing approach must permeate whole company	Power of defence/energy • strengthen the internal structure to defend oneself • all troops must cooperate to achieve better results
*S*trategic • probing analysis leading to a winning strategy	Laying plan • thorough analysis of environment and competitors before laying plan
*E*ffectively executed • strong and disciplined executed on a daily basis	Waging war • act quickly once decided to wage war

need to focus on the heart, and not on the mind of management. He pointed out that in war, the general cannot rely on material benefits to motivate his troops. Instead, he has to appeal to their sense of national pride and loyalty. He exemplified this point by generalizing that Japanese and many Asian companies tend to focus more on managing the hearts of their employees. In contrast, Western companies, largely due to their cultural influences, tend to focus more on managing the minds by offering higher salaries and perks. However, most of the literature still remains at an early stage of development and further validations are required.

Management tools developed through Sun Tze's ideas

These are practical and ideal packages for management to employ since they are normally developed into models or frameworks that provide step-by-step procedures for achieving success in business. This approach takes into account the parallels and similarities that exist between the *Art of Warfare* and business practices (Yuan, 1991). Unfortunately, literature in this category is extremely limited and usually not tested with Western business practices. This presents barriers for Western management to effectively implement such methods.

Table 3.3   Differences Between *Art of Warfare* and Western Business Strategies

	Art of Warfare	Western business strategic theories
Contents	*Wider:* not only cover strategy and management, but also human resources, leaderships, finance, etc.	*Focused:* mainly on strategy and management
Description	*Specific:* details in both strategy and tactics, suggested to leaders what they should do when facing certain situations and environment	*General:* details in strategy only, provide a framework for management but not the skills
Focused	*Competitors:* As warfare is all about winning strategy, no consumers are involved	*Consumers:* play an important part as they buy the products. Also easier to manage and obtain information from them compared to competitors
Decision making	*Generalship:* General is the heart of command, so rely very much on his ability	*Top management with consultation:* involve more staff at junior level, good communication structure required

Similarities and Differences with Western Business Strategies

Hugh Davidson (1987), in his book on offensive marketing mentioned that adopting offensive marketing, can make the switch from losing to winning. He used POISE (*P*rofitable, *O*ffensive, *I*ntegrated, *S*trategy and *E*ffectively Executed) to elaborate the elements for carrying out offensive marketing which has found many similarities to Sun Tze's *Art of Warfare*. Their similarities are summarized in Table 3.2.

Since Sun Tze's *Art of Warfare* is a treatise originally designed for warfare strategies, it obviously has some distinctions when compared with current Western business strategic theories. The major differences are briefed in Table 3.3.

"WINNING MODEL" TO ACHIEVE BUSINESS SUCCESS

In order to provide effective guidelines on the deployment of Sun Tze's *Art of Warfare* in business, a framework called the "winning model" is proposed in Figure 3.1, with the details explained as follows.

Aim and Structure of the Model

The aim of the model (winning model) is to describe a winning business strategy against competitors, in a step-by-step procedure, based on Sun Tze's philosophy. The model is divided into two parts. The first part is the "outer ring" which is meant to be functional and directly linked to day-to-day operations. The second part is the "inside chain" which is more specific for formulating a particular winning strategy, for instance, entering into a new market.

Winning Model — Outer Ring

Analyses of situations

Analyses of the external and internal environments are always essential steps before laying down a detailed plan since better decisions may be achieved through a thorough understanding of the situation. This is of great importance in the modern business environment — in order to gain success it is vital to do the right thing the first time. Thus, reliable and detailed market knowledge is essential. Sun Tze proposed the same ideas. In *The Art of Warfare*, chapter III, he mentioned the importance of understanding the environment, the enemy and oneself, as a key to winning a battle. He stated:

> The one who has a thorough knowledge of himself and the enemy is bound to win in all battles. The one who knows himself but not the enemy has only an even chance of winning. The one who knows not himself nor the enemy is bound to perish in all battles.

In other words, the more analyses that have been carried out, the better the chances of winning. In respect of knowledge of the external business environment (which is akin to climate and terrain), Sun Tze said in chapter X that:

> Know your enemy and yourself, your victory will not be threatened; know the climate and terrain, your victory will be assured.

Thus the initial step towards success is to be clear-minded and gain a thorough understanding of the current and future business environment. The purpose of doing this is to compare the strengths and weaknesses between oneself and the

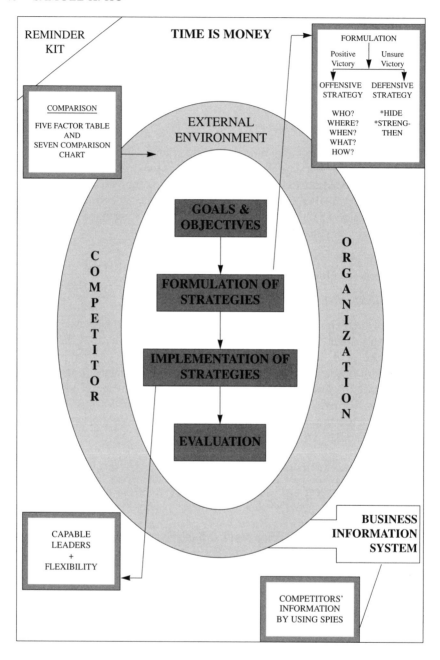

Figure 3.1 'Winning Model' — Achieve Business Success Through Sun Tze's *Art of Warfare*

Table 3.4 'Five Factors' Table—Five Areas to be Considered

Five factors	Areas to be considered	
	In war	In business
Morality	• Moral of the ruler	• Moral of the key management • Social responsibility of the organization
Climate	• Climate nature	• Business climate, e.g. recession
Terrain	• Terrain of battlefield	• Industrial environment, e.g. competitiveness
Generalship	• Ability of generals	• Quality of staff and management
Doctrine	• Discipline of the troops • Execution of laws and instruction	• Government regulations and organization discipline

enemy and calculate the chances of winning so as to make a decision of whether or not to proceed with combat.

Comparison checklist

Unlike the Political, Environmental, Social and Technological (PEST) and strengths, weaknesses, opportunities, and threats (SWOT) analyses, Sun Tze provided a more detailed checklist on what should be considered before making an important decision. In chapter IV of his book, he used "Five Factors" (Table 3.4) and "Seven Dimensions" (Table 3.5) to further elaborate upon what can lead to a victory. In business, these five factors and seven dimensions can be considered to be a checklist and evaluation tool for reference by management before making a decision.

The questions posed by the Seven Dimensions may be modified to fit the nature and needs of the organization. They are only listed as a guideline to explain further the meanings of the dimensions. The Seven Dimensions are not necessarily weighted equally—they can be allocated "weight factors", depending on the needs of the organization. After allocating a mark for each dimension (maximum 100%—note only one score is required although some of them have posed two questions), the overall percentage is:

$$\frac{\text{Total score}}{700} \times 100\%$$

According to Sun Tze, if the total score is over 60%, planning of warfare should be continued because the internal resources and external environment

Table 3.5 "Seven Dimensions" Chart[1]

Seven dimensions	Weigh factor (WF)[2]	In war[3]	In business	Score max. 100%	Total (WF × score)
Moral influence of ruler		• Is the type of leadership morally accepta- ble (in order to gain support from troops)	• Is the organiza- tion socially responsible? • Are the staff commited to the organization?		
Ability of generalship		• Which general is the most capable?	• Are there any suitable managerial staff in charge of the project?		
Advantage of climate and terrain		• Who has the advantages of climate? • Who is able to obtain better terrain?	• Is the current economic environment of benefit to the project?[4] • Who has better informed industrial terrain?[4]		
Execution of law and instruction		• Who has effective execution of laws and instruction?	• Are current government regulations favourable? • Which organiza- tion has better discipline?		
Size and number of men		• Which troops have the greater number of soldiers?	• Which organiza- tion is the largest?[5] • Who has better human resources?		
Training		• Which army is better trained?	• Who has better trained staff and quality management?		
Reward and punishment		• Which army has given reward and punishment properly?	• Who has the better policy towards motivation of staff?		

Total score = >

[1]Overall % = (Total score/700) × 100%.
[2]This column should be used when necessary.
[3]This column should be omitted when this chart is used for business purposes.
[4]Based on Michael Porter's Five Forces, the competitiveness of the industry is decided on the barrier of entry and exit, power of suppliers and buyers. Industrial terrain refers to how well these factors are developed.
[5]Usually, a large firm has better human and financial resources. Comparing its resources with competitors, a higher mark should be given if the firm has more and better resources.

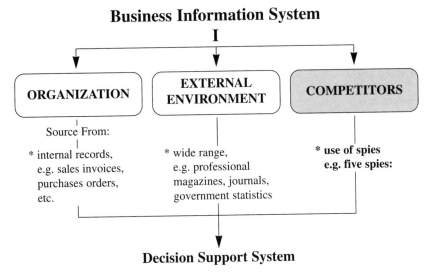

Figure 3.2   Business Information System

are more favourable than for competitors. Therefore, the higher the score, the greater the chance of winning.

Business information system

In order to obtain quality information to make decision and comparisons, a well organized and managed business information system is required. Currently, an increasing number of organizations are setting up "marketing information systems" or "consumers and competitors databases" which perform functions similar to a business information system.

In general, three types of information can be classified within the business information system. They are the "organization', "external environment" and "competitors" (Figure 3.2).

The most useful and influential information is usually the most difficult to obtain. In chapter XIII of the *Art of Warfare* Sun Tze suggested the use of spies to gather top secret information from competitors (Table 3.6). This can be of great value in determining the relevant strengths and weaknesses of an enemy or competitor. However, it also involves controversial ethical issues. Therefore, it is up to the organization itself to decide whether or not it should engage in this activity.

Table 3.7 gives an example to show the relative importance of information obtained from the three main sources of the outer ring of the winning model. As an illustrative example, achieving success in the record industry is explored.

Table 3.6   Sun Tze's Five Types of Spies[1]

(1) Local spies	Live in the opposing nation
(2) Insider spies	Officials in the enemy's courts and palaces
(3) Converted spies	Enemy intelligence whom you have bought over
(4) Deadly spies	Supply the enemy with false information or risk losing their lives working in the opposing nation
(5) Secure spies	Can return safely to make reports after a successful spying mission abroad

[1]Source: Sun Tze's *Art of Warfare*, chapter XIII.

Reminder kit

The reminder kit is a reminder for management to speed up the decision making and planning processes which are normally expensive human and financial resources and could delay the implementation of a project. Delaying the commencement of a project might affect the likelihood of success of the selected strategies because the environment and situations might have already changed due to the time gap between planning and execution. This was inherited from the idea in chapter II of Sun Tze's book:

> If war is prolonged or delayed, the army's vigour and morale will be dampened. A long battle will also deplete the country's reserves.

Winning Model — Inside Chain

Once it has been decided to enter into competition, a move should be quickly made towards the centre part of the model — formulating the winning strategy. Since Sun Tze did not mention the sequences of formulating strategy, the inside chain is adopted from the Western strategy formulation framework instead.

Goal and objectives

Sun Tze said that the aim of battle was not just for winning but also for profit. The goal of running a business is somewhat parallel to warfare because the objectives of a project or programme are usually related to a profit increase. Also clear and well-defined goals and objectives can not only ensure that all staff have a common understanding, but also provide a guideline for evaluation at the final stage of the model.

Formulation of strategies

Sun Tze stated in chapter III of the *Art of Warfare* that the best strategy is to win without fighting. Thus, during the formulation of strategies (Figure 3.3), it

Table 3.7 Relative Influence of Information for Achieving Success in the Record Industry

	Influence[1] of information obtained from		
Critical success factors	External environment	Competitors	Organization itself
To be able to identify and foresee technological developments such as digital compact cassette (DCC), mini-disc etc.	✓✓✓✓	✓✓✓	✓✓
To be able to identify, nurture and promote a wide range of 'new talent' which includes artists, songwriters, singers and composers	✓✓✓	✓	✓✓
To be able to strengthen their position in the established markets	✓✓✓	✓✓✓	✓✓✓
To be able to maintain a good relationship with the influential mass media organizations such as TV broadcasts, radio stations etc.	✓✓	✓	✓✓
To acquire extensive and cost-effective distribution channels	✓✓	✓	✓✓
To be able to identify future trends and preferences in the music industry	✓✓✓✓	✓✓	✓✓
To have a cost-conscious management to balance out the success and failure of artists			✓✓✓
To be able to identify the potential for a new global market	✓✓✓✓	✓	✓✓✓
To secure profit from copyrights	✓✓		✓

[1]Scale of influence: ✓ = unimportant; ✓✓✓✓ = important.

should be borne in mind that a surprise attack on the competitor's plan may yield precious results. For example, consider the bucket-flight shop selling cheap flight-only tickets within Europe: it is better to offer package holidays (flight plus accommodation) which would be of benefit to the consumer rather

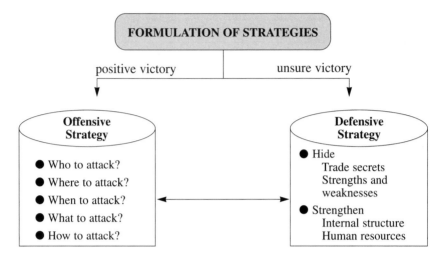

Figure 3.3   Tool for formulation of strategies

than offering simply the same product at a slightly discounted price. This would also represent an attack on the competitor's strategy.

Offensive Strategy

- What to attack?

According to Sun Tze, concentration of effort to attack the weaknesses of competitors is often the most effective strategy. He also emphasized the importance of confusing the enemy because this not only acts as a defensive strategy, but could also divert their efforts on defending themselves elsewhere.

Case example.   A decade ago, Coca Cola identified the weaknesses of other soft drinks manufacturers in that their competitor's products did not cater for people who were on a diet or those who wanted to reduce their calorie intake because of health reasons. They then introduced a product—Diet Coca Cola—which combated against the weaknesses of existing products from other manufacturers. However, consumers generally found that the overall taste of the new product was slightly lacking when compared to the original Coca Cola. This therefore represented a weakness in the marketing of Coca Cola. Ten years later, Pepsi Cola (Coca Cola's main competitor) also employed similar tactics and introduced Pepsi Max which is totally sugar-free and claims to have the original taste of cola.

- Where to attack?

In war, the battleground and the environment could affect the choice of strategies. Those who arrive earlier in the battleground not only can have a better understanding of the environment, but also can occupy the best position in preparing to challenge their enemies. Therefore, in a similar vain, organizations should enter a new market or new market segment before their competitors, so that their position can be secured and a substantial market share obtained. Innovation is one of the essential elements to lead competitors.

Case example. Gillette UK Ltd is a company that traditionally produced shavers for men. Recently, they entered a new market segment — women. Sales of women's shavers are tremendous so the company gained considerable reward while they were monopolizing the market. Inevitably, other companies started to enter this new market but Gillette remained market leaders and, with their experience and benefit of low cost of production together with their favourable household name recognized by consumers, continued to make profit.

- When to attack?

The best time to attack competitors is when they have lost their direction and when they are hesitant as to the correct response to the market. Fighting at the right time is the key otherwise the whole plan will go to ruin. Organizations should have a good sense of timing on launching different products to fit into the trends of the target market.

Case example. In summer 1995, McDonald's Restaurant promoted their "Batman Menu" to run alongside the screening of the film *Batman Returns*. The film was targeted principally at young people — also the major target segment of McDonald's. McDonald's created this new menu which directly matched the trend of the market. Obviously, it was a short-term exploitation of the market segment whilst this particular fashion was in vogue.

- Who to attack?

The *Art of Warfare* never specifically mentioned the best target to attack. However, throughout the treatise, Sun Tze highlighted the advantages of having the greatest possible manpower since it can represent strength and a greater chance of winning. The power of an army is akin to the size and resources of an organization: if the strength of an organization is greater than their competitors, a challenge for market share should be a relatively easy affair. To attack competitors, choose those who have the least power or influence if the organization's existing resources and power cannot compete with the market leader.

● How to attack?

According to Sun Tze, the strategy on how to attack competitors depends on the size and power of the army. In business, competition with others should be undertaken only when there are sufficient human and finance resources. If resources and power are fewer than competitors', tactics should be used that exploit the weaknesses of the opposition. Sun Tze (chapter I) listed some tactics for use in war which could be applied into business, they are as follows:

1. to avoid an open clash if the opposing force is united or strong;
2. to stir up the emotions of the opposing force so that an attack can be staged when it is emotionally unstable;
3. to exhaust the enemies;
4. to create distrust among the leaders, officers and soldiers of the opposing camp;
5. to wait for the moment when the enemies are not prepared and then attack.

Defensive Strategy

Defensive strategy is used when the enemy is stronger and the organization is not ready or prepared to go to war. It would also be used as a defensive measure whilst launching the offensive strategy. Strictly speaking, a defensive strategy should be in use at all times.

● Hide

—   Hide the strengths and weaknesses of the organization. This can avoid competitors gaining an understanding of the weakest part of the organization.
—   Hide trade secrets and important information concerning the organization and its business.

● Strengthen

—   The organizational internal structure needs to be strengthened in order to increase the commitment and morale of employees.
—   Strengthening human resources means having better training for employees and recruiting quality management to improve the human aspect of the organization because Sun Tze emphasized throughout the treatise that a capable general is the fundamental element in winning the battle.

Table 3.8 compares EMI Music strategies with the winning model. It can be seen that EMI Music adopted both types of strategies, offensive and defensive, to launch an attack against competitors and also continuously strengthened their current position in the marketplace (Thorn EMI, 1994).

Implementation of strategy

According to Sun Tze, capable leaders and flexibility are the two basic requirements for implementing strategy. A general is the heart of the troops. Just like the management of a business, they are directing and controlling the development of the whole organization. Therefore, having capable managers and quality staff represents a definite advantage for the success of a business.

Flexibility means to be able to adapt to the changing situations by using tactics because competitors might respond differently resulting in an unpredictable situation. In chapter V, Sun Tze used water to describe the flexibility of implementing strategies:

> Just as water shapes itself according to the ground, an army should manage its victory in accordance with the situation of the enemy. Just as water has no constant shape, so in warfare there are no fixed rules and regulations.

Evaluation

Although there is no mention in Sun Tze's *Art of Warfare*, evaluation is an essential and important part of the strategic formulation process. The information gathered is valuable for formulating further strategies in the future and reflects the effectiveness and efficiency of employing the winning model. Also, it provides information to the organization in order to modify the model to fit its specific needs.

NINE STEPS TOWARDS WINNING STRATEGIES

The following nine steps are based on the theories developed in the winning model. An example (entering into a new market for computer products) is used to show the practical procedures of formulating winning strategies. The information in steps 1–3 are to be extracted from the "business information system'. The first four steps are related to the outer ring of the model which aims at understanding the corporate external and internal environment; the last five steps are concerned with the development of specific strategies for entering the new market.

Step 1

According to Sun Tze, one has to understand one's mission, resources, and implication before attacking

Table 3.8   Comparing EMI Music to Winning Model (Thorn EMI, 1994)

EMI Music	Sun Tze's *Art of Warfare*
Strategies used	*Offensive strategies*
1 • introduce innovative technology, extend this to new delivery systems, new formats and new sound and production techniques	• *Where to attack* — *lead the competitors to where you are familiar with, have more experience and are better researched; innovation leads competitors to where you want them to fight and make them followers*
• e.g. invest in 'music television', audio and video in CD-ROM technology	*EMI* — secure better position and gain first profit in the new market
2 • extend repertoire of sources by making small but strategic acquisitions	• *Who to attack* — *attack the competitors whose size is smaller in order to strengthen competencies*
• e.g. acquisition of Virgin Records Ltd and Chrysalis Group Plc	*EMI* — acquire small companies to strengthen existing competencies in order to compete with the bigger and stronger competitors such as Polygram
3 • extend repertoire of sources by alliances with competitors to form a new music publishing agreement • e.g. EMI joined partners with Sony, Polygram and Warner Music Group in a German start-up called VIVA, which focuses on the development of local talent	• *How to attack* — *avoid an open clash if the opposing force is united or strong* *EMI* — Polygram, Sony and Warner Music Group have comparatively stronger power in the industry, form an alliance with them to avoid an open clash
4 • identify future trends particularly in technological development	• *When to attack* — *wait with patience, fighting at the right time*
• e.g. they have identified the 'digital superhighway' that will become popular in the future, therefore they entered the business of digital cable radio by becoming a partner in Music Choice US. This service offers a wide range of advertisement-free, CD quality music to home subscribers	*EMI* — start to invest in 'digital superhighway' — related business, developing the appropriate networks, to wait for the time when 'digital superhighway' becomes commonplace
5 • explore the global market, maximizing the potential artists on a global scale. Develop certain artists to a multi-cultural appeal, with fans stretching from Southeast Asia to Latin America • e.g. in recent years, EMI acts from Sweden's Roxette to the Ivory Coast's Alpha Blondy have become international stars	• *What to attack* — *a market or segment can be seen as the target to be attacked. This is also the opportunities of the market* *EMI* — there are still many potential markets around the world and their music trends are strongly influenced by US and European countries. With competition high in the US and European countries, EMI explores new defensive strategies potential markets to 'attack'

Continued

Table 3.8 *(continued)*

EMI Music	Sun Tze's *Art of Warfare*
	Defensive strategies
6 ● strengthen its position in an established market by investing in and acquiring small independent record companies	● *Strengthen* —*strengthen their internal human and financial resources in order to compete with future competitors*
● e.g. acquisition of a German independent record company, Intercord Tongesellschaft mbH in March 1994	*EMI*—acquisition of Intercord can explore new talents and the overall increase in size could help EMI to improve its sales and profitability
7 ● cost management on distribution operating system	● *Strengthen* —*strengthen the internal financial situation in order to be stronger*
● e.g. use the 'just-in-time' (JIT) system to meet customers' demand and achieve efficiency	*EMI*—JIT improves not only the efficiency of operation but also the quality of services which gives the company greater credit
8 ● alliances with competitors to form new music publishing organizations	● *Hide* —*hide the strengths and weaknesses of organizations to confuse the vision of their competitors*
(same as number 3)	*EMI*—alliance with competitors is also a strategy by putting a cloud over their heads to confuse competitors on whether they should cooperate or compete with each other

[1]Source: *Financial Report*, EMI Music, 1994.

The organization itself

● What resources and finance are available to develop a new market?
● Are there sufficient personnel on hand to cope with entering the new market?
● Which departments will take charge of the new project and who will head them?
● What will be the implications for the organization?
● Does it meet the mission of the organization, etc?

Information can be obtained from financial reports, ratio analysis, company profile and data, employees, observation, etc.

Step 2

On the basis of the information determined in Step 1, identify which markets are suitable for the existing capacity and competencies. In order to do so, a comprehensive understanding of the external environment is essential.

External environment

- Study the national statistics of countries that might have the possibility to enter. Obtain information such as Gross National Product (GNP), population, economic environment, culture, technological development, consumption power, etc.
- Specifically analyse the development of the computing industry in the potential new market(s).
- Analyse whether any other primary data are needed in order to determine which are the most suitable countries to target.
- Obtain information that could predict the technological development in the next five or ten years, etc.
- Examine the existing products in the potential new market. Can they be further modified and developed, etc?

Step 3

Investigate relative strengths and weaknesses of competitors. A thorough understanding of competitors should be gained both in the UK and overseas.

UK competitors

- Are they operating in overseas markets?
- Which countries have they chosen for further expansion?
- What (if any) successes or progresses have been achieved?
- What tactics or strategies were employed?
- What products are they offering for these markets?
- What are their planning and development strategies for the next 5 and 10 years?

Overseas competitors

- Who are already in the market?
- Who are the market leaders and why?
- What are their relative strengths and weaknesses?
- What financial and human resources do they have?
- Which is the strongest company?
- Do they have strong management teams or effective styles of management?

Step 4

Consider the "Five Factors" and by using the "Seven Dimensions" chart evaluate the likelihood of success of entering into a new market.

- If the total score of the comparison is over 60%, it means the likelihood of successfully entering into the market is high. The organization should enter into the new market.

Step 5

Specify concise goals and objectives in such a way that progress may be continuously charted. This will subsequently provide an easier means of evaluation. Goal and objectives can be set as both long term and short term, as follows:

Short term (first year)

- Obtain at least 15% of the market share.
- Improve at least 10% profitability.
- Explore the right image of the products and organization for the new market.

Long term (second and third year)

- Gain more than 40% of the market share by the third year.
- Improve profitability at least 20% each year.
- Build up the selected and appropriate image to the public.

Step 6

Assuming that a high score was achieved in the prementioned "Seven Dimensions" chart, which represents a stable internal climate, the next priority is to formulate an *offensive strategy*.

The 5 Ws need to be answered

What to attack

- Identify opportunities within the new market.
- Identify strengths and weakness of the competitors.

Where to attack

- Are there any market segments or niches unexplored by the competitors?
- Can computing technology be developed for any other purposes? Are there other industries that would benefit from computerization?
- Which countries possess the greatest potential for exploitation and development?

When to attack

- Determine the most popular products and topics at the present time within the computing industries.
- How are these products used within everyday society?
- Discover what is currently in fashion, especially with the younger generation, what they like or dislike?
- Would the launch of a new product fit in with, or go against, current trends?

Who to attack (finding the target)

- Identify the relative sizes and power of existing competitors.
- Grade them as to whether they are weaker, comparative or stronger than yourself.
- Single out those where a defeat (merger or takeover) would be possible and produce a beneficial result on the overall business.

How to attack

- Identify what tactics would be effective against competitors.

Step 7

It is imperative to gather together defensive strategies — the organization must guard its business ventures at all times

Hide

- Key management personnel should remain alert regarding the possibility of "spies" within the organization.
- Confidential company information should be accessible only by those staff on a "need to know" basis. Security passwords should be used wherever possible for accessing computer databases. Staff identity cards should be worn at all times.
- Sometimes it is possible to let some unimportant or irrelevant data leak from the company in the hope that it will cause a degree of confusion amongst competitors.
- Attempt to impress upon employees the importance of confidentiality at all times, for example, not to disclose any details of company's business to anyone outside the organization such as current research and development, any inner strengths or weaknesses, plans for the future, etc. Generally, such factors rely on the overall commitment of the staff.

Strengthen

- Recruit high-calibre qualified people if additional human resources are required.
- Provide suitable training for relevant personnel, some of whom may be sent to work overseas under a totally different environment and culture, etc.
- Motivate employees by the appropriate methods. Set up "Quality Circles" to improve the overall efficiency of operation, make them feel proud of the successes of the company and understand the importance of their contributions to the successes.

Step 8

Throughout the implementation period, capable leaders and flexibility to deal with the situation are required. Make sure that the team is cohesive and motivated, and that management and employees have the essential skills to cope with the sudden changes during implementation. Otherwise, measures need to be taken to improve the situation.

Step 9

A full evaluation at the end of the implementation stage should be undertaken. Mid-term evaluation is often useful if substantial changes have been made to the original plan. Evaluation should not be treated as marking the end of a project but the beginning of the development phase in that particular country.

CONCLUSIONS

Sun Tze's *Art of Warfare* has long been proven to be successful as warfare strategies. Many marketing strategists have tried to apply its principles in modern day businesses, but few have developed a systematic approach. The winning model is developed based on the essence of Sun Tze's teaching in warfare strategies. Some figures, tables and short case examples have been used to illustrate his teaching and a major case study has been used to illustrate the effectiveness of the model. It provides a guideline for management to practise Sun Tze's proven strategies in business. Although his *Art of Warfare* is for military strategists, it can be adapted for marketing applications with minor modifications. For example, the use of spies has been seen as an effective and efficient way of collecting the top secrets from competitors in war, but in business, this has been considered unethical. Nevertheless, organizations can modify the use of model in order to fit its particular needs. Finally, the model will provide a unique competitive advantage, especially when your competitors are not aware of such strategies and the associated tactics.

REFERENCES

Cheung, M. (ed.) (1990). *Sun Tze's Art of Warfare in Business Practice*, Cheung Moon Publishing, Taiwan.

Chow, H. W. (1994). Sun Tze's Art of Warfare; selected applications, In: D. E. Hussey (ed.) *International Review of Strategic Management, Vol. 5*, John Wiley & Sons, UK.

Chung, T. C. (ed.) (1991). *Chinese Military Classic: The Art of War*, Asiapac Publication, Singapore.

Davidson, H. (1987). *Offensive Marketing or How to Make your Competitors Followers*, Penguin Books, UK.

Lee, Z. C., Yeung, S. K. and Cham, K. C. (1995). *Sun Tze Art of Warfare in Practice*, Yuen Lau Publishing, China.

Lip, E. (1989). *The Chinese Art of Survival*, EPB Publishers, Singapore.

Thorn EMI (1994). Playing a part in your life, *Financial Report 94*.

Yuan G. (1991). *Lure the Tiger Out of the Mountains: The 36 Stratagems of Ancient China*, Judy Piatkus Ltd., London.

4

A MODEL OF STRATEGY DECISION MAKING

Gordon E. Greenley

Birmingham Business School, University of Birmingham

There is still a lack of agreement on how future strategies should be formulated in companies. In this chapter, a simple model is given, which explains a range of five fundamental decisions that need to be addressed when formulating strategies within a company. The focus is on the nature of strategy decisions, with the aim of alleviating some of the confusion surrounding the formulation of strategy.

INTRODUCTION

Managers will be aware of the confusion that surrounds the formulation of strategies for the future. No doubt they will also be aware that reference to the literature for guidance reveals similar confusion. Many different types of strategy are also talked about in corporate circles, while a similar array of types are advocated in the literature. Common to both these sources is a lack of agreement in defining these strategy types.

Another contentious issue is that these different types of strategy are assigned to different levels within a company's organizational structure, to give a hierarchy of strategies. Again, there is confusion as a wide variation can be found in the way that companies organize this hierarchy, while different writers give different views on how the strategies ought to be organized.

The Strategic Decision Challenge, Edited by D. E. Hussey
© 1998 John Wiley & Sons Ltd

In this chapter, an attempt is made to alleviate some of this confusion. A simple model is proposed, which aims to show the range of fundamental decisions that need to be addressed when formulating strategies within a company. This model is about the type of decisions to be made, but not about how to make them. However, if managers are to formulate strategies that are meaningful and effective, then they must be couched in a model or scheme that is readily understood and which will give a common perceptual framework. The model that is given in this chapter is based on only five major decisions, which capture the range of strategies that need to be tackled throughout a company's hierarchy.

THE PROBLEM OF CONFUSION

This lack of consensus in agreeing explanations of different types of strategy has been noted by several observers, such as Carroll (1982) and Wind and Robertson (1983), who have also pointed to the use of the word strategy in the wrong context. For example, readers are likely to have experienced its use as a substitute for the word important. In developing this scheme of decision making, the starting point has been three base levels of strategy, which seem to be more or less universally accepted. Hofer and Schendel (1978), for example, give these three levels as follows:

Corporate strategy. the level at which decisions are made about the range of businesses in which the company will compete

Business strategy. the level that concentrates specifically on the manner in which the company is to compete with respect to each business

Functional strategy. the level that concentrates on the use of each of the business functions, such as marketing and production.

Although the above is conceptually quite simple, the problem of confusion arises in the way firms address strategy decisions at these levels, through the different labels that they use to identify these strategies, and the different ways that they extend this simple hierarchy, both vertically and horizontally. Similarly, writers also vary in the way that they describe these issues. Indeed, looking through the literature one finds many labels, a selection of which includes: organizational strategy, generic strategy, strategic business unit (SBU) strategy, strategic management, strategic planning, strategic marketing, master strategy, grand strategy, composite strategy, root strategy, strategic posture, programme strategy, operational strategy and marketing strategy. This situation is at the heart of the problem of confusion, although obfuscation is added by the process that is used for decision making when formulating strategy and the management of implementation of the chosen strategies.

Process and Implementation Issues

In this chapter, I differentiate between three major aspects of strategy in companies:

- the nature of strategy decisions
- the management process that is required in order to make these decisions
- the implementation of the formulated strategy decisions.

As implied above, this chapter is concerned only with the nature of strategy decisions. However, the discussion will be enhanced by briefly dwelling on these other issues. Both these sets of issues, management process and implementation, are concerned with managerial behaviourism, whereas the nature of strategy decisions is descriptive. These behavioural issues are obviously couched in the irrationality of human behaviour, while personal values and expectations strongly influence managers' performance, and indeed may result in a conflict of interests between individual managers and the objectives of the company.

Central to these two aspects are the abilities of managers to understand the nature of these decisions, to participate effectively in the process that actually leads to making them and to implement them effectively. The willingness, as opposed to the ability, of managers to participate in all these aspects is also of central importance. Again, the irrationality of human behaviour can result in managers not participating effectively, or managers often operating at a suboptimal level for several reasons. Readers wishing to pursue these behavioural issues further are referred to Ansoff (1984), Buchanan and Huczynski (1985) and Sturdivant et al (1985).

Although this chapter is concerned only with the nature of these decisions, they are of course part of this total system. Therefore, these behavioural issues contribute to the total confusion within the overall domain of strategy, exacerbating the obfuscation.

THE STRATEGY MODEL

The model proposed in this chapter for understanding the nature of strategy decisions is based on five central decisions. These are fundamental to the strategy hierarchy, from those at the very top that determine the long-range posture of the company to operational strategies needed to achieve performance. However, this is not the complete set of decisions; rather, they represent the five central decisions that lead to an understanding of the nature of strategy formulation. These decisions are presented in Figure 4.1. However, the model assumes that a set of organizational objectives has already been established, which specifies long-range aspirations in terms of performance measures such as growth of sales, market spread, profitability, margins and efficiency.

DECISION 1: DO WE WANT THE COMPANY TO PURSUE GROWTH OR STABILITY OF PERFORMANCE ?

DECISION 2: HOW MANY BUSINESSES OR SBUs DO WE WANT TO BE IN ?

Growth; through additional SBUs by
  * diversification or
  * forward/backward integration

Stability; stay in existing SBUs through
  * holding or
  * harvesting

DECISION 3: FOR EACH OF THESE BUSINESSES OR SBUs DO WE WANT TO PURSUE GROWTH OR RETAIN STABILITY ?

Growth; alternatives of market penetration, horizontal integration, market development, and product development

Stability; alternatives of holding and harvesting

DECISION 4: FOR EACH MARKET IN EACH SBU, HOW MANY SEGMENTS DO WE WANT TO BE IN ?

Growth; through positioning in additional market segments

Stability; holding in current market segments

DECISION 5: HOW DO WE WANT TO USE THE ELEMENTS OF THE MARKETING MIX IN EACH OF THE MARKET SEGMENTS ?

Growth; aggressive use of the mix elements in the market segments

Stability; passive use of the mix elements in the market segments

---

Figure 4.1   The Five Fundamental Strategy Decisions

The rest of this section explains the nature of each of these decisions. They are illustrated with reference to a publishing company that participates in a number of businesses, which have been established as follows:

Business 1 — books
Business 2 — newspapers
Business 3 — magazines
Business 4 — academic journals.

Decision 1

The answer posed by the first question should have already been answered when establishing the objectives. However, for many companies the objectives are implied rather than being explicit. While growth is often seen as being essential for the future, for some companies this may not always be appropriate. Stability of output and sales revenue in the immediate future may be necessary in order to concentrate on building profits, which in turn can be used to generate growth in future years. Alternatively, market conditions may not be favourable for growth. However, if growth is to be pursued then the question becomes one of magnitude.

For the publishing company, the following questions need to be addressed: is growth by incremental development over the next five years appropriate, is a quantum leap aspired to at some stage, or can major advances be achieved only beyond five years?

As well as being based on environmental issues in the publishing industry, the answers to these questions are also related to behavioural issues, and in particular to the aspirations of managers and owners for the long-term future of the company. However, major advances in growth may not be possible in the publishing industry, depending on the phase of its industry life cycle. Despite industry conditions, a clearly planned path of growth or stability is essential for strategy formulation, as all the remaining decisions are dependent on it, and as long-run company success is more likely with such planning.

Decision 2

Currently, the publishing company participates in four different businesses or SBUs. These are clearly separate SBUs as the needs and requirements of different groups of people for books, newspapers, magazines and academic journals are obviously different. The common thread across these SBUs is communications, but in the printed word or hard copy. For future growth, this publisher has two broad alternatives. First, to find additional SBUs that require traditional printing. Second, to move into electronic forms of publishing, such as satellite broadcasting or electronic data transmission.

While potential for growth within these two opportunities needs to be assessed, behavioural issues are also important. As the second alternative would take the company away from its existing field of knowledge, it may be perceived as being too high a business risk. Alternatively, it may be seen as a huge opportunity for growth; the point is that it will depend on managers' perceptions, their aspirations for the future and their acceptance of change and associated risk.

Decision 2 will also affect the future size of the company and its domain of operation, as well as its potential to achieve growth. While the addition of SBUs can clearly allow for major advances in growth, it must be remembered that it is not the only way. Growth within the SBUs is also possible; for example books and magazines may still be growth businesses, but newspapers may be in decline, while academic journals may be static. Allied to this decision on additional SBUs is the state of competitive rivalry. In industries that are static or in decline competition is likely to intensify, whereas in newly developing industries there is likely to be little competition. However, the situation can quickly change. A declining industry may see firms withdrawing, leaving an opportunity for the remaining companies, while a new but expanding industry will very rapidly attract new competitors.

Growth alternatives

As shown in Figure 4.1, there are two alternatives for moving into additional businesses. Diversification implies that it would be a new area of operation for the company, in a new industry. For the publishing company, satellite broadcasting would certainly be diversification, in that it would take them into new realms of production and technology, and into new markets requiring new knowledge and expertise. Some writers differentiate between related diversification and conglomerate diversification. The difference is perhaps slightly academic, but the point is that both require managers to attain new skills and knowledge.

While integration at this level is concerned with new businesses, they are within the distribution chain of the existing industry. The publishing company could achieve forward integration by moving into printing or even retailing, while backward integration could be achieved by moving into the literary agency business, or even into paper manufacturing. Here, the risk can perhaps be seen to be less than that for diversification, in that the company will still be operating in the same industry, albeit in a different business, where different knowledge and expertise are needed. The opportunity is with respect to now supplying competitors in the case of backward integration, while supplying final customers in the case of forward integration. However, both alternatives should lead to greater competitive domination within the industry.

Stability alternatives

Here, the decision probably implies that the company is satisfied with projections for growth within books, newspapers, magazines and academic journals, being consistent with objectives and aspirations for the future. However, it could also imply that managers are not willing to take the risk associated with moving into new SBUs. For the publishing firm, it could be the view that non-printed forms of communication are too far from the existing domain of the company, representing too great a risk in terms of both technological acquisition and competitiveness, in an unknown industry. Whatever the reason, the two alternatives for stability are holding and harvesting. The former means that existing SBUs will continue to be developed, with sales and profit objectives being consistent with appropriate growth within each respective SBU, and with incurring costs for new product development and other ways to improve the effectiveness of serving the industry.

Harvesting, however, changes the overall aim within a particular business. This is to attempt to maximize profits gained, by reducing costs and possibly increasing prices to generate these extra profits. In publishing, this may be possible in the specialist academic journals business, generating cash to finance future developments in this business, or indeed some of the other SBUs. However, in most cases this would be a short-term alternative, and is often appropriate where the industry is in maturity and/or where withdrawal is anticipated in the medium term. Continued cut-backs in expenditure on education may have prompted such a planned withdrawal from academic journals.

Decision 3

Having decided on the range of businesses in which to participate, attention is now diverted to a strategy within each of these businesses or SBUs. Again, the fundamental decision is one of growth or stability, but being specific to competitive rivalry in each of the SBUs. Taking as an example two of the businesses of the publishing company, the markets in which they participate in these SBUs are as follows:

magazines — consumer, childrens, industrial and professional
books — fiction, reference, academic and school.

For each of the SBUs, this third decision revolves around a business strategy for tackling the markets of the industry to which each SBU relates. For growth, there are several alternatives, as shown in Figure 4.1, which are discussed below.

Market penetration

This alternative is to pursue more market share within the markets of the respective business, obviously to the detriment of competitors. In the industrial and professional markets of the magazine business, it may be that the publisher is particularly strong and therefore will be able to penetrate further into these markets. However, in the books business this may be possible only in the reference books market, where there is less competition and where the company has established market leadership.

Horizontal integration

This is an alternative that may be feasible for fiction books. Here, the company would acquire competitors in this market, thus gaining additional market share through acquisition of existing product lines. Unlike integration at the higher level decision, the company remains in the same business achieving growth across the same market.

Market development

This alternative involves taking existing products to new markets. A simple example would be to market some of the existing magazines in new countries as new markets. However, it could also be achieved by marketing some professional magazines into academic institutions, or using some appropriate school texts for the adult literacy market.

Product development

This final alternative concerns developing new products for existing markets. While this alternative could be viable for any market in any SBU, there are many limiting constraints. Of prime importance is the number of products that already serve the market, trends in their relative market shares, the trend of growth in the market and any changes in customer requirements. In the books business, product development will be a continuous strategy in that new titles will be continuously added to the product lines, while near-obsolete titles will be regularly deleted. However, in the magazines business, particular magazine titles will last for many years before coming to the end of their life cycles.

For stability at the SBU level, there are again the alternatives of holding and harvesting. However, it could be that one of these alternatives has already been designated in Decision 2 for a particular SBU, but if not it can certainly be selected at the business level. For a holding strategy, the existing allocation of resources would be retained in order to maintain or hold the existing market share. However, if the market size is growing the result could still be a growth of sales revenue, albeit with the same market share. Such an alternative may be appropriate in the newspapers SBU, where the industry is nearing maturity with high levels of competition from a few large competitors, resulting in the need for high levels of expenditure to gain small increases in share, and which is therefore cost prohibitive.

Harvesting is again the option of maximizing profits, with the aim of generating cash that can be used for future developments. Within an SBU, this may be valuable in that cash generated in one market, say fiction books, can be used for product development in markets for other books, or indeed to enter new markets.

Decision 4

The penultimate fundamental decision is, for each market, to select the number of segments in which the company is to participate. For the consumer market of the magazines SBU, segments will be fashion, hobbies, outdoor pursuits, sports, home and garden, women and animals. Here, the decision is one of whether to participate in all segments or to concentrate on a selected number. This decision will, of course, be required for all markets in each of the SBUs. These decisions are often referred to as market positioning, and are generally seen as being part of marketing strategy. Therefore, there will be a separate marketing strategy for each market in each SBU. For consumer magazines, the market positioning strategy may be in fashion, hobbies, and home and garden, while for the professional magazines, the market positioning strategy may be based on accountancy, marketing and engineering.

At this level of decision making those to be made are very much dependent on the previous higher level decisions (Decisions 1 to 3 inclusive), and are therefore subservient to these decisions. However, this does not mean that they are any less important. Indeed, the outcome of positioning decisions will represent major ramifications to a company. In the publishing example, sports and outdoor pursuits magazines are given as being new to the company. There is obviously risk attached to entering these segments in that new products will have to be developed or acquired, while knowledge of the requirements of consumers in these segments will also need to be understood. Therefore positioning in segments should be based on available resources for exploitation, the relative growth potential in all the segments of the market, consumer requirements and the degree of competitive rivalry.

Decision 5

The last of the five fundamental decisions is within each of the market segments. These decisions need to be addressed for each segment of each market in which the company is positioned, and they should be repeated across all SBUs. Again, the major split is between growth and stability within each segment. Where competition and segment size will allow for growth, then this will be pursued through an aggressive use of the elements of the marketing mix. Here, the simple principle is that there needs to be specific tailoring of the elements for each of the segments. The approach taken for consumer magazines will clearly be different from that taken in the professional market. However, there still needs to be fine tuning between the segments, as promotions and pricing, for example, will be different with respect to fashion magazines as opposed to hobbies magazines.

Where segments are static and/or where there is excessive competition, but the company decides to retain positioning, it is likely that a passive use of the elements is appropriate. In professional magazines, the trading conditions may be such that aggressive advertising would not achieve significantly higher market shares, while a new pricing policy may do little for brand switching. Consequently, this leads to a holding strategy for expenditure on the marketing mix, where levels are set to retain existing sales and market shares. The utilization of the elements of the marketing mix in this way is also generally seen as being part of marketing strategy, along with the decisions on market positioning.

SUMMARY

In this chapter, a simple model has been given, which explains a range of five fundamental decisions that need to be addressed when formulating strategies within a company. The chapter differentiated between three major aspects of strategy in companies:

- the nature of strategy decisions
- the management process that is required in order to make these decisions
- the implementation of the formulated strategy decisions.

The thrust of the chapter was to focus on the nature of strategy decisions, with the aim of alleviating some of the confusion surrounding the formulation of strategy. The importance of the other two aspects of strategy was acknowledged, and the influence that they also have on strategy formulation.

Ensuring that managers understand the nature of strategy decisions is essential for the future success of a company. Managers must be able to identify just where in the hierarchy their decision contributions are located, how they are framed by higher level decisions and how in turn their decisions will affect those of other managers who are lower in the hierarchy. Such an understanding should also help to reinforce the vital importance of the two central outcomes of long-range planning. These are, first, the long-term commitment of resources to particular business ventures, which are likely to be decisions that are not easily reversed. Second, long-term commitment to serving the needs and requirements of particular industries and their markets, where failure affects, of course, not only performance but total credibility as an organization.

REFERENCES

Ansoff, H. I. (1984). *Implanting Strategic Management.* Prentice-Hall, Englewood-Cliffs.

Buchanan, D. A. and Huczynski, A. A. (1985). *Organizational Behaviour*, Prentice-Hall, London.

Carroll, P. J. (1982). The link between performance and strategy. *Journal of Business Strategy*, **2** (4), 3–20.

Hofer, C. W. and Schendel, D. (1978). *Strategy Formulation; Analytical Concepts, West.* St Paul, USA.

Sturdivant, F. D., Ginter, J. L. and Sawyer, A. G. (1985). Managers' conservatism and corporate performance. *Strategic Management Journal*, **6**, 17–38.

Wind, Y. and Robertson, T. S. (1983). Marketing strategy: new directions for theory and research. *Journal of Marketing*, **47**, 12–25.

5

THE EMPHASIS ON VALUE-BASED STRATEGIC MANAGEMENT IN UK COMPANIES[1]

Sylvia A. Handler

Associate Director, Harbridge Consulting Group Ltd, London

Recent research into UK publicly traded companies reveals that corporate UK managers are focusing their efforts toward creating and enhancing value for shareholders. Advocates of value techniques believe that managing for shareholder value provides managers with a more appropriate yardstick for measuring their companies' performance. Here Sylvia Handler reveals some of corporate UK's experiences with value-based strategic management.

Research in 1990–91 into the UK's largest publicly traded companies explored their awareness and use of value-based strategic management (VSM). The research discovered that, although corporate managers have long emphasized the importance of their shareholders' interests, the poor stock market performance of many UK companies in the recent past shows that shareholder objectives are not being met. Even when increasing shareholder wealth takes priority, corporate managers may still fail to meet this objective because they cannot see a consistent relationship between their corporation's strategic and financial performance and the company's share price. Understanding how the stock market values a company's shares, and managing that value, may have a significant influence on the future of the company and its managers.

---

[1] This chapter is based on 1990–91 research by Harbridge Consulting Group Ltd. The full text of the research report is available from Harbridge Consulting Group Ltd, 3 Hanover Square, London W1R 9RD.

The Strategic Decision Challenge, Edited by D. E. Hussey
© 1998 John Wiley & Sons Ltd

Creating and enhancing value for shareholders is becoming the primary focus of an increasing number of present-day UK managers. Some major UK companies, such as Blue Circle, British Petroleum, Dixons Group plc, Lloyds Bank and TSB Group, all advocates of value techniques, believe that managing for value provides managers with more appropriate yardsticks for measuring their companies' performance. This article begins by exploring VSM generally, and then looks at the experience of three UK corporations with the "value" approach to corporate decision-making.

WHAT IS VSM?

Value-based strategic management (VSM) is a strategic management process for building shareholder value. Its advocates believe that the most important focus for management at every level must be to maximize the firm's current market value. The obvious objective of this focus is a greater reward for a company's owners, its shareholders. And even wider benefits to society at large are derived from a more robust economic growth and improved living standard when scarce resources are used most productively.

The success of the process is measured by growth in shareholder value (the growth over time in share price appreciation plus accumulated gross dividends). This value approach to strategy formulation and implementation integrates financially-oriented value-based planning (discounted cash flow) techniques into the traditional strategic management process. It is, therefore, a technique which forces decision-makers, including investors, to look to the future cash flows of the firm rather than just to the past profit performance of the company.

Corporate UK is continually forced to reassess its business position due to the turbulence of the modern-day economy and, in some instances, the crumbling of the latter-day advantages of vertical and horizontal integration. Today's manager is aware that shareholders have become less tolerant of weak performers, and the market for corporate control (the market for buying and selling companies) is a constant threat. VSM has been seen by some to be a potential weapon for waging the corporate control battle, for it focuses attention on the concerns of shareholders: that is, how to maximize the long-term returns to the shareholder. It seeks to balance the development of long-term business strategies (strategies which have been chosen based on their ability to maximize shareholder value) with value strategy implementation.

UK managers who advocate VSM believe that VSM can help to ensure that the financial markets fairly value their shares, in other words that business-level competitive strategies are linked with company-level portfolio planning, and that this integration is then reflected in the share price. VSM is, therefore, also seen by an increasing number of companies as the only appropriate method for measuring company performance.

Those who prefer the value method over more traditional accounting based methods of performance measurement do so because they hold the following beliefs.

- The stock markets are concerned with the long-term economic value of management decisions and how those decisions are implemented, not just the more traditional short-term measures, such as profit growth and earnings per share. VSM, because it relates directly to shareholders' objectives, will help planners and managers to understand investors' expectations and communicate company performance in terms of those objectives. VSM managers are convinced that stock market myopia is a myth.
- VSM provides a better mechanism, whereby strategic decisions at the corporate level (concerned with the right mix of businesses) and business level (concerned with competing the right way within the industry) are actually implemented at both levels. This involves the key concern of resource allocation to various business and functional areas, involving all levels of management in both formulation and implementation.
- VSM helps to eliminate the problematic dichotomy between the economic approach to strategic decisions at both corporate and business levels, and the accounting approach to measuring the performance of the managers who will implement that strategy. The conflict, illustrated in Figure 5.1, occurs when managers make decisions to maximize performance based on ROCE or some other accounting measurement, but investment decisions are based on economic measures (discounted cash flow, net present value, IRR).

THE "MYTH OF MARKET MYOPIA"

Value advocates believe that it is pure myth that the stock market is myopic or short-term in its method of setting share prices. Rather, it is the maximization of free or distributable cash flow that drives share price, not some method of

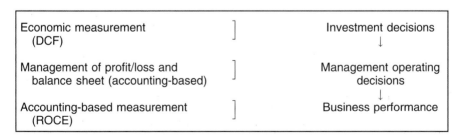

Figure 5.1 Conflicts Between Measurement Systems

present earnings capitalization. Because managers are often confused as to what investors really want, business decisions involving acquisitions, divestments, business strategies, dividend policy and even management compensation become difficult and distorted.

Paul Marsh, in his excellent work in this area, presents a strong 'case for the defence' of market myopia (Marsh, 1990).

> The crime of which the stock market stands accused is that of mispricing shares. . . . What is directly at issue, however, is not how analysts and fund managers talk, or appear to behave, or even how they actually behave. Instead, the question is one of *how share prices behave*, and whether they fairly reflect *both* short- and long-term prospects, or whether they tend to overvalue the short-term and undervalue the long. No reliable evidence has yet been put forward to support the claim of short-termism in shareprices.

Marsh goes on to build a sound defence of the stock market, as outlined here in Figure 5.2. The question "market myopia — myth or reality?" is really one about market efficiency: can the stock market be trusted to set market prices that reflect fairly all the information available at the time of the deal? Research into equity markets has therefore focused on whether the market is efficient and share prices fair.

Empirical evidence in the case to prove market myopia, gathered in both US and UK stock market analysis, does not favour the prosecution.

1.   Evidence on *dividends* shows that the market has had a preference for capital gains rather than dividends and that high yielding shares have been more lowly valued.
2.   Evidence on announcements of *capital expenditure*, *R&D* and *investment in new products*, all of which will reduce short-term ROE, indicates that reactions, on average, are favourable and result in increased share price.
3.   Evidence on differential *reactions by different groups of companies to various types of announcements* has a direct bearing on the short-termism debate. One study showed that announcements of capex by US utilities companies who are constrained to make only "normal profits", had no effect on share price as would be expected. The same study examined the effect on capex announcements in industrial firms, which showed significant increases in share valuation.
4.   Indirect evidence, related to the way the market reacts to earnings and dividend announcements, changes in accounting policies, fund-raising, and mergers and acquisition policy, all supports "the general hypothesis that the stock market is broadly efficient, and that it is concerned with, and on average correctly discounts, the long-term as well as the short-term implications of relevant news items and key events" (Marsh, 1990).

Figure 5.2   Evidence in favour of market efficiency

THE QUEST FOR VALUE: THE ACCOUNTING MODEL *VS.* THE ECONOMIC MODEL

VSM managers believe that in the search for shareholder value, the economic model provides the better method for making business decisions and measuring business performance. The following briefly explains each approach.

Accounting Model

The traditional accounting model which relies on some method of reported earnings (after-tax profits), contends that the stock market sets share prices by capitalizing a company's earnings per share (EPS) at an appropriate price/earnings multiple (P/E). If, for example, a company has a P/E of 15 (selling at 15 times earnings) and EPS of £0.50, the predicted share price would be £7.50. If earnings rise to £1.00, the share price would be expected to rise to £15.00.

One fallacy of this model is that it assumes that P/E multiples never change. In fact, P/E ratios are constantly adjusting to account for changes in the "quality" of a company's earnings in the wake of acquisitions, divestments, future investment opportunities and changes in financial structure and accounting policies. That adjustment makes EPS an unreliable measure of value.

Growth in EPS is almost universally used to measure management performance and return to shareholders. Those who make business decisions based strictly on the accounting model believe that if EPS is growing, shareholder value is assumed to be enhanced (although not necessarily maximized). But in relying on growth in EPS managers are ignoring the element of risk and the time value of money. And equally invalid, they are relying on the inadequacies of some basic financial accounting precepts in searching for shareholder value. The conflict between economic and accounting models is highlighted in Figure 5.3, which looks at several management decision issues.

Economic Model

The research upon which this chapter is based revealed that the majority of the business educators and company managers surveyed feel that the economic model is the correct model for measuring business performance. The economic model forces business decisions based on the discounting of future cash flows by an appropriate cost of capital (a required return on investment, both equity and debt, which considers the inherent risk of the investment). The economic model of value holds that share price is determined by investors who care about two things: the cash to be generated over the business life, and the risk of the cash flows. The model is not subjected to accounting profit distortions. In addition, it considers the time value of money, which means it is concerned

Changing inventory valuation methodology, i.e. from FIFO to LIFO inventory costing in times of changing purchasing power. In times of rising prices the change from first-in first-out to last-in first-out inventory costing will reduce a company's earnings, at the same time reducing cash tax payments. Does the stock market focus on the reported change in earnings or the change in cash as a result of tax saved?

Writing off of goodwill which arises from a premium paid over book value of a seller's assets. In the accounting model this amortization of goodwill, often in the year of purchase, reduces earnings, but is of no consequence in the economic model because it is a non-cash expense. How often are decisions made to 'not purchase' because of a concern over the short-term impact on profits of a one-time write-off of goodwill against earnings? And what does this do to the long-term value for shareholders?

Research and development: capex or revex? Although unpredictable, R&D spending, like any capital expenditure, is expected to create a lasting value. Yet standard accounting principles require R&D to be expensed as if its potential value is exhausted in the period of outlay.

Full cost vs. successful efforts approach to asset valuation. With successful efforts accounting, used frequently in oil and mining industries, the costs associated with finding the minerals or oil/gas are capitalized only if the results are successful. Although the policy reduces earnings when the costs are written off, permanent asset values are reduced, eventually leading to overstated ROI. Full-cost accounting requires, for example, that a gold mining company capitalize all exploration and mining outlays, and then amortize them over the lives of all its successful operations (in the belief that part of the cost associated with finding gold is the cost of mining exploration that has been unsuccessful). Writing off unsuccessful investment will overstate ROI and possibly encourage future investment in business units which are not as 'valuable' in reality as they are on paper. The share market is seldom a fool — it uses full cost to judge performance. (Stewart, 1991.)

Figure 5.3   Management Decisions: Accounting Model or Economic Model?

with the timing of all cash flows, particularly investment and reinvestment of fixed and working capital.

The limitations of the economic approach relate mainly to its practical application, for its usefulness relies heavily on making correct assumptions about the future.

MANAGING AND MEASURING VALUE FOR THE LONG TERM

For most managers it makes good sense to use the economic model for making strategic portfolio decisions involving acquisitions, disinvestment and investment in assets and strategic focus. Management of these decisions becomes difficult, however, when return on the investment in assets is measured using the accounting model and some measures of ROE or ROI (see Figure 5.1). What is needed is a return that measures the productivity of capital employed without regard to financing method and free from accrual accounting distortions and understated capital—a cash-on-cash after tax yield earned in the business.

Net Operating Profit After Tax (NOPAT) Return

There are many variations on the theme of:

$$r = \frac{\text{NOPAT}}{\text{Capital}}$$

However, all such measures of value return must both be deleveraged (the effect of gearing up the capital structure with debt removed) and have other financing and accounting distortions eliminated. Because the effect of financial structure is entirely eliminated, this rate of return is a much clearer measure of operating performance than the standard return on equity, and it is one that can justifiably be compared year by year for an individual company and among companies in the same year (Stewart, 1991).

G. Bennett Stewart III (1991), in his very practical book *The Quest for Value, A Guide for Senior Managers* (required reading for all students of value), recommends the procedure shown in Figure 5.4. Some explanation is given below.

- *Income available to common shareholders* is assumed to equate to cash-in from operations.
- When *interest expenses net of taxes saved* is added back to profits, the earnings are similar to what they would be if the company's capital had come solely from common equity. Although leverage is important, the benefit achieved when debt shelters operating profits is incorporated in the weighted average cost of capital.
- Adding the equity provided by *preferred shareholders* and *minority investors* to capital and adding *income diverted to these equity sources* back to NOPAT eliminates other financial distortions.
- *Equity equivalents* (EEs) gross up the standard accounting book value into economic book value, which is intended to be a truer measure of the cash which investors have put at risk and upon which they expect to accrue returns. EEs eliminate accounting distortions by adding back to capital such items as deferred taxation, inventory valuation resource, the cumulative amortization of goodwill, expenditure on R&D (and other market-building outlays) and cumulative unusual net after-tax write- offs. Adding change in EEs to reported earnings bring reported earnings closer to a firm's true economic profits.

$$r = \frac{\text{NOPAT}}{\text{capital}}$$

where NOPAT =

Income available to common shareholders
+Interest expenses after tax
+Preferred dividend
+Minority interest equivalent
+Increase in equity equivalents

and capital =

    Common equity
+Debt
+Preferred stock
+Minority interest
+Equity equivalents

Figure 5.4   Adjustments to Reported Earnings and Capital for Deriving Economic Return

- *The NOPAT return* can be compared with the weighted average cost of capital, the absolute standard of performance.

NOPAT return can be further broken down by examining operating profit margin (OPM) derived from net operating profit before tax (NOPBT), capital (or asset) turnover (CT) and the effective cash tax rate on operating income (CTR), therefore:

$$r = \text{OPM} \times \text{TO} \times (1 - \text{CTR})$$

$$R = \frac{\text{NOPBT}}{\text{sales}} \times \frac{\text{sales}}{\text{capital}} \times 1 - \frac{\text{Cash operating taxes}}{\text{NOPBT}}$$

where OPM is the ratio of pretax economic earnings to sales, TO is the ratio of sales to beginning capital and CTR is the tax payable in cash on operating profits expressed as a percentage of pre-tax operating profits (the rate at which NOPBT would decrease in the absence of debt financing). The components of NOPAT return have a useful purpose in that they can be compared to prior levels, pre-set targets and to those from a peer group.

Economic Value Added (EVA)

Earning an attractive value rate of return is, of course, very important for attracting capital and building a premium-valued company. But it may send the wrong signals to operating people. Already profitable businesses may pass up attractive investment opportunities and unprofitable businesses may seek more capital, hoping to earn better returns. So NOPAT return may be flawed as a performance measure for an entire company or business unit. Stewart suggests that *economic value added* (EVA) is the one performance measure that accounts properly for all of the ways in which corporate value may be added or lost (Stewart, 1991).

EVA is a residual income measure that subtracts the cost of capital from the operating profits generated in the business. EVA (calculated and illustrated in Figure 5.5) will increase if one or all of these strategies is adopted.

- Operating profits are grown without additional capital investment; and/or
- New capital is invested in *any and all* projects that earn more than the cost of capital; and/or
- Capital is diverted from business assets that do not cover their cost of capital.

EVA is computed by multiplying the economic book value of a firm's capital by the spread between the return on capital (r) and the cost of capital (c).

$$EVA = (r - c) \times \text{economic capital}$$

So, for example, if NOPAT is £1,000, economic capital is £3,000, and the cost of capital is 20%, then:

$$EVA = \left[\frac{£1,000}{£3,000} - 20\% \right] \times £3,000$$

$$EVA = (33\% - 20\%) \times £3,000$$

$$EVA = £400$$

Or alternatively, if EVA is defined as residual operating profit (operating profit less a charge for the use of capital), then:

$$EVA = NOPAT - (c \times \text{economic capital})$$

$$EVA = £1,000 - (20\% \times £3,000)$$

$$EVA = £400$$

Figure 5.5   Calculating EVA

The real value of EVA is its abilty to tie directly to the share market value of the company, for when EVA is projected and discounted to present value it equates to market value net of the capital it has employed, i.e.:

MVA = market value − capital

MVA = present value of all future EVA

MVA is therefore a measure of the spread or "gap" between a company's market value and its book economic capital. For those companies concerned with creating values for its owners, maximizing MVA will be a primary objective.

VALUE SHARING: MOTIVATING MANAGERS FOR VALUE CREATION

In one of my business school courses I had to debate the pure side of the argument that "money *is always* a motivation for work". I think I probably had the easiest side of the debate, for although one can present other motives, most people will eventually be disinclined to work unless there is some financial reward.

One of the most important implications for the value company is finding the best way of putting value theories into practice. Rewarding managers and staff for making the best long-term value decisions instead of just traditional short-term performance rewards becomes a perplexing, but not insurmountable problem. But it is an issue that must be properly sorted (value reward system designed and accepted) before any firm can truly consider itself a "value" company.

In addition to traditional targets which are basically related to accounting-derived turnover and/or profit return, i.e. growth in sales and/or margins, and some definition of targeted return on profit, many managers and employers are rewarded with stock options, gain-sharing and profit-sharing plans and the like. These last rewards all involve the issue of ownership, which is key to the development of a value compensation system, one that makes all workers partners in the process of adding to shareholder value. The idea is to reward managers for reaching or exceeding targeted performance measures that run parallel to the creation of value on an annual basis.

Keying bonuses to EVA

Because EVA is the fuel that fires a premium (or accounts for the discount) in the market's valuation of any business, what better measure for connecting performance and value (Stewart, 1991). Managers are rewarded for increasing EVA relative to target and are penalized for falling short. EVA forms the foundation of the reward system of many notably successful companies. Coca-Cola is a fine example.

In recent years each of Coke's 19 division presidents has had to present annual 3-year projections of the "economic value" he expects to add to the corporation. Says [Chairman Roberto] Goizueta: "Adding economic value to the company is the key to rewarding shareholders in the 1990s" ("Leaders of the Most Admired", *Fortune*, 29 January 1990).

With EVA as each manager's goal, clear links are forged between operating and strategic decisions and the subsequent evaluation of managers' performance.

CORPORATE UK'S EXPERIENCES WITH VSM

Interest in VSM started in the mid-1970s in the US, when the then popular portfolio planning techniques were modified to focus on the goal of creating economic value for a company's shareholders. The 1980s saw value boom in the US, and for those who have been successful in implementing this approach — Coca-Cola, Disney, Pepsico, GE, Westinghouse, to name but a few — the results have been impressive. Westinghouse, for example, which saw its share price increase 2 ½ times between 1988 and the end of 1990, gives much of the credit to VSM.

The 1990–91 UK research conducted by Harbridge Consulting Group, MORI (MORI and Coopers & Lybrand Deloitte, 1991) and 3i (Graham Bannock & Partners Ltd, 1990) revealed that a keen interest in VSM is shared by many major UK companies. In fact, an estimated 60–70% of top UK companies now make use of some concept of VSM. And although most UK value advocates admit to minimal VSM experience, several companies in cameo appearance below (Figure 5.6) are notable exceptions.

BRITISH PETROLEUM PLC

The first issue of *Value Forum* (March 1990), a BP internal publication, provides a quotation which sums up BP's view of VSM.

Oscar Wilde defined a cynic as one who knows the price of everything and the value of nothing. If you substitute the word 'profit' for 'price' you'd have a good definition of a manager whom the value revolution has passed by.

Creating value for the shareholder is now, without question, the over-riding corporate objective at BP, and its executive management believes that it is on course to meet the challenges and opportunities of the 1990s and beyond.

BP's journey along the value road has been rapid (since 1987), but not easy. The cause of its focus on value was not unlike those of other value-oriented companies: the 1980s wave of mergers, the development of leveraged buy-outs and, for BP, the sale of the Government's shareholding. It has precipitated a

---

The British Petroleum Company plc. BP's core businesses relate to oil exploration, production, refining and marketing, and chemicals. It began exploring the use of VSM in 1987, and has used its techniques to make recent portfolio decisions, such as divestment of BP Minerals. It has also attempted to push VSM to the strategic business unit level with varying degrees of success.

Dixons Group plc. The fall of Dixons' share price in late 1989 and the subsequent hostile takeover bid from Kingfisher crystallized Dixons' attention on the nature of the group's business and its problems and left it wondering how it might avoid such challenges in the future. Management's lack of awareness of what was driving value in the business, plus poor communications with shareholders and analysts, depressed Dixon's share price well below its discounted cash flow value. Dixons became determined to eliminate the value destroyers of the past — lack of long-term value consideration, and short-term return focus — and concentrate on long-term investment to achieve customer satisfaction.

Lloyds Bank. The value methodology has been used at Lloyds since 1986 for major strategic decisions and at the business unit level. VSM has helped Lloyds focus on the strengths of the markets which it serves, both at home and abroad, and has led it successfully through the 1990–1991 downturn in the banking industry.

Figure 5.6   Three UK "Value" Companies

reappraisal of the relationship between managers and shareholders, and although BP finds a significant and legitimate conflict of interest between managers in general and shareholders, it believes that good value-based management must aim to establish procedures and frameworks which wherever possible align the two interests.

The History of VSM in BP

As early as 1985, BP's executive managers recognized that maximizing quarterly or yearly EPs was often done at the expense of future profits, and that the investment decisions being made by BP, based on economic principles, just did not equate to the output measurements in accounting terms.

Management was not convinced that the value approach was the way to go, but it was willing to consider the case for value. Marakon Associates, a consultancy specializing in value analysis, was hired to help to make that case and to help BP with the value analysis process. A first-cut analysis was made in 1987. The success of the process in convincing management was a combination of rigid methodology on how to value strategies, and strong arguments that capital markets are rational and think long-term. Marakon's approach provided a number of insights as to which businesses provided most value to the Group. Top management accepted the technique, and authorized further study on how the value approach could be used in BP.

BP's chairman, Robert Horton, understands the theory of value and believes in it, although he is the first to comment that value is not a "black box" and is only there to help in decision-making. Horton is experienced in using value. In the turnaround of BP Chemicals and BP America which Horton directed, value was implicit in his approach. He is now creating a culture in BP where value can thrive, and where change and challenge are welcomed and encouraged.

With all this enthusiasm from the top, those with responsibility for value implementation within BP feel that it is still miles away from where they want to be: "There is grass roots enthusiasm in some areas, but grass roots scepticism in others".

BP defines its value approach as using the insights given by the discounted cash flow (DCF) method to help manage a company. If the overall financial objective is maximizing value for shareholders, it is an important way in which BP feels it can measure and successfully compete with other major oil companies, and similar types of investments.

The emphasis it places on shareholder value does not mean that other stakeholder interests (customers, suppliers, governments, society, employees) are excluded. BP believes that the shareholder is in the middle and only gets his or her return if all stakeholders are considered. More specifically, it feels that all stakeholders will be let down if strategy decisions are made and implemented with only accounting objectives in mind. It emphasizes the shortfalls of accounting objectives as ignoring future earnings prospects, the risk of earnings, the quality of reinvestment, the time value of money, and dividend/reinvestment policy, to name but a few. The fact that over the 1980s the oil industry gave good returns to its shareholders without growing real earnings per share gives additional proof of how shareholder returns and accounting ratios are not related.

BP believes that there is ample proof that it is often impossible to tell whether, at the margin, profit increases are good or bad for shareholders. It is even so bold as to comment that quick fixes for profit are almost always bad for value. Figure 5.7 shows that a profit increase may have a neutral or bad, rather than a good, effect.

Profit	Value		
	Bad	Neutral	Good
Increase	Cut R&D	Change depreciation policy	Cut bureaucracy
Decrease	Cut margins	Increase dividends	Re-image
Source: *BP Value Forum*, March 1990			

Figure 5.7   The Effect on Value of Decisions Affecting Profit

The point about dividends reducing profit is that after the company has paid an increased dividend it earns less money on its reduced pool of cash. BP believes that the DCF model underpins stock market prices — that is, the market price is influenced by an unbiased market perception of the estimate of a company's economic value. BP sees the implications for management as a need to take decisions from the perspective of shareholders wanting value, not accounting results, to manage over the full time span and to take account of the time value of money. The biggest limitations it feels are obvious: projecting the correct cash flows and estimating the correct risk ("garbage in = garbage out").

Senior management, who fully support the VSM approach, advocate the use of the value technique in BP in a number of ways.

- In choosing between strategies and evaluating business unit plans.
- In revenue expenditure control — the target for cost control should be value, not minimization.
- In performance analysis, not just based on value return (funds generated/ opening value) but questioning the reasons behind it (was the return due to controllable or uncontrollable factors?) Managers are urged to use a value rational basis to reconcile the changes between one business plan and the next.
- In providing the basic framework for resource allocation by allocating resources to maximize the value of strategies, not projects. The ultimate aim for VSM is a BP with no capital constraints. This would require that only good projects and good strategies are proposed. But there will still be an important constraint to consider, namely BP's ability to identify and implement value-creating investments.
- In determining dividend and financing policy, VSM will assess these issues from a shareholder value perspective. Figure 5.8 illustrates that considering the flows of money to shareholders and not just to the company often gives a quite different view of a financing scheme's attractiveness. Paying dividends to shareholders, for example, is cash going out of the system.
- In minimizing the differences of purpose between shareholder and manager, the difficulty is usually that the company system and structure enable managers to benefit from non-value maximizing actions. BP is working on minimizing this effect, but admits it has a long way to go.
- Senior manager value proponents advise their managers to make value the consistent theme in their decision-making, not to be blinded by the numbers, and to manage for the *full term*, not the long or short term.

Implementing VSM within BP Oil

Once group senior management approval was achieved for VSM, it became important for BP to achieve successful use and implementation of the techniques and procedures as quickly as possible within the business units. BP

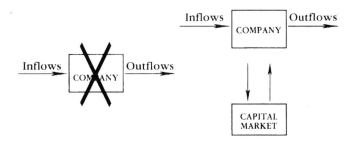

Source: *BP Value Forum*, March 1990

Figure 5.8 Dividend and Financing policy

Oil is recognized by senior management as the business unit which has taken the lead among BP's business in using the value approach.

Implementation began with an attempt to categorize its different function sectors (refining, retail, lubricants, etc.) relative to dividend yield and equity growth, which provided fresh insight into the structure of the business and a valuation for BP Oil as a whole.

The next step was to improve the understanding of VSM by BP Oil's managers and planners, particularly in the functional Business Development Units (BDUs). The process was met with some scepticism: difficult arithmetic, no earth-shaking revelations to prove that they had been doing the wrong thing all along, difficult external imponderables such as Green pressures, and the BP culture, which normally demanded a concentrated focus on short-term financial results. Managers, however, were hopeful that the value approach would reduce the emphasis on calendar year targeting and favoured the examination of performance over longer time periods.

In the initial stages of implementation BP Oil felt that its progress and success with the techniques had been mixed, but that the real benefits of the longer-term (value) perspective would lie in the use of the management balance sheet (MBS). The MBS is an initiative expected to change the way in which BP manages and controls itself, for the value principles and the focusing of longer-term performance are the foundation stones of MBS.

The MBS is a business- or company-specific balance sheet which includes not only that entity's assets, but also imputed debt and share equity, therefore including both accounting and economic values of assets, equity and debt. The MBS was originally introduced to help the Group manage the businesses. However, equal in importance to its use by the businesses in managing themselves is its use in managing the strategic business units (SBUs) within each business. The VSM proponents within BP Oil see the MBS as a tremendous opportunity to strengthen commitment within an SBU by extending accountability for decisions to the longer term. Particularly attractive is the prospect of replacing the current process of financial control, based on individual calendar years, with a continuously updated approach. BP believes that the MBS framework creates three important linkages

- It bridges the gap between value-based and accounting measures of performance.
- It links planning and control in a common reporting framework.
- It links one year to the next through the debt level, thus allowing continuity between consecutive planning periods.

The BP advocates of the MBS see many benefits, but particularly the linking of value-based planning and financial control systems, permitting more delegation and decentralization, and providing a framework for consistent measurement of economic performance.

DIXON GROUP PLC

Dixons Group's value focus involves long-term investment to develop a mature base of operations, centred on customer satisfaction. It believes that striving for customer satisfaction will drive value across the entire business, a congruence which will be achieved by building long-term customer confidence. The Group believes that the success of VSM and its benefits will depend in part on developing sales staff rewards based on customer satisfaction rather than short-term sales targets. Its considerable progress with its focus on value led in part to a 75% increase in its share price through 1991, a difficult time for retailers as many endured horrific recessionary setbacks.

Dixons Group plc is an international group specializing in the retail sale of consumer electronics, photographic products, domestic appliances and related services (profiled in Figure 5.9). It trades through Dixons, Currys and Supasnaps in the UK, and Silo in the US. The Group is also engaged in

---

Dixons. Retails consumer electronics and photographic products through high street stores.

Currys. Retails a wide range of domestic electrical products through superstores and high street stores.

SupaSnaps. Offers film processing services and photographic accessories.

Silo. Retails a wide range of consumer electronics and domestic appliances through superstores in the US.

Figure 5.9   Profile of Dixons Group Companies

property development and trading in the UK, Belgium, Germany, France, Luxembourg and Portugal through Dixons Commercial Properties International.

The consumer electronics and domestic appliance sectors, although generally regarded as long-term growth markets, are cyclical. As a result, business is subject to considerable fluctuations in demand, which tend to be exacerbated by new product introductions and shifts in economic climate.

This had led to a number of problems.

- In the mid-1980s, when demand was strong and sales of new products such as VCRs, microwaves and computers were growing rapidly, Dixons made a number of investment decisions based on what turned out in the short term to be unsustainable levels of sales. Because the "brown goods" (TV, audio, video, camcorders) sector is very prone to such investment "traps", making investment decisions on the basis of high short-term profitability can lead to problems in later years as demand declines, particularly when costs are also rising rapidly.
- The integration of Dixons' and Currys' logistical support and the realization of the synergy between the two businesses was delayed because the short-term buoyancy of the market obscured the underlying problems.
- Currys' competitive position was eroded because of its structure of small stores, and at the same time its cost base was high due to the location of its shops on the high street. The strategic response to the problem, the move to edge-of-town superstores, was slow to implement.

These problems were tackled in 1988 and 1989, but the solutions were poorly communicated to shareholders and analysts, and the results were not immediately apparent due to the weakness of the market and the timescale for implementation. Dixons' market share growth rate began to slow down, with a simultaneous cost escalation. As a result, the share price fell sharply, and in December 1989 Kingfisher made a hostile bid for Dixons Group. Although this offer was unsuccessful, it focused Dixons' management's attention on its failure to communicate with the investment community and led to a considerably better perception of the nature of the group's business, its problems and the solutions being implemented.

The group's 1990s plan for creating shareholder value is a many-faceted strategy for building long-term customer satisfaction. Dixons Group firmly believes that value in its businesses is created when long-term customer loyalty is created. This involves not only an up-market push for Dixons and the expansion of Currys Superstores, but also the emphasis of new concepts in systems, service, merchandising, product improvement and innovation, and staff development and compensation.

Expansion of Currys Superstores

Currys, in shifting away from the high street to edge-of-town superstores, hopes to give customers a far better shopping experience, i.e. a large range of white goods (washers and dryers, refrigerators, freezers, cookers, small appliances), larger, more comfortable stores with a relaxed atmosphere, longer opening hours and convenient parking. This move has led to improved sales, up by 11% like-for-like against a 4% reduction in its high street store sales. The group expects that Currys Superstores will account for 35% of retail space by April 1992, at least equal to Currys' High Street stores.

Up-market Push for Dixons

Dixons' attack on margins focuses on upgrading the mix of its merchandise to achieve higher average prices. Between 1988–90 Dixons saw a 24% ticket price improvement in real terms as average prices were decreasing. This meant that the volume of goods handled dropped sharply while it managed the same turnover. This had a significant effect on its cost base. Retailers of white and brown goods traditionally sustain high overheads to deal with large volumes of sales, i.e. warehousing, delivery, administration, after-sales service. Smaller investment in inventories has not only reduced investment in working capital, but Dixons finds itself discounting less because of obsolete and warehouse-worn merchandise.

Modernized Information Systems

The group is currently making considerable investment (£10m) in a sophisticated branch PC network designed to provide branches with up-to-date stock availability information as well as store profitability. It provides instant information about previously evasive issues such as discount origin, customer service history, and inventory and service parts availability. The system will eventually allow instant access to credit and repair organizations, and detailed product specification data which will give sales personnel more authority in dealing with customers' hi-tech equipment.

Improved Merchandizing

In addition to improved merchandizing of white goods in Currys Superstores and upgraded Dixons merchandizing of brown goods, the group has opened new specialist departments on a trial basis, particularly at Dixons stores. More space and a wider range of computer game hardware and software is catering to the growth of the computer game market. Other specialist departments group together low-ticket merchandise like films and video tapes as well as general brown goods accessories on a self-service basis.

To improve its already impressive 33% of the UK camcorder market, 300 Currys High Street stores have installed camcorder centres through the summer of 1991, with very encouraging results. In addition, Currys High Street stores have begun a trial (10 stores at end 1991) to reduce the space given to big white goods. Instead it sells them through an in-store catalogue centre, and focuses much more in store on small appliances. It is hoped that this move will improve its presence and market share in small appliances, while the large Currys Superstores in cheaper, cost-efficient locations handle a larger than ever market share of the larger white goods.

Product Improvement and Innovation

Historically, electronic goods have been made with two points in mind: the ease of manufacture and the number of features. "User friendliness" has until recently not been a priority. Consumer complaints range from complex and contraruction booklets to £2,000 systems that are packaged without plugs. Figure 5.10 outlines some significant Dixon initiatives guaranteed to please any customer who has to install his/her own TV, stereo or VTR. In addition, with the average cost of servicing a VTR at approximately £30, eliminating an estimated 30% of unnecessary service callouts will mean significant financial benefits to Dixons as well as improving customer satisfaction.

The product innovation cycle has been quiet since 1983 since the peak of the VCR boom. The expected launch in 1992 of CDI (interactive compact

---

Joint customer satisfaction projects with Sony, Hitachi, Panasonic and Matsushita have been initiated to respond to calls for simpler technology.

- Circuit boards, which formerly had to be soldered out, now clip out, enabling repair to be done in the customer's home with minimal fuss.
- Instruction bookets, with large easy-to-follow diagrams with colour coding for cables and plug points have been rewritten to improve former badly translated Japanese to English and to correct contradictions.
- More care is being given to make sure that bits that go into holes in other bits are all compatible.
- Design initiatives are under way for future electronic equipment which will have four or five diagnostic points built in to enable engineers to find faults quickly. 90% of engineer time is spent now in locating a fault and only 10% in fixing the fault.
- Packaging is being redesigned to make life easier for the consumer, so that spending 45 minutes getting a TV out of a box may soon be a thing of the past.

Figure 5.10   Dixons' Initiatives to Simplify Consumer Installation and Engineer Repair of Electrical Goods

disk) as well as the DCC (digital compact cassette), a 16×9 picture format colour TV and high definition TV are all expected to boost the innovation cycle. Although the innovation in products is not expected to be really buoyant until 1994–95, Dixons is projecting that its market share will continue to move upwards.

Staff Development and Compensation Programmes to Build Shareholder Value

In 1990–91 average branch staff numbers fell by 5% in Dixons and 14% in Currys (which translated through to 12–14% increases in sales per employee). Distribution employees were also significantly reduced (16%), and branch pay increases were modest. How then does Dixons Group account for the results of a 1991 employee survey that showed a sharp drop in staff turnover and that employee perceptions of the company and motivation to create value through retaining customer loyalty have never been higher?

Clear career structure, trust of managers and a sharp drop in the level of customer complaints (40% drop in the 18 months to September 1991) are credited for this remarkable improvement in perception. The group's plans for developing and keeping "value"-oriented staff, as outlined in figure 5.11, are all based on its belief that staff give better care to customers when they have been with the company for some time, when they are better trained and when they are compensated for the long-term sales, not just immediate sales that may not create customer loyalty.

---

1. The compensation system is based in part on commissions focused not just on sales (except for Christmas sales bonuses), but on margin improvements, add-on products, housekeeping (credit agreements, etc.) and care to stock (significant drop in lost and damaged stock in 1990–91).
2. Compensation is also keyed to staff development so that those who partake of offered training programmes are eligible for bonuses. Training in two key areas — product knowledge and selling skills — is carried out both in-house and through distance learning programmes, often with major input from manufacturers. Training is primarily focused toward value creation, as it is directed towards solving customer problems. Training is structured with milestone targets, at which staff qualify for extra pay.
3. Staff pay is also tied to employment longevity, based on Dixons Group's firm belief that loyalty for service (and presumed improved performance) must be rewarded.

Figure 5.11   Dixons Group's Plan for Developing and Keeping 'Value'-Orientated Staff

Substantial Improvements to Customer Service

Dixons/Currys central service organization, Mastercare, has improved out of all recognition. Its "same day service" really works, and engineers even call the customer directly before a visit to check on the time of appointment. With its desire to deliver consistently the best service possible, Dixons/Currys is installing in-store repair centres for quicker turn-round times for customers. The concept, which is being introduced into 30 Currys Superstores around the country, is also expected to substantially reduce the group's costs of repair while reinforcing its fundamental philosophy of building trustworthiness.

In summary, Dixons Group's concentration on building shareholder value through customer satisfaction and loyalty has captured investors' attention, as evidenced by its significantly improved share price. The message from the analysts: It is not too late to buy!

LLOYDS BANK PLC

> Lloyds Bank's primary objective is to create value for its shareholders—by increase in the dividend and appreciation in the share price. This is the driving force behind our decisions and actions. . . . We rank each business on the basis of the shareholder value they create; each activity is viewed as a creator or destroyer of value. Businesses which consume cash and destroy value are targeted for divestment. (CEO's Report, 1989)

Lloyds Bank were one of the success stories of the 1980s, with a compounded growth rate of 27% (on January 1981 investment with dividends reinvested), a performance not matched by any other UK bank. During 1991 its business mix enabled Lloyds to achieve a return on assets 50% higher and dividend growth 37% higher than the peer group. Its distinct structural advantages with focus on high-margin, low-capital-intensive domestic businesses, together with its philosophy of maximizing shareholder value, have made it the core bank holding of an increasing number of investment portfolios.

The group's three basic strategies, responsible for its remarkable results, reinforce its belief in what drives value for shareholders (Figure 5.12) and its sub-targets for creating shareholder value:

- to achieve a net ROE greater than 18% (Lloyds' cost of capital)
- to increase the dividend payout ratio
- to maintain a strong balance sheet with equity grown from retained earnings.

The objectives and methodology of value strategy and management have been debated and agreed with the bank's senior management. The methodology is used for major strategic issues, and to a lesser extent for

From a practitioner's point of view, Lloyds believes that identification and management of 'value drivers' should be left to the business units. Generally, though, it feels that a significant number of factors drives the value to its shareholders:

- The ROE of each business unit.
- Avoiding strategic mistakes (in other words, "getting it right the first time")
- Projecting the right image in the right market.
- Avoiding bad debts.
- Targeting customer groups prepared to pay a premium for Lloyds' service.
- Quality of service to the customer: "It is cheaper to retain existing customers than to get new ones".

Figure 5.12   Value Drivers in Lloyds' Business

business unit strategies. Below this level the approach is simplified to the objective of achieving a sustainable after-tax return (equal for all business units) on equity, which will at least equal its cost of equity. Nevertheless, Lloyds believes that there is still plenty of scope for extending the full approach to lower levels within the organization.

With the 1990 economic fluctuations out of the way, the benefits of the approach are clearly shown in the growth in shareholder value of Lloyds Bank compared with its peer group (which includes a 35% + growth in share price during 1991). The philosophy of shareholder value, which was formulated and propagated by the current CEO, Brian Pitman (appointed December 1983), places primary emphasis on creating distributable returns (free cash flow) for shareholders via profitable non-capital-intensive businesses.

Lloyds Strategies for Creating Shareholder Value

Lloyds implements three basic strategies to achieve the goals stated above

1. *Reallocation of assets.* This strategy for creating shareholder value has transformed Lloyds from a diversified international bank into a focused domestic bank. Lloyds's policy is to focus on the strengths of the market, not necessarily domestic investment vs. international activities. Although it has recently disposed of some UK assets (selling its stake in Yorkshire Bank and closing its gilts and eurobond operations) and acquired others abroad (Abbey Life in Ireland and Germany), the larger proportion of its business is in the UK.

   Its 62% international assets in 1981 had been reduced to 28% by the end of 1990. The significantly wider domestic net interest margins reflect a large component of consumer and small business lending funded from a base of cheap retail deposits. The international segment was wholesale in orientation, geared to low margin, new-currency and large corporate lending. Now this is focused on international private banking in those countries where Lloyds is not a major player in the retail market.

Lloyds has moved away from low margin euro-currency lending and sold international offices in the US, Canada and Portugal. It has also enhanced value to shareholders by recognizing that growth, to compensate for declining (at the time) corporate loan margins, must come from other areas, such as increasing arrangement and lending fees, and enhancement of the personal customer base (thus Lloyds' acquisition of Abbey Life).

Lloyds estimates that its interest margin is almost 25% higher than the peer group average because of its low percentage of international assets.

2. *Seeking selective market leadership.* Lloyds' second strategic principle concerns competitive advantage. Its stated policy, which underlies its switch from international to domestic assets, is to seek selective market leadership and to avoid those markets and products where it cannot obtain a strong position. It pulled out of gilts and euro-bond operations in 1987, for example, because 'markets were overcrowded and we were marginal players'.

3. *High margin/low capital intensive businesses.* In keeping with its policy of producing high affordable dividends (distributable returns), Lloyds has sought balance sheet growth by moving away from low-margin commodity lending into risk management and fee-based services. Development of its life assurance subsidiary, Black Horse Life, began with the acquisition of a 57% stake in Abbey Life, projected to generate significant cash flow from its existing client base. This is expected to prove extremely effective in terms of capital cost regulatory requirements (cash holdback), as requirements are minimal in relation to the costs of lending under the BIS rules. Although embedded value life profits are not technically distributable, they can be included within the group's capital and effectively free up banking-derived earnings for distribution.

Lloyds' focus on high margin areas like personal and small business lending has resulted in a higher yield on its domestic assets and stronger net interest margin than its peers.

The results of Lloyds' adherence to its strategic principles has produced amazing results since 1986 (see Table 5.1): pre-tax return on assets 185% better than peers in 1990 vs. 33% in 1986.

Table 5.1 Comparison of Lloyds with Peer Groups

	Lloyds	Barclays	NatWest	Midland
Return on earning assets, 1986				
Net interest income	3.82	3.78	3.54	3.27
Other income	1.85	1.91	1.55	2.05
Costs	−3.60	−3.82	−3.25	−3.93
Subtotal	2.08	1.87	1.84	1.39
Bad debts	−0.50	−0.64	−0.52	−0.70
Investment gains	0.00	0.06	0.01	0.10
Associates	0.05	0.11	0.09	0.05
Pre-tax	1.62	1.41	1.41	0.85
Return on earning assets, 1990				
Net interest income	4.29	3.07	3.34	2.74
Other income	2.84	1.97	1.88	2.45
Costs	−4.62	−3.31	−3.69	−4.00
Subtotal	2.50	1.73	1.52	1.20
Bad debts	−1.76	−1.08	−1.07	−1.17
Investment gains	0.04	0.00	−0.01	0.05
Associates	0.04	0.03	0.02	0.04
Exceptional	0.29	0.00	0.00	−0.09
Pre-tax	1.11	0.67	0.47	0.02

Source: UBS Phillips & Drew, October 1991.

Difficulties in Implementing a Value Approach

The problems experienced by Lloyds in implementing VSM were primarily technical and involved retraining its own financial experts and those within the investing community to think of cash flow in terms of "free cash" or "affordable dividends" to shareholders, rather than cash flow in the traditional sense. Lloyds' experience with the investing community was that, with a few notable exceptions, there was little awareness of, but a lot of interest in, the value techniques. Its regular meetings with analysts and fund managers has succeeded "only up to a point" in educating and convincing the investing community of the benefits of managing for value; "They [the investors] are convinced by the results, but not by the theory".

In summary, Lloyds feels its value strategy can be encapsulated in three points.

- Ensuring profitability of ongoing businesses without going to its shareholders for more capital.
- Reducing investment in those parts of the business which cannot realistically expect long-term returns exceeding the cost of equity.
- Increasing investment in high return businesses.

Overall, Lloyds' objective is to maximize shareholder value, which means "maximizing the present value of (estimated) future affordable dividends". It does not attempt to maximize ROE but instead attempts to take on all business which at the margin will generate 18% ROE. Lloyds believes that maximizing ROE does not maximize shareholder value. Rather, it feels that success is better measured by the actual change in shareholder value over time.

When asked if it felt it would be a takeover target in the future, Lloyds' opinion was that it would not: 'Management is already maximizing returns for shareholders'.

Indeed, if the sentiments of many of the analysts surveyed are to be believed, it is a share to buy.

CONCLUSION

Although some UK companies have already gained considerable 'value' experience, the value-based approach in UK companies is seen to be only in its infancy, with expectations for considerable growth in the next 5–10 years.

Projections of 30–40% per annum growth in their value business by value consultants leads to the conclusion that there is great expectation of a wider acceptance of the value theories by UK companies in the future. But "value" longevity will depend on successful implementation and demonstrable results to the investing community. Some UK companies are already making considerable strides in that direction, determined not to be left behind in the race to maximize shareholder value.

REFERENCES

Bowditch, Gillian (1991). User-friendly Dixons aims to take the science out of its appliances. *The Times*, 23 October.

Day, George and Fahey, Liam (1988). Valuing market strategies. *Journal of Marketing*, July, 45–66.

Fahey, Liam (1988). Linking product-market analysis and shareholder value. *Planning Review*, March/April, 18–21.

Graham Bannoch & Partners Ltd (1990). *3i plc Shareholder Value Survey: Corporate Attitudes to Stock Market Valuations*, London.

Marsh, Paul (1990). *Short-termism on Trial*. Institutional Fund Managers' Association, London.

MORI and Coopers & Lybrand Deloitte (1991). *Shareholder Value Analysis Survey*. London.

Rappaport, A. (1986). *Creating Shareholder Value*. Free Press, New York.

Rappaport, A. (1987). Stock market signals to managers. *Harvard Business Review*, Nov–Dec.

Reimann, Bernard C. (1988). Managing for the shareholders: an overview of value-based planning, *Planning Review*, February, 10–22.

Reimann, Bernard C. (1989). Managing for value, a guide to value-based strategic management. In *The Planning Forum* in conjunction with Blackwell, Cambridge, USA.

Stewart, G. Bennett III (1991). *The Quest for Value*. Harper-Collins, New York.

Value Forum. British Petroleum Co. Plc. (Internal Publication.)

6

THE PARADOX OF COMPETITIVE ADVANTAGE

Frank L. Winfrey

*The Clark N. and Mary Perkins Barton Associate Professor of Management,
Division of Business and Economics, Lyon College*

Michael D. Michalisin

Assistant Professor, Department of Management, South Illinois University

William Acar

Associate Professor, Graduate School of Management, Kent State University

- Sustained competitive advantage in a turbulent environment requires the simultaneous achievement of strategic fit and strategic flexibility.
- Attaining competitive advantage is affected by the firm's competitive arena, its position within the arena, and the firm's array of resources.
- A strategic asset neutralizes a threat or allows the firm to exploit an opportunity.
- A firm can create strategic, specialized assets by configuring in bundles, appropriate elements of unspecialized resources.

A firm achieves superior performance by aligning its strategy and resources with the environment. This alignment is termed strategic fit (Venkatraman and Camillus, 1984; Drazin and Van de Ven, 1985; Venkatraman and Prescott, 1990; Chorn, 1991; Nath and Suharshan, 1994). In past decades when

The Strategic Decision Challenge, Edited by D. E. Hussey
© 1998 John Wiley & Sons Ltd

competition was limited, product life-cycles were long, and technological change was slow, achieving strategic fit was not a particularly difficult task. However, companies in the 1990s are confronted with intense domestic and foreign competition, short product life-cycles, rapidly changing technology, and a growing demand by customers for greater product variety at lower prices (Harrigan and Dalmia, 1991; Goldhar et al., 1991). In this hyper-competitive global environment, achieving strategic fit becomes considerably more challenging to management.

The ability of a firm to adjust to changes in the environment is referred to as strategic flexibility (Harrigan, 1985; Noori, 1990; Harrigan and Dalmia, 1991; Goldhar et al., 1991; Sorge, 1991; Parthasarthy and Sethi, 1992; D'Aveni, 1994). This chapter extends the resource-based view of the firm (RBV) to suggest how firms can sustain strategic fit with flexibility in a hypercompetitive environment. The first part of the chapter draws from the RBV to examine how firms use flexible resources (physical, human, organizational) to buttress environmental change. The second part of the chapter delineates how the firm can achieve both flexibility and fit by strategically configuring unspecialized assets into strategic, specialized bundles of assets.

CONCEPT OF COMPETITIVE ADVANTAGE

Competitive advantage is regularly used in strategic management to describe a critical phenomenon in business, yet management scholars do not appear to agree as to the composition of this transient phenomenon. This first section examines the phrase "competitive advantage" by analysing its components — competition and advantage. Specifically, the two parts include defining the competitive arena (identifying the competition) and identifying factors that affect firm performance.

A firm's competitive advantage is affected by its competitive arena (Porter, 1980 and 1985; Powell, 1992; Moore, 1993; Normann and Ramirez, 1993), its position within the arena (Porter, 1980 and 1985; Powell, 1984; Harrigan, 1985; Hansen and Wernerfelt, 1989), and its resources (Wernerfelt, 1984; Rumelt, 1984; Barney, 1991; Conner, 1991; Collis, 1991; Tallman, 1991; Mahoney and Pandian, 1992; Robins, 1992). The competitive arena can be described broadly or narrowly such as business ecosystems, industries, industry segments, or products. The firm's competitive position is a function of its intended strategy and the arena's competitive forces. The ability of the firm to achieve superior profits relative to its competitors is a function of its resources (Peteraf, 1993; Amit and Schoemaker, 1993). Resources that are valuable, rare, imperfectly imitable, and have no strategic equivalents are capable of providing the firm with superior profits.

Defining the Competitive Arena

Competitive advantage is derived from having resources superior to one's competitors (Barney, 1991; Peteraf, 1993). Superior resources allow the firm to capitalize on market opportunities and neutralize threats in ways that competitors cannot (Porter, 1985; Mahoney and Pandian, 1992). Thus the initial task in developing an advantage is to first identify one's competition. This section describes alternative levels of defining the competitive arena.

Business ecosystems

Moore (1993) notes that successful companies do not view themselves merely as members of a single industry, but rather as members of ecosystems. He notes that competitive advantage is derived through the creation of customer value and that today's successful organizations cultivate superior value through cooperative networks that span multiple industries.

Firms join cooperative networks across industries in a process referred to as *systematic social innovation* to form complex business systems (Normann and Ramirez, 1993). In working together on technologies central to the network, the group can create greater levels of value for its customers than may be possible by the individual firms. The ability to coproduce greater levels of customer value gives each of the firms in a network a competitive advantage.

Industries

Porter (1980; p. 5) describes an industry as a

  group of firms producing products that are close substitutes for each other.

He (1985) proposes the use of the five-forces model to assess the attractiveness of this competitive arena. The critical purposes of this analysis are to: (i) identify the threat of existing competitors, (ii) assess the potential threat of new competitors entering the arena, (iii) identify means to manipulate the competitive forces in the firm's favour; and (iv) thus determine the overall attractiveness of the industry.

However, Porter's approach (1985) has two important weaknesses. First, his framework for identifying industry boundaries is an arbitrary process. Second, it does not address the relative proximity of competitive threats. Grouping competitors on the basis of generally related products or services does not provide in itself a clear sense of the degree of threat that a particular competitor may pose.

Strategic groups

Porter (1980) suggests that clustering firms based on some significant competitive criteria can aid in the identification of those firms within the industry that constitute direct competitors. A cluster of related firms is referred to as a *strategic group* (Dess and Davis, 1984). The competitive criteria bonding a strategic group can vary based on specialization, technological leadership, range of products, customer service and price policy.

While members of strategic groups represent a firm's most immediate competitive threats, the unspoken agreements among "good" competitors in the group may protect each firm's market share and profit levels (Porter, 1985). The stability and profitability of the strategic group can exist due to differences in the products offered by the group members and the reluctance of group members to engage in direct competition (Powell, 1992).

Generic strategies/subsegments

Porter (1985) identifies four types of competitive strategies (referred to as generic strategies) that are capable of achieving above average profits among competitors: cost leadership, differentiation, cost focus and differentiation focus. Porter uses the four generic strategies to classify competition across an entire industry.

Porter has suggested that these are the only types of competitive strategies that are capable of achieving above average industry profits. However, other scholars have subsequently challenged Porter's assertion, noting companies that have achieved above average industry returns while simultaneously pursuing both cost leadership and differentiation strategies (Murray, 1988; Hill, 1988).

Products

Companies that manufacture more than one product are commonly referred to as "multiproduct" firms. Some firms pursue more than one competitive strategy through their multiproduct offering (Nayyar, 1993). Spurred by the debate over whether companies could simultaneously pursue more than one generic strategy (Murray, 1988; Hill, 1988), Nayyar analysed a profitable large multidomestic firm that produces over 2000 products worldwide. His study found that although the company uses more than one generic strategy, it only uses one strategy per product. The company is able to profitably produce and sell products that are cost leaders and differentiated ones due to economies of scope and the ability to deter competition through extensive presence in the market.

Nayyar concluded that competitive strategies are applicable at the product level. According to this view, competition should be analysed according to individual product markets. Thus, the competitive profile of a multiproduct firm would be a basket of competitor groups that are related within each group but can vary across groups.

Factors Affecting Firm Performance

This section focuses on firm performance because the objective of a competitive advantage is to earn above average industry profits (Porter, 1985). Hansen and Wernerfelt (1989) identified three economic and organization factors that determine firm performance: (1) industry characteristics; (2) competitive position; and (3) firm resources.

Industry characteristics

The attractiveness of an industry refers to the opportunities that it presents for achieving an acceptable return on investment (Porter, 1980 and 1985; Harrigan, 1985; Hansen and Wernerfelt, 1989). A firm may have resources that provide it with a competitive advantage in any particular industry, but if the industry is unattractive, even above average profits may be low relative to other strategic options.

The factors affecting industry attractiveness are referred to as industrial forces. These forces include key participants in the competitive arena: buyers, suppliers, competitors, potential entrants, and substitute products. It is the amount of bargaining power each of the forces has over the firm that makes the industry attractive or unattractive (Powell, 1984; Porter, 1985; Harrigan, 1985; Hansen and Wernerfelt, 1989).

The determinants of customer bargaining power can be classified as bargaining leverage and price sensitivity (Porter, 1985; Harrigan, 1985). Determinants of customer bargaining leverage include buyer concentration versus firm concentration, buyer volume, buyer switching costs and buyer information. The supplier's bargaining power over the firm is affected by the switching cost of the buyer, the existence of substitute products, the differentiation of inputs, and the size of the firm's order relative to the output to the supplier (Porter, 1985).

Existing and potential competitors can affect the profitability of an industry. Such rivalry determinants include industry growth, fixed costs, product differences, brand loyalty, and concentration and balance within the industry. The existence or lack of entry barriers can affect industry attractiveness including economies of scale, property rights, capital requirements and access to distribution channels (Porter, 1985; Harrigan, 1985; Hansen and Wernerfelt, 1989).

Competitive position

Identifying an attractive industry is only half of the challenge. The other half of the challenge involves competitively positioning the firm so as to achieve above average industry profits (Powell, 1984; Hansen and Wernerfelt, 1989).

As previously noted, Porter (1985) identifies two types of competitive strategies that are capable of positioning the firm so as to achieve above average industry profits: cost leadership and differentiation. He notes that these strategies actually arise from firms attempting to cope with industry forces.

Underlying the ability to achieve a competitive advantage are the firm's resources. Resources provide the firm with the wherewithal to achieve a strategic position within an industry (Mahoney and Pandian, 1992). Resources can also affect the degree to which industry forces can threaten or exert bargaining power over the firm. The RBV is described in the next section.

Firm resources

The RBV describes the firm as a bundle of resources with the nature of the resources as the key determinant to achieving a competitive advantage and thus above average industry returns (Barney, 1991). Thus, the differences in firm resources across an industry explain the variability in profits. The ability of resources to account for differences in firm profits across an industry is based on two assumptions. The first assumption is that resources are asymmetrically distributed across the industry and competitive advantage is derived from the heterogeneity of resources (Barney, 1991; Collis, 1991; Tallman, 1991; Peteraf, 1993; Amit and Schoemaker, 1993).

The second assumption is that the sustainability of competitive advantage is a function of resource immobility (Wernerfelt, 1984; Barney, 1991; Mahoney and Pandian, 1992; Robins, 1992; Amit and Schoemaker, 1993). A firm will continue to earn above average profits from superior resources until competitors gain access to the resource and implement similar strategies.

Firms attempt to block or slow the dissemination of critical resources through developing mobility barriers and entry barriers (Porter, 1980; Conner, 1991; Mahoney and Pandian, 1992; Amit and Schoemaker, 1993; Peteraf, 1993). These isolating mechanisms impede the mobility of critical resources and deter the entry of potential competitors.

Strategic assets

Firms achieve a competitive advantage by identifying, selecting, and implementing superior resources that are heterogeneous and immobile in an industry. Superior resources are characterized along the following dimensions: value, rarity, imperfect imitability, no strategic equivalents, and affordability (Amit and Schoemaker, 1993).

A resource is a strategic asset if it is valuable to the firm. It is valuable to the firm either because it neutralizes a threat in the competitive environment or allows the firm to exploit an opportunity (Barney, 1991). An important factor in asset value is its *specificity*. In general, specialized assets are more capable of achieving higher profits than assets that are more general purpose in nature (Mahoney and Pandian, 1992).

The degree of specialization is also a function of the firm's existing resources. It may be that an asset is specialized for one firm's unique bundle of resources but less specialized to all other firms in the industry. Such differences in firm resource bundles tend to create the heterogeneity of resources within an industry.

An asset is only capable of providing a firm with an advantage if it is rare among its competitors (Barney, 1991). If an asset is not scarce within an industry it is not capable of providing a firm with a competitive advantage. Additionally, the sustainability of the firm's competitive advantage will also be affected by the availability of the resource outside the industry (potential entrants).

Strategic assets provide the firm with a competitive advantage because they are imperfectly imitable (Barney, 1991; Peteraf, 1993). Imperfect imitability may result from the competitor experiencing causal ambiguity (Barney, 1991). In examining the firm's complex bundle of resources, the competitor may be unable to determine the cause and effect relationship between firm assets and the resulting competitive advantage, thus making it difficult to replicate the strategy (Reed and DeFillippi, 1990). The competitor may also be unable to replicate the firm's asset base due to other factors such as path dependency, bounded rationality, social complexity, and high transaction costs.

An asset is only capable of providing the firm with a competitive advantage if there are no strategically equivalent substitutes (Mahoney and Pandian, 1992). Strategic equivalence refers to the ability of another asset to assist the competitor in achieving a similar competitive advantage in the industry. In addition to imperfect substitutability, the firm must be able to acquire the strategic asset at a relatively low cost. The ability to achieve high net profits from the resource is a function of the acquisition cost of the needed resources (Porter, 1980; Wernerfelt, 1984). One way to achieve a competitive advantage is to anticipate future strategic asset needs and position the firm to acquire and control needed resources (Amit and Schoemaker, 1993).

In this section, it is argued that a firm's performance is affected by its competitive arena, its competitive position within that arena, and its resources. But can any resource be used to achieve a profitable and defensible competitive position? The concept of strategic fit attempts to address these issues.

STRATEGIC FIT

The purpose of strategy is to align firm resources to exploit opportunities and minimize threats (Venkatraman and Camillus, 1984; Porter, 1985). The notion of strategically aligning firm resources with the competitive environment underlies the concept of strategic fit. Specifically, strategic fit is the degree alignment between the competitive situation, strategy, firm culture, leadership style and other firm resources (Chorn, 1991; Nath and Suharshan, 1994).

Perspectives of Strategic Fit

Venkatraman and Camillus (1984) note six perspectives on strategic fit. Each perspective of strategic fit describes how firm performance is affected by firm and environmental variables. Thus, each perspective provides insight regarding firm performance in terms of the fit and the interaction of clusters of different sets of variables.

Strategic formulation perspective

The strategic formulation perspective denotes that a firm's performance is contingent on its environment. Accordingly, managers formulate strategies based on the current competitive environment as well as anticipated changes (Venkatraman and Prescott, 1990; Chorn, 1991). The firm has some influence on the environment (primarily the strategic group) through its strategic actions (Venkatraman and Camillus, 1984; Porter, 1985).

Strategic implementation perspective

According to the strategic implementation perspective, firm performance is a function of the fit between strategy and internal elements. High-firm performance is achieved through the composition and fit of resources supporting the firm's strategy. This is similar to the RBV (Barney, 1991) in that it relates performance to firm resources but differs due to the emphasis on fit rather than resource acquisition and control.

Integrated formulation–implementation perspective

The integrated formulation–implementation perspective underscores the interdependence of strategy formulation and integration. Strategic fit is viewed as a linear relationship between context and structural variables.

Interaction perspective

The interaction perspective describes how a firm can anticipate, control, and influence a competitor. This approach considers the threats and opportunities of existing or potential networks of firms in its strategic analysis and formulation and encompasses firm advantages derived from membership to business ecosystems (Venkatraman and Camillus, 1984; Venkatraman and

Prescott, 1990; Normann and Ramirez, 1993; Moore, 1993; Nath and Suharshan, 1994).

Strategic choice perspective

According to the strategic choice perspective, fit is not merely a matter of accommodating contingencies but rather a strategic choice. As such, managerial focus is on the interactions of firm resources and resource constraints in formulating a strategic plan. Its primary difference from the other perspectives is in that it is proactive rather than reactive in its approach.

"Overarching Gestalt" perspective

The overarching Gestalt perspective is perhaps the most comprehensive of the six perspectives because it accommodates fit among firm variables and environmental variables, including business ecosystems. Because organizations are not autonomous entities, this perspective embraces multiple contingency configurations derived from the set of possible strategic responses by competitors (Venkatraman and Camillus, 1984; Drazin and Van de Van, 1985; Venkatraman and Prescott, 1990).

Regardless of the approach, empirical studies have found that firms exhibiting strategic fit consistently outperform firms that appear less strategically fit (Chakravarthy, 1986; Venkatraman and Prescott, 1990; Sorge, 1991). However, scholars have noted that future research must address the difficulty in achieving strategic fit in a volatile environment (Venkatraman and Camillus, 1984; Chakravarthy, 1986; Sorge, 1991). Chakravarthy (1986) notes that an excellent firm improves its strategic fit in volatile environments through adaptive specialization and adaptive generalization. Adaptive specialization is the use of slack resources to improve the firm's current fit, while adaptive generalization involves using the firm's slack resources to improve the firm's flexibility.

STRATEGIC FLEXIBILITY

Achieving strategic fit among firm resources, strategy, and the environment over extended periods of time is difficult when firm resources are not capable of adjusting to rapid technological change and short product life-cycles, customers demanding variety, customers demanding quick response, customers demanding higher levels of quality, and customers demanding a low-cost product (Harrigan and Dalmia, 1991; Goldhar et al., 1991). This section discusses how flexible resources (physical, human, and organization) promote the maintenance of organizational advantage in a hypercompetitive environment.

Physical Resources

Physical resources include land, equipment, buildings, raw materials, and the physical technology used in a firm (Barney, 1991). In stable environments, firms often employ fixed equipment that performs single repetitive operations yielding consistency, efficiency and volume (Parthasarthy and Sethi, 1992). Such specialized equipment is effective in producing low-cost standard products that capitalize on economies of scale and learning-curve effects; however, it is notoriously difficult and expensive to modify such dedicated equipment (Noori, 1990; Goldhar et al., 1990, 1992; Sorgi, 1991).

Flexible automation systems utilize general purpose, computer-controlled devices that can be quickly adjusted without significant cost to accommodate changes in either the product design or the process design (Noori, 1990; Goldhar et al., 1991; Parthasarthy and Sethi, 1992). System flexibility allows the firm to quickly create batches of unique products at relatively low cost (Parthasarthy and Sethi, 1992). Thus, such systems provide multiple sources of competitive advantage: spreading fixed costs over more units (standard and differentiated products), eliminating the competitors learning-curve advantages, gaining first-mover advantages due to design-engineering-production-delivery speed, cost effectively customizing products to meet special customer needs, and reducing labour costs (Noori, 1990; Goldhar et al., 1991; Sorgi, 1991; Parthasarthy and Sethi, 1992).

Galbraith (1990) notes that flexible systems can be valuable resources through their transferability. Referred to as "floating factories", entire production facilities thus transcend being inert, fixed assets, and become flexible systems that can be expanded, disassembled, relocated, and reconfigured. These floating factories can be described as technological bundles transferable to other geographical locations with favourable labour costs, in closer proximity to customers, in closer proximity to technology centres, or providing other strategic benefits (Goldhar et al., 1991).

Human and Organizational Resources

Congruent with the concept of strategic fit, a firm's competitiveness can be assessed by comparing its resource profile to market requirements (Amit and Schoemaker, 1993). As such, the organizational and human resource requirements to be successful in a hypercompetitive environment should be different from those required in a stable environment. Thus, it is not surprising to suggest that a fast-paced environment noted for introducing low-cost, innovative products would require flexible workers and organic structures (Harrigan and Dalmia, 1991).

In a hypercompetitive environment, organizational structure plays a crucial role in development and maintenance of a firm's competitive advantage

(D'Aveni, 1994). In turbulent environments where task uncertainty is high, the appropriate organizational structure should facilitate speed in the sharing of critical information among its members, de-emphasize specialization, and promote employee discretion (Drazin and Van de Ven, 1985; Nemetz and Fry, 1988; Chorn, 1991; Goldhar et al., 1991; Parthasarthy and Sethi, 1992; D'Aveni, 1994).

The employees in successful firms, technically competent and well versed in a diversity of subjects, are often referred to as "knowledge workers" (Harrigan and Dalmia, 1991; Parthasarthy and Sethi, 1992). Knowledge workers are often moved around the organization to focus their creative and technical skills on those issues critical to the firm's competitive advantage. By having such employees interact with one another in various contexts of the organization, the firm reaps synergistic benefits from their trans-organizational knowledge.

To develop strategic flexibility in their organizations, managers must instill culture based on individualism, creativity, and quick response (Noori, 1990; Chorn, 1991). The firm maintains this culture by hiring workers who have vision, can tolerate ambiguity, and are flexible (Nemetz and Fry, 1988; Chorn, 1991). The firm's leaders perpetuate such culture by opening lines of communication in the organization, empowering workers to perform their roles, and rewarding workers based on creative, proactive behaviour.

PARADOX RESOLVED

According to the resource-based view, a firm's profitability is a function of its resources (Rumelt, 1984; Barney, 1991; Peteraf, 1993; Amit and Schoemaker, 1993). Specifically, the firm's relative profits are based on how well its resources match the requirements of the market given the processes with which it has equipped itself (Barney, 1991). Thus, to gain a competitive advantage, the firm should strive to acquire assets specific to certain market requirements (Rumelt, 1984). However, in a hypercompetitive environment, identification of requisite assets is subject to change and rapid turnover (Harrigan and Dalmia, 1991; Goldhar et al., 1991; D'Aveni, 1994).

Specialized assets that are dedicated to specific functions are notoriously inflexible toward accommodating requirements arising from significant market changes. Unspecialized assets are suitable for the demands of an unknowable future market, but are less efficient and effective in meeting current market requirements than specialized assets. Thus, the strategist is confronted with the compelling and competing demands of strategic fit and strategic flexibility.

Resolution of the simultaneous demands would require resources that are capable of both achieving and perpetuating a competitive advantage. In a hypercompetitive environment, resolution requires resources that are flexible

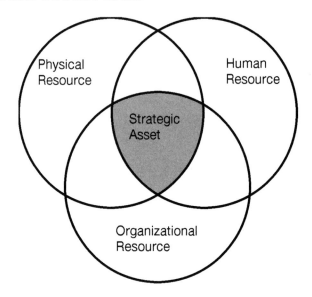

Figure 6.1   Strategic, Specialized Bundle

but that can perform specialized functions. The basic premise of this chapter is that a firm can enhance its competitiveness by configuring unspecialized resources in ways that achieve a specialized purpose. Competitive advantage is achieved by arranging unspecialized resources into strategic, specialized bundles of assets.

The Venn diagram intersection in Figure 6.1 represents a single strategic, specialized bundle. The strategic asset is a combination of a human resource, a physical resource, and an organizational resource. Each of these resources alone is an unspecialized asset. The bundle is a unique combination of the resources forming a strategic asset that serves a specialized purpose. This unique strategic, specialized bundle thus forms the basis for achieving a competitive advantage.

As the environment changes, unspecialized firm resources can then be reconfigured to achieve high levels of synergy thus maintaining competitive advantage. The reconfiguration may be in response to changes in market requirements or it may be an offensive posture to throw the market into disequilibrium (D'Aveni, 1994) (Figure 6.2). In either case, the complexity of the bundle and the frequency of its change can lead the competitor to experience causal ambiguity (Reed and DeFillippi, 1990). First, the complexity of the strategic asset configuration itself can make it difficult for the competitor to replicate. Second, through frequency of change, the competitor may not have adequate time to unravel or develop an advantageous

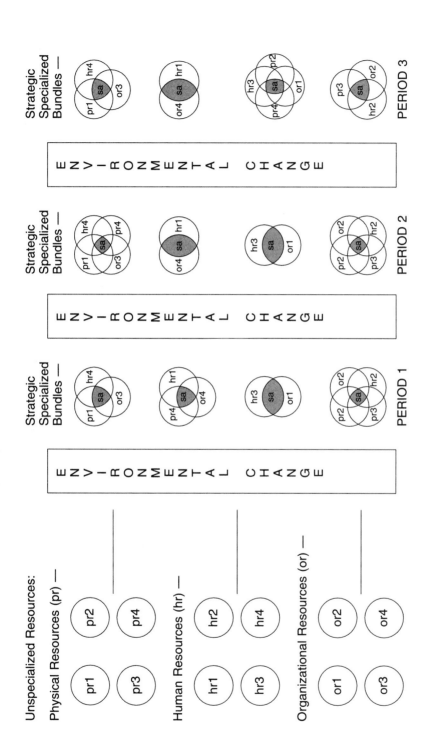

113

Figure 6.2 Dynamic reconfiguration of strategic, specialized bundles in a hypercompetitive environment. pr(i) = unspecialized physical resource; hr(i) = unspecialized human resource; or(i) = unspecialized, organizational resource; sa = strategic asset

configuration. Thus, the firm uses speed and surprise to sustain a competitive advantage (D'Aveni, 1994).

The individual assets comprising the unique bundle can also be a source of sustainable competitive advantage (Barney, 1991; Collis, 1991). Because the configuration of a particular firm's resource bundle is unique, a given asset may be a strategic asset to that firm but not to its competitors. Furthermore, through the combination of speed, surprise, and financial wherewithal, the firm with flexibility and fit can shape the competitive arena to its advantage and can define which future resources will constitute the basis for strategic advantage.

CONCLUSION

A firm achieves superior profits by competing in an attractive industry, pursuing a competitive strategy that best fits the needs of the market, and having the appropriate resources to implement the strategy. This alignment of resources–strategy–environment is called strategic fit.

✗ The ability of the firm to adjust to changes in the environment is referred to as strategic flexibility. Firms buttress environmental changes with flexible, unspecialized assets; however, unspecialized assets typically cannot meet market requirements as effectively as specialized assets.

The notion that a firm's success is a consequence of choosing competitive positions in attractive industries that best match a firm's resources is problematic in today's hyper-competitive environments (D'Aveni, 1994). Traditionally, such turbulent markets would have been labelled as unattractive.

In recent years, firms have attempted to maintain their competitiveness in turbulent environments through the acquisition of flexible assets. However, the widespread availability of flexible assets undermines their role in providing the firm with a competitive advantage (Jensen and Meckling, 1976; Barney, 1991; Peteraf, 1993).

The ability to achieve a competitive advantage through strategic fit in a hypercompetitive environment can be accomplished through strategic bundles. Depending on the significance of the required change, strategic bundles may accommodate changes in customer demands during one or more cycles in a hypercompetitive market.

This chapter has delineated how strategic fit and strategic flexibility can be achieved by configuring unspecialized assets into strategic, specialized bundles. This chapter describes how, with the flexibility to frequently reconfigure the strategic bundles, the firm can use speed and surprise to sustain a competitive advantage.

From the practitioner's perspective, the concept of creating strategic, specialized bundles provides an additional technique for achieving a competitive advantage. For the scholar, this reconceptualization extends the concept of synergy and economies of scope in new directions. Future research might involve empirical studies of firms within specific hypercompetitive environments to measure the ability of this strategy to provide a sustainable competitive advantage in different contexts.

REFERENCES

Amit, R. and Schoemaker, P. J. H. (1993). Strategic assets and organizational rent, *Strategic Management Journal*, **14**, pp. 33–46.

Barney, J. (1991). Firm resources and sustained competitive advantage, *Journal of Management*, **17**(1), pp. 99–120.

Chakravarthy, B. S. (1986). Measuring strategic performance, *Strategic Management Journal*, **7**, pp. 437–458.

Chorn, N. H. (1991). The 'alignment' theory: creating strategic fit, *Management Decision*, **29**(1), pp. 20–24.

Collis, D. J. (1991). A resource-based analysis of global competition: the case of the bearings industry, *Strategic Management Journal*, **12**, pp. 49–68.

Conner, C. R. (1991). A historical comparison of resource-based theory and five school of thought within industrial organization economics: do we have a new theory of the firm? *Journal of Management*, **17**(1), pp. 121–154.

D'Aveni, R. A. (1994). *Hypercompetition: Managing the Dynamics of Strategic Maneuvering*, The Free Press, New York.

Dess, G. G. and Davis, P. S. (1984). Porter's (1980) generic strategies as determinants of strategic group membership and organizational performance, *Academy of Management Journal*, **27**(3), pp. 467–488.

Drazin, R. and Van de Ven, A. H. (1985). Alternative forms of fit in contingency theory, *Administrative Science Quarterly*, **30**, pp. 514–539.

Galbraith, C. S. (1990). Transferring core manufacturing technologies in high-technology firms, *California Management Review* (Summer), pp. 56–70.

Goldhar, J. D., Jelinek, M. and Schie, T. W. (1990). Flexibility and competitive advantage-manufacturing becomes a service industry, *International Journal of Technology Management, Special Issue on Manufacturing Strategy*, **6**(3/4), pp. 243–259.

Hall, R. (1992). The strategic analysis of intangible resources, *Strategic Management Journal*, **13**, pp. 135–144.

Hansen, G. S. and Wernerfelt, B. (1989). Determinants of firm performance: The relative importance of economic and organizational factors, *Strategic Management Journal*, **10**, pp. 399–411.

Harrigan, K. R. (1985). *Strategic Flexibility: A Management Guide for Changing Times*, Lexington Books, Lexington.

Harrigan, K. R. and Dalmia, G. (1991). Knowledge workers: the last bastion of competitive advantage, *Planning Review*, November/December, pp. 4–9, 48.

Hill, C. W. (1988). Differentiation versus low cost or differentiation and low cost, *Academy of Management Review*, **13**(3), pp. 401–412.

Jensen, M. C. and Meckling, W. H. (1976). Theory of the firm: managerial behavior, agency costs and ownership structure, *Journal of Financial Economics*, **3**(4), pp. 305–360.

Mahoney, J. T. and Pandian, J. R. (1992). The resource-based view within the conversation of strategic management, *Strategic Management Journal*, **13**, pp. 363–380.

J. F. (1993). Predators and prey: a new ecology of competition, *Harvard Business Review*, **71**(3), pp. 75–86.

Murray, A. I. (1988). A contingency view of Porter's 'generic strategies', *Academy of Management Review*, **13**(3), pp. 390–400.

Nath, D. and Suharshan, D. (1994). Measuring strategy coherence through patterns of strategic choices, *Strategic Management Journal*, **15**, pp. 43–61.

Nayyar, P. R. (1993). On the measurement of competitive strategy: evidence from a large multiproduct U.S. firm, *Academy of Management*, **36**(6), pp. 1652–1669.

Nemetz, P. L. and Fry, L. W. (1988). Flexible manufacturing organizations: implications for strategy formulation and organizational design, *Academy of Management Review*, **13**(4), pp. 627–638.

Noori, H. (1990). Economies of integration: a new manufacturing focus, *International Journal of Technology Management*, **5**(5), pp. 577–587.

Normann, R. and Ramirez, R. (1993). From value chain to value constellation: designing interactive strategy, *Harvard Business Review*, **71**(4), pp. 65–77.

Parthasarthy, R. and Sethi, S. P. (1992). The impact of flexible automation on business strategy and organization structure, *Academy of Management Review*, **17**(1), pp. 86–111.

Peteraf, M. A. (1993). The cornerstones of competitive advantage: a resource-based view, *Strategic Management Journal*, **14**, pp. 179–191.

Porter, M. (1980). *Competitive Strategy: Techniques for Analyzing Industries and Competitors*, Free Press, New York.

Porter, M. (1985). *Competitive Advantage: Creating and Sustaining Superior Performance*, Free Press, New York.

Powell, T. C. (1992). Organizational alignment as a competitive advantage, *Strategic Management Journal*, **13**, pp. 119–134.

Reed, R. and DeFillippi, R. J. (1990). Causal ambiguity, barriers of imitation, and sustainable competitive advantage, *Academy of Management Review*, **15**(1), pp. 88–102.

Robins, J. A. (1992). Organizational considerations in the evaluation of capital assets: toward a resource-based view of strategic investment by firms, *Organizational Science*, **3**(4), pp. 522–536.

Rumelt, R. P. (1984). Towards a strategic theory of the firm in: B. Lamb (ed.), *Competitive Strategic Management*, pp. 566–570, Prentice Hall, Englewood Cliffs, New Jersey.

Sorge, A. (1991). Strategic fit and societal effect: interpreting cross-national comparisons of technology, organization and human resources, *Organization Studies*, **12**(2), pp. 161–190.

Tallman, S. B. (1991). Strategic management models and resource-based strategies among MNEs in a host market, *Strategic Management Journal*, **12**, pp. 69–82.

Venkatraman, N. and Camillus, J. C. (1984). Exploring the concept of "fit" in strategic management, *Academy of Management Review*, **9**(3), pp. 513–525.

Venkatraman, N. and Prescott, J. E. (1990). Environment-strategy coalignment: an empirical test of its performance implications, *Strategic Management Journal*, **11**, pp. 1–23.

Wernerfelt, B. (1984). A resource-based view of the firm, *Strategic Management Journal*, **5**, pp. 171–180.

7

THE NOBLE ART AND PRACTICE
OF INDUSTRY ANALYSIS

Per V. Jenster

Professor, IMD, Lausanne, Switzerland

Peter Barklin

Partner, The Senior Management Company, London

The purpose of strategic marketing in any organization is through a thorough analysis of the firm's market opportunities and challenges, to determine the optimal way in which the firm can channel resources to increase the value for its share holders.

Therefore, the starting point for any strategic marketing problem is to solve business problems of strategic importance. Although much has been written on strategic marketing models, little has been written on how to actually carry out the work leading to a conclusive analysis.

This article takes the point of view of a management team undertaking a strategy development process. It investigates the practical work the strategic market analyst should go through to arrive at useful results.

As a generic prescription, the strategic market analysis is divided into three parts.

- Overview of the general market.
- Driving forces which impact industry relevant activities serving customer segments; we call this transvection process, the "business system". Originally developed and used by consultants, such as McKinsey & Co., this approach

---

The Strategic Decision Challenge, Edited by D. E. Hussey
© 1998 John Wiley & Sons Ltd

to studying industries has gained popularity also amongst academics. At IMD, scholars such as Professors Bouvard, Boscheck, Gilbert, Kubes and Strebel have further developed the academic side of business system analysis.
- Competitive dynamics, including analysis of players and the different ways of competing profitably.

Following this "road map" in the analytical process, there are three key sets of questions which must be answered.

1. Is the industry attractive? Why or why not?
2. If attractive, how do the economics work, and what issues threaten attractiveness? If not attractive, which opportunities exist to improve attractiveness?
3. Which strategy can competitors pursue?

In order to illustrate this approach, we will use the European soft drinks industry as a practical example. In addition to this methodology, we will also summarize how data can be gathered from a wide variety of sources, and explain some of the specific data gathering techniques and sources used in the process.

STEP 1

Determining the Current Attractiveness of the Industry

An industry's attractiveness depends on a specific company's point of view. A capital rich, but slowly growing corporation may look for capital intensity (to keep competition out) and absolute size (to be worth the effort). A smaller entrepreneurial company may look for requirements of special skills and emerging technologies (that the company masters). With only a few exceptions, all companies seek profitability and growth.

The criteria described in Table 7.1 can be used as a checklist. The list is not complete but provides a good starting point for your analysis. The further you

Table 7.1   Factors Indicating Level of Industry Attractiveness

Profitability	The financial return on capital to competitors in the industry
Growth	The opportunity to grow businesses organically by keeping up with basic demand
Size	The industry must be large enough to be significant to 'serious players'
Customer/risk	The more customers the less risk
Barriers to entry/exit	The difficulty for new competitors to enter the industry or old ones to leave
Capital intensity	The relative amount of capital required to support revenue

go down this list, the more the criteria tend to be determinants influencing profitability and growth — the most critical factors. Arguably, the shortest possible list includes only profitability and growth. After all, who would not be happy to compete in a highly profitable and strongly growing industry?

The soft drinks industry has been very profitable and consistently so (Figure 7.1). The industry has also been growing very fast compared with most other related industries. Ask now 'So what?'. Maybe the industry is very profitable, because it is growing so fast? Or are there other explanations? Are all product categories equal in development (see Figure 7.2). Can it continue to grow at these rates? The industry is clearly very attractive, but are there any threats to this?

Let us first examine the prospects for future growth. While this type of analysis should never be turned into a forecasting exercise, it is clearly useful to

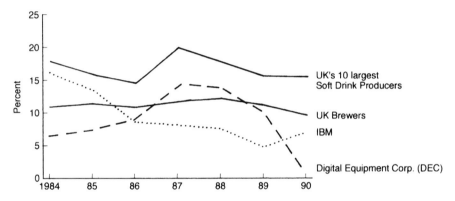

Figure 7.1   Return on Capital (profit before tax/capital) Employed. (Source: Market Reports, Annual Reports)

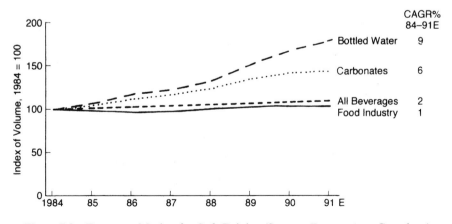

Figure 7.2   European Market for Soft Drinks. (Source: *Euromonitor*, Canadean)

assess the likelihood of future growth. Ideally, you want to identify the growth driver(s), the factor(s) determining why growth is so high, and then try to explain growth prospects through an understanding of the driver.

The question to follow, then, must be *what is driving growth?* At this stage of the analysis you may not even have a clearly articulated hypothesis, and the best advice is therefore to turn to industry experts or veterans. Simply start to place telephone calls to people in the industry asking:

why has demand for soft drinks grown so rapidly?

In this case, we listened to as many different answers as the 20 people we interviewed. This is also a good illustration of how an unaware analyst, by applying this structured approach, can actually 'add value' through highlighting different perspectives to decision makers who have spent a lifetime in an industry. Typical answers were:

the changing lifestyle of consumers, the ease-of-use of the product, the advertising we do, the Americanization of our society and our ability to develop products consumers want.

How can these influences be quantified — let alone be predictors for the future? They cannot. While they may all be true, you will have to find some tangible benchmark against which to judge future growth. We were able to identify three such pieces of "hard data".

First, growth in consumption of soft drinks has historically been at the expense of other drinks (Figure 7.3). The underlying growth driver is not just

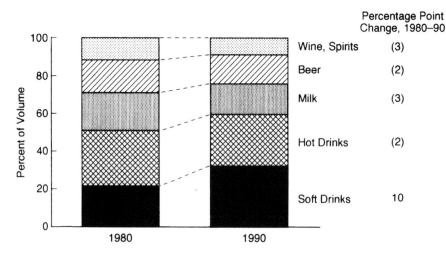

Figure 7.3   Consumption of all Beverages in Western Europe. (Source: Canadean)

population growth, but a trend explained by various changes in consumption habits, driving consumers away from traditional beverages and over to soft drinks.

Secondly, it appears that there is a relationship between national wealth and consumption of soft drinks (Figure 7.4). The richer the country, the higher the consumption per capita.

Thirdly, while European consumption averages 200 litres per capita per year and is still growing, US consumption averages 300 litres per capita per year and is stagnant. What is more, US consumption seems to be on a different relationship "curve" between national wealth and consumption.

We then *hypothesized* that all the factors affecting consumption in Europe had already been "discounted" in the per capital consumption in the US.

Using this information, we can start building scenarios for future growth of the European industry. If we believe that the relationship between consumption and gross domestic product (GDP) per capita will continue to be true and that the US market represents the highest possible consumption per capita and the US market is saturated, then it is easy to calculate how much growth there is left in the European market. It works out to approximately six years at present growth rates, assuming Europe will reach the full US level. To 'close half the gap', Europe has three years of high growth left. The calculation is illustrated in Figure 7.5.

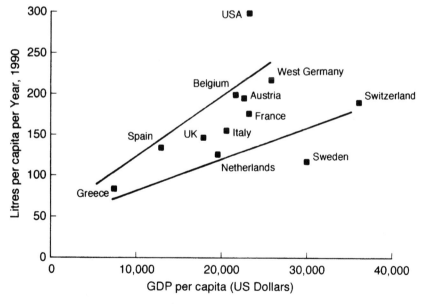

Figure 7.4 Soft Drinks Consumption *versus* GDP. (Source: *The Economist*, Key Note Report)

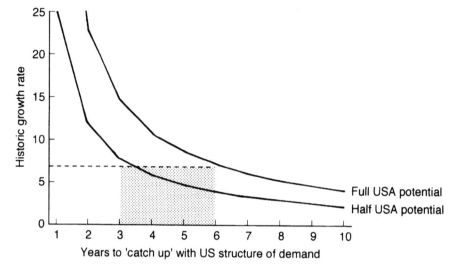

Figure 7.5   Relationship between annual Growth Rate of and Demand for Soft Drinks. (Source: SMC Analysis Assuming no Growth in the USA)

Without attempting to make exact predictions, we have built a likely growth scenario; that the European soft drink market has about three to six-years of high growth left. Regardless of exactly when growth slows, the issues of strategic importance are as follows.

a.   How will slower growth change the ways of competition in the industry?
b.   What will that mean to profitability?
c.   Which actions can competitors take to prepare themselves?

In other words, we need to dig deeper into the dynamics of the industry in order to understand exactly how economic value is created and what changes are happening to threaten and to provide opportunities.

STEP 2

Analysing the Business System

The vehicle we chose to do more detailed analysis has been termed the "business system" (an old consulting tool, popularized by academics). It very simply consists of the chain of the major relevant activities necessary to develop, produce, market and distribute products to end users. Once you have mapped out the chain, you have an analytical tool that will help ensure that no activity within the playing field is forgotten. Figure 7.6 shows the business system for the soft drinks industry.

As one examines each of the boxes of the business system, it should be kept in mind that costs are added to the final product at each step of the way. "Costs" are distinctly different from the "value" created in the eyes of the customer. This is one reason why we prefer not to use the term "the value chain". These costs can be accounted for (the number on top of the boxes indicates how much *cost* is added at each stage — shown as a percentage of price paid by the consumer). Ask:

what is happening to influence the size and variations of the costs?

Consumers are generally ignorant of the physical activities of bringing a product to market and only perceive the final attributes of the product/service bundle. Each competitor must manage the business system to create as much perceived value as possible, while incurring as little cost as possible. Ask:

is the cost added at each stage justified by the value perceived by the customer, and what is the opportunity at each stage to create more perceived value at the same, or lower, cost?

Changes happening in each of the "boxes" must be analysed, and the impact on the industry as a whole considered. The strategic importance of each issue should be evaluated so that issues not affecting value creation can be disregarded.

Usually, you will start by analysing the "consumers box". For the soft drinks industry, we have already identified the threat to continued growth.

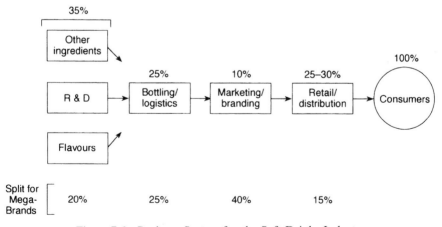

Figure 7.6   Business System for the Soft Drinks Industry

Whenever you analyse food-based industries the health trend is likely to appear. The soft drinks market has seen a high differential growth in diet (low-calorie) products. But what is the strategic impact of this trend? We would argue that when (some) consumers demand sugar-free drinks, competitors simply have to respond by launching sugar-free drinks. *Doing so is not a strategic decision* — merely a response to a change in what customers want!

What then is a strategic issue? For European soft drinks customers, the most important issue is that they keep demanding more but will probably only do so for another three to six years. That is the issue which the strategy must address, as it is likely to significantly change the rules of competition!

Without dealing with each strategic issue in great detail, here is a list of the most important ones this business system analysis uncovered.

- The issue of private labels in the retail sector. For some products, mainly low-growth products, the share of private labels has grown to over 90%, posing a powerful threat to producers. If private branding of soft drinks really takes off, there will be pressure on margins, advertising will become less important, and hence require different competitive strategies.
- General concentration in distribution is intensifying, especially in Northern Europe, giving retailers additional power. The strategy must address how to secure retail distribution as chains become less dependent on choice of brands, more dependent on private labels and more powerful in deciding who should be their favoured suppliers.
- As margins come under pressure, competitors will seek to improve profits through more efficient operations. For producers of branded products this means focusing on marketing expenses as these represent the largest part of their cost structure. Producers who do not rely solely on branded products must focus primarily on production and cost of logistics. The pressure to operate more efficiently can be responded to by traditional cost cutting and by increasing the scale of operations.
- In the branding function of the industry activity chain there has been a lot of takeover activity. This has happened in the belief that there are economies of scale to be achieved, a belief which is probably true (Table 7.2). This trend could easily intensify, especially when demand and hence organic company growth slows down.
- Competitors must consider what would happen if their relative cost position becomes eroded by other competitors' activities to create scale.

At this stage of the analysis, you have now created a good helicopter view of the trends in the industry. To summarize, the industry is very profitable and rapidly growing but over the next three–six years growth will probably slow down. Margins will probably come under pressure because of the private label threat and the growing power of retailers due to concentration. The best

Table 7.2 Apparent Competitive Strategies (Source: GENSTRAT. GGM)

	Type 1: "Mega-branders"	Type 2: "Premiums"	Type 3: "Low-cost producers"
Anticipation of lower growth	Expansion in developing geographical areas such as China, South-East Asia and Eastern Europe	Segment/niche focus	Price competitiveness
Threat of private labels and brands	Reinforce own branding	Segment/niche focus	Subcontracts to owners of own brands
Growing retailer power	Securing HoReCa through acquisitions and alliances. Stimulates consumer demand through 'pull' advertising	(not observed)	Tries to secure long-term contracts
Pressure to be more efficient	Persistent cost-focus culture. Outsourcing and contracting	(not observed)	Low-cost focus in raw materials, processing and marketing
Strong branding through marketing	"Mainstream" pricing through life-style advertising	Premium pricing through image of health/life-style	Cost focus. No branding, only selling (not observed)
Merger activity	Acquires bottlers around the world	(not observed)	(not observed)

players in the industry should respond by becoming more efficient which, in addition to traditional cost reduction measures, could lead to merger and takeover activity in order to take advantage of economies of scale.

So, if the above represents the issues and general trends in the industry, what then should a company do to compete successfully and profitably? Which competitive strategy should be pursued? Are alternative strategies equally viable?

The answer, of course, depends on specific, company-related factors that are unique to each competitor. An industry analysis should therefore not seek to answer that question for individual competitors. Rather, it should identify generic strategies that could be pursued by types of competitors. Strategies must then be "fine-tuned" at later stages in the strategic process involving detailed company analysis.

STEP 3

Competitor Analysis

We believe it is critical to study existing ways of competition by examining activities and results of the industry's competitors and their evolution. In doing so, one should focus on how the key issues identified earlier are addressed by the various competitors.

Analysing competition is an exhaustive and time-consuming process. First, one must understand the "apparent" strategy followed by each competitor. Then the analyst must assess the degree of success each competitor has achieved.

The apparent strategy describes how the competitor addresses each of the key issues we identified in the business system analysis. After a thorough analysis of all competitors, one should try to group them into meaningful clusters as we did for the soft drinks industry (Figure 7.7). "Mega-branders" are the very large brand based companies such as The Coca-Cola Company and Pepsico. "Premiums" sell specialized brands, typically with health and/or sports claims. "Low-cost producers" sometimes have their own brands, but are primarily producing for retail chains' own labels. There is a fourth group that appears to be "doing everything"; the companies in that group pursue very confusing strategies. An analysis of performance success shows that these companies are not very profitable and in some cases even loss-making.

We prefer to conduct a performance assessment which includes: (1) market performance, (2) operational performance, and (3) financial performance. It should be carried out in order to deepen the understanding and assessment of the success of each of the above strategies.

a.   Market performance must include an assessment of absolute size and development in market share, growth relative to the total market, price

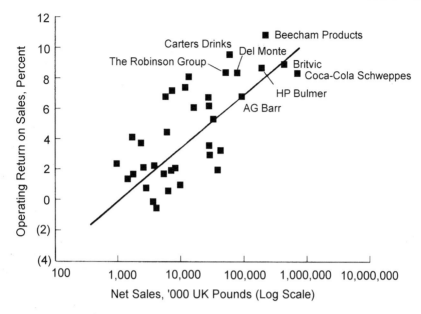

Figure 7.7 UK Soft Drinks Manufacturers 1990/91. (Source: ICC Business Ratios Ltd)

realization, product range, consumer awareness and relations to distribution channels.

b. Operational performance looks at productivity, capacity utilization, and other internal factors such as organization and management.

c. Financial performance includes study of key indicators. In the soft drinks industry, it seems more to be a function of size than of strategy. All categories, "mega-branders", "premiums", and "low-cost producers", are making healthy profits. Companies without clear strategies are not very profitable which is hardly surprising — this is the case in most industries we have analysed.

At this stage of the analysis, you may find information that contradicts your initial hypothesis. If, for example, we had found that some competitors were addressing issues that we had not anticipated, we would have had to go back to the business system analysis and, maybe, completely revise our earlier conclusions. Fortunately, that did not happen in this case.

Generating Strategic Options and Generic Strategies

In the final phase of the industry analysis, you should also apply "wisdom" based on your findings in the preceding two parts. You need to make sense of the generic strategies in a way that will help you check consistency and spell out the actions of individual competitors in the context of the industry as a whole. For this you need a framework. Clearly, many frameworks exist in books written on this subject, and there is no guide to help you pick the right one. Sometimes you can borrow from similar situations, other times you need to develop one from scratch. Our analysis uses, the so-called **HPV-LDC diagram**, an analytical tool refined at **IMD**.

As mentioned earlier, customers trade-off perceived value of a product against its cost. Fortunately, not all customers make the same trade-offs so they can be grouped into segments. To illustrate, one group of customers is willing to pay a higher price for drinks with a health claim. Others simply go for the lowest price. Still others may be somewhere in between.

Figure 7.8 shows two viable strategies. The "premium" companies (illustrated by the upper left circle) are able to create high-perceived value, although at a relatively high cost. These firms are still able to maintain attractive margins. Because there are customers willing to pay a premium price for that company's products, the company is able to make good profits following this strategy.

In contrast, "low-cost producers" (illustrated by the lower right circle) focus primarily on costs, and may not be highly regarded for product quality, innovation etc. However, because of the low-cost position, the company can sell products at cheaper prices, thus attracting a particular consumer segment. Although prices are low, so is the cost position gained through volume advantages, providing healthy margins with good profits as a result.

The mega-brand companies such as Coca- Cola and Pepsico are probably positioned somewhere between our two focused companies. Coca-Cola and

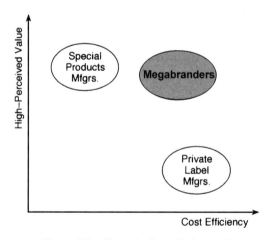

Figure 7.8   Organic Growth Strategies

Pepsico may not have the lowest possible unit costs (because of large marketing expenses) and their perceived value may not be the highest in the industry (because others can emphasize specific product attributes such as health/sports), but because they can be almost as cost-efficient and deliver almost as high value as the best in the industry, they are able to sell at high prices leading to very high profitability, and as the customer segment is so large, this leads to large absolute size (Figure 7.8)!

The mega-branders are almost outpacing competition but as long as focused competitors can find ways to create more value or produce at lower costs, they still can make money in their segments.

As our competitor analysis showed, it is the unfocused businesses — companies trying to be everything to everybody — that are in trouble (Figure 7.9). Because of scale disadvantages, nobody will be able to do what mega-branders do.

Trying to create "branded value" will definitely lead to higher costs. Trying to compete on price at the same time will lead to lower gross margins. In total, profits will be eroded and survival will be high on the company's agenda.

GROWTH THROUGH ACQUISITION

As organic growth in existing markets slows down, competitors will seek to grow through entry into other markets and through acquisition of competitors upstream and downstream in the business system.

Let us examine some "alternative" growth strategies, as these will affect every competitor — even the one who chooses not to pursue them (they may

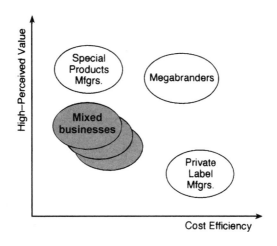

Figure 7.9 Organic Growth Strategies

get their relative cost position eroded). Figure 7.10 shows the business system once again and looks particularly at the strategies followed by the mega-branders. The activities of mega-branders should be interesting, not only for the ideas they can provide, but also because their actions are likely to affect the rest of the industry.

As market growth slows down in Coca-Cola's and Pepsico's traditional markets, these companies repeat their successes in emerging geographical markets throughout the world, leveraging off their core marketing skills. We have already discussed this "option" which need not be acquisition-led.

The business system in Figure 7.10 can be used to think about possible directions the "mega-branders" can take when making acquisitions. Pepsico is probably the best example of a "mega-brander" trying to control distribution, simply by buying restaurant chains. Pepsico and Coca-Cola are both very actively running "armies" of vending machines.

Coca-Cola has begun to buy into its own bottling licensees in some highly developed European markets, and indications are that Pepsico will be pursuing a similar strategy. The cost structure suggests that Coca-Cola potentially can capture another 25% of the retail revenue for its sales, which in itself is a growth opportunity. The real question is: Does Coca-Cola plan any restructuring opportunities such as mergers, closures etc. that could threat other competitors on both cost structure and access to distribution?

OPPORTUNITIES FOR NATIONALLY BASED COMPETITORS

Figure 7.11 shows the business system for nationally based competitors. There is evidence that mergers have already taken place between nationally based

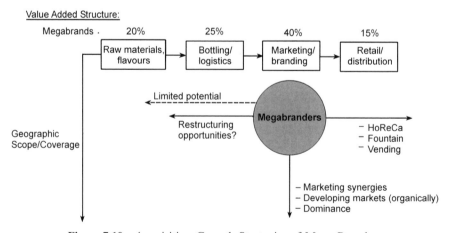

Figure 7.10   Acquisition Growth Strategies of Mega-Branders

(smaller) competitors, and the number of competitors in the marketplace has certainly gone down.

Before thinking about growth through acquisition, the smaller player must be clear on which organic growth strategy he wants to pursue. How else can a company's strategy be consistent?

The "low-cost producer" can think about further defending and improving his cost position through consolidation by acquisition of scale and subsequent realization of synergy potential in production, sourcing, logistics and administration. It may even be possible to build a transport shield within a geographical area by building a dominant position in that area.

The nationally based "low-cost producer" is probably too small to acquire distribution outlets but may seek to establish alliances with retailers by creating value for the retailer at low cost to the competitor.

The "premiums" rely on marketing and may be able to exploit their brand names in a wider geographical area, thus achieving synergies by spreading expensive selling costs over a larger revenue base.

In addition, as we have shown, companies focused on specially branded products have an equally strong need to keep costs down, so most of the elements of low-cost strategies will apply to them as well.

SUMMARY

The European soft drinks industry is currently very profitable and demand for such products is growing. However, growth is not expected to continue at these high rates forever, and when growth slows, competitors will be exposed to a

Figure 7.11 Acquisition Growth Strategies of National Competitors

number of issues that will put pressure on their margins and threaten their sales volume.

Every competitor should start preparing for these structural changes by first deciding which organic strategy to pursue and second considering how to respond to a likely wave of mergers and acquisitions.

The analytical process competitors should undertake (in continuation of this industry analysis) is as follows.

(i)   Refine and expand this industry analysis to include the geographical area in which they compete.
(ii)   Perform in-depth analyses of each competitor within that area.
(iii) Analyse in-depth, their own company in order to decide which strategy is the right one given that company's situation.
(iv)   Formulate action plans and start implementation immediately. The advantage of being the "first mover" often determines the difference between success and failure, and the opportunity to move first will not reappear.

CONCLUSIONS

As mentioned in the beginning of this article, a strategic marketing analysis is the starting point for phases in a, say, strategy development project. What follows must consider the situation of the specific company as an integral part of the strategy process; its strengths and weaknesses as well as its general position in the marketplace.

This follow-on phase often uncovers important issues the company needs to address before it can implement a certain market strategy. This is because few companies are perfectly positioned to the realities of the market segment(s) it chooses to serve. These issues represent specific decisions that need to be taken in areas as diverse as marketing, product development, production, finance and general management. Examples of such issues are organizational adequacy, depth/width of product range, pricing policy, choice of distribution channels, structure of capitalization and even ownership decision.

It is the hope of the authors that this article will help initiate the strategic process and that it in turn will help management make better choices.

8

STRATEGIC ANALYSIS FOR AN INFORMATION BUSINESS — A CASE STUDY

Sebastian Crawshaw

Infomat Ltd

In times of crisis, information, particularly reliable timely information, is at an absolute premium. The use of military satellites and on the ground reconnaissance enabled commanders to have precise knowledge of Iraqi movements during the Gulf War. Comparable information about allied movements was denied to the Iraqis due to their absence of air power. Similarly, during the recent coup in the former Soviet Union, access by Yeltsin to sympathetic parties within the capital's KGB enabled him to take steps which otherwise might not have been possible. At these times, the challenge is to resolve the different sources of conflicting data to gain real insights into the underlying processes which are taking place.

The Information Industry has not changed as rapidly as the events in August 1991 in the former Soviet Union. However, for an outsider it can be singularly confusing, since many of the competitors offer intangible products derived from licensing of information from apparently rival organizations. Clear understanding is also confused by different interpretations of words like 'database' (is this the software or the information stored on that software?).

The Strategic Decision Challenge, Edited by D. E. Hussey
© 1998 John Wiley & Sons Ltd

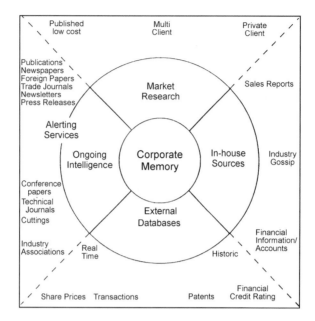

Figure 8.1   Corporate Information Requirements and Sources

THE MARKET

Setting aside demand for entertainment services, the demand for corporate information is illustrated by Figure 8.1.

All companies require some combination of information services illustrated in this figure. These can be segmented into three main areas.

Repeated transaction support.   The financial services sector, with its plethora of products for foreign exchange, share transactions, futures, commodities, etc., illustrate this sector.

Specific decision support.   Demand here is for use of databases (in-house or external), consultants, market research specialists, information brokers, etc.

Ongoing scanning or corporate radar.   This involves monitoring a defined brief, whether it is for the PR department (press clippings) or for strategic planning and competitor analysis work.

The first of these segments, *transaction support*, is at present the most developed. Any purchase of information can be directly linked to a trading decision, either foreign exchange, commodity or even purchase of airline tickets. The highly developed businesses of Reuters, Telerate and the other Financial Information Service organizations attest to the success of this sector.

The second segment, *decision support*, represents the need to gather information for decisions which are not normally repeated, e.g. acquisition of a specific business, purchase of new equipment, entering into a new market. This sector is supplied by a range of management consultants, market research specialists, information brokers, etc., who will use their own resources and a wide spread of database products available on the open market.

The third segment, *ongoing scanning* or *corporate radar*, represents the little pieces of a jigsaw which, when assembled, bring together the big picture. When decisions are made managers rely on their judgement, which is really an assessment of the expected outcomes and their associated probabilities. This is a cumulative process, built layer on layer, rather than satisfying an immediate demand. While this is clearly highly significant, the direct linkage between the information provision and the profit and loss on a specific transaction is less well defined. Based on this guiding principle, it is not surprising that the largest segment is the area supporting repeated transactions and those supporting specific 'I need to know now' types of decisions.

COMPANY BACKGROUND

Infomat operates within the information industry, supplying a daily tailored alerting service on a contract basis to large companies. Working with clients we identify their information needs, i.e. construct a profile. We then read over 600 journals, newspapers and trade magazines in 12 languages. The analysts select from these publications the articles which we believe our clients will find useful and abstract the key information — in English. We are, in effect, a professional information-gathering organization.

Started in 1981, Infomat now employs around 40 staff, mainly multilingual graduates, and services over 100 leading companies, including ICI, Shell, British Telecom and Rolls Royce. Initially the service was paper-based. In 1984–85 electronic delivery was started for a few clients who did not trust the post!

Electronic delivery is now available via PSS (Packaged Switch System) into boardroom systems or clients' software. Alternatively, we can supply Infoman, a specially modified text retrieval software package, which enables clients to build their own in-house database and handle the information we supply more efficiently.

In December 1985, the full Infomat database was licensed to Pergamon Infoline (now Maxwell Online) and Infomat entered the electronic publishing business. Other hosts were licensed later, including Dialog, Data-Star and BT/Dialcom. In early 1986 90% of the revenues were paper-based. Electronic delivery now accounts for over 50% of a substantially larger revenue base.

TAILORED ALERTING SERVICE

Our primary driving force has been the tailored alerting service, i.e. delivering the right information to the individual manager every day or every week.

The information is required within organizations for decision support to brief (other) executives who are planning an activity, be it visiting a client in Germany, deciding to build a new plant or deciding to enter a market.

Infomat's alerting service clients typically have an outward focus. They need to monitor market trends, competitors, new product launches, potential acquisitions, etc. They may also use the service for ideas generation or to create specific business opportunities. Above all the service acts as a way of building and maintaining a picture of their product/marketplaces.

The cost of a service varies with requirements, but the normal range is £5000–10,000 per annum. The buying cycle is fairly long, on average six months.

OBJECTIVES OF COMPETITOR ANALYSIS

In 1988, Infomat had experienced a rapid phase of growth, with turnover quadrupling in three years. The emergence of the single European market had produced a spurt to this growth, but the underlying uncertainty due to the 1987 crash meant that we wished to establish a clearer understanding of the market dynamics. The information industry had been growing at around 20–30% per annum and, following the 1987 crash, it was likely that markets would be changing.

The objectives of the analysis were:

1.   to clarify our understanding of the industry;
2.   to define competitors strengths and weaknesses;
3.   to sharpen Infomat's positioning and product offerings; and
4.   thereby to improve our competitive position.

METHODOLOGY

The work was undertaken by senior Infomat staff. The information was gathered by desk research, published market research, some database searching and use of in-house documents, including minutes of previous planning sessions.

We also collected competitors' brochures and information at the industry exhibitions — utilizing a specially designed form for recording data. We subsequently set up specific contacts with competitors, via consultants, to gain detailed knowledge of their activities.

Step 1

At the time when we had just started this work, we were asked to experiment with a workbook on competitor analysis being developed by a firm of management consultants, ultimately for use by their clients. This consisted of an approach to competitor analysis, supported by a generic questionnaire to aid collation of the necessary information. The workbook provided a way of mapping the key elements in the structure of an industry, approaches to competitor profiting, and some concepts to building competitive advantage. To this we added some ideas of our own on value chain analysis. This approach stimulated questions and kept them in a structured form. Inevitably not all the questions were relevant, e.g. plant capacity. A lot of the information was not immediately available (neither did we go and seek it at that stage). However, by making a few telephone calls and checking publicity material we were able to infer capacity data.

Step 2: Market Size

We identified that the target market could be between £5 million and £100 million per annum (see Table 8.1).

This may appear simplistic, but when no data is available, reasonable guesstimates have to suffice. This quantified the gross value associated with this type of service, even if at this stage most of it was inaccessible.

Step 3: Industry Analysis

The information industry is highly labour-intensive, but with a high cost of entry. During the 1980s there was a shift from the technology-driven businesses selling to the publishing-driven businesses. For example, Thorn EMI's Datasolve service was sold to the *Financial Times* and renamed Profile. Lockheed, the aerospace contractor, sold Dialog to Knight-Ridder. The ever-acquisitive Maxwell purchased Infoline, Orbit, BRS and OAG (Official

Table 8.1 Target Market for Alerting Services

Infomat target market = times 1000 companies.	
100% penetration @ £5k p.a. (average)	= £5 million
Across Europe, 4000 companies	= £20 million
For fully developed clients paying £20k p.a.:	
UK market	£20 million
European market	£80 million
	£100 million

Airlines Guide). The *Financial Times*, having missed the main market place in financial services, is trying to recover its position by acquiring McCarthy, and more recently Analysis, to combine with its Profile activities. Other players have fallen out of the marketplace, having failed to make an impact, e.g. GAS (Global Analysis Systems, purchased by Maxwell and shut), BT's Hotline service, which was a late entry into a crowded database hosting market. This has been shut and converted into a gateway service, providing additional information facilities for electronic mail users on BT Gold. Indeed, the late 1980s and early 1990s have shown every indication of an industry entering maturity, with the weaker players failing to survive and late entrants failing to enter. Having completed the initial workbook sections, we had identified a number of points.

- Buyers' views vary dramatically by segment.
- We have no standardized competition.
- Numerous substitutes exist.
- Products can be differentiated if you are knowledgeable.

Based on the analysis of each group (publishers, vendors or retailers, abstractors, Telecom operators), we built a model of the industry structure (Figure 8.2). Each horizontal line represents a competitive source of information.

We also identified some major trends which are likely to impact us in the future:

- globalization of publishing
- forward integration by publishers
- more full text publishing online
- continued industry consolidation
- growing impact of personal computer-based software.

Step 4: Competitor Analysis

Buyer behaviour

Information requirements vary by job function, and we built a matrix of job functions vs. information needs.

The actual information content changes according to the industry sector. Since publications tend to be targeted at specific industries, the competition varies by sector. This was a key realization — albeit an apparently obvious one.

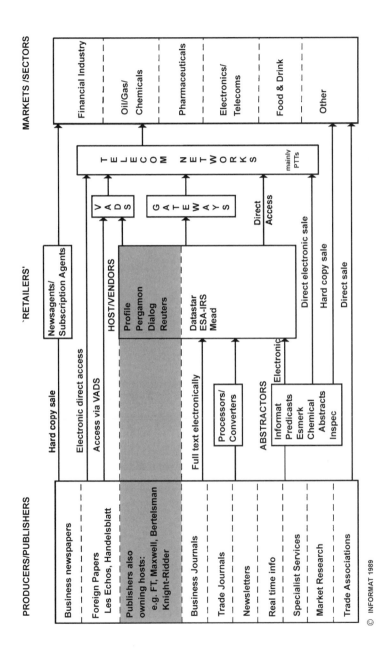

Figure 8.2 Structure of the Information/Publishing Industry. VADS = Value Added Data Service; PTTs = Post & Telecommunications Authorities

Competitors

The competition was also analysed by content, means of availability or publication (i.e. paper or electronic) and by type of publication (i.e. daily paper, weekly, journal, monthly, etc.). (See Figure 8.3.)

Publishers

For each sector there is a different set, although the main national newspapers — e.g. *Financial Times, International Herald Tribune, Wall Street Journal, Les Echos, Handlesblatt, El Pais*, etc. — crop up in all sectors.

Specialist newsletters occurred in each industry; some of these may be parts of major groups, e.g. Fintech, IDB, while others are selectively small operations.

Abstractors

Within the abstracting and specialist services producers, there are only two or three organizations, Esmerk, Reuters/Textline and Predicasts (Infomat's parent), which compete in abstracting capability across a wide range. But again, in different sectors there are specialist services (see Table 8.2).

Consequently, we analysed each of the major sectors and started assessing the data we had on competitive operations.

In-house competition

We concluded that the main competitor to our tailored alerting service was press clippings, 'do it ourselves' or blind ignorance. Apart from budgetary constraints we tend not to compete with the other abstracting services.

While the main competitor analysis work was being undertaken we met to brainstorm our service offering and re-examined each step, identifying where we added value. This worked as an excellent management training exercise and also generated:

• shared understanding
• development of a new mission statement.

This process prompted evaluation of all of Infomat's competitors against the criteria which clients would use in deciding whether to buy our service. It also provided the basis for subsequent quality improvement actions.

We then set about analysing all the parameters which could be utilized for segmenting our markets. The most appropriate emerged as being the purchase selection criteria applied by clients or potential clients (see Table 8.3). We evaluated our performance as we thought clients would perceive it (recognizing the risk of bias).

Source \ Information Requirements	Company News UK	Company News Europe	Company News R.O.W.	Credit Rating/ Co. Accounts	Share Prices	Foreign Exchange	Stockbroker Research	Product/Market Info UK	Product/Market Info Europe	Technology Projects Planned	Technology Innovations	Technology Patents	Economic Information	Country Analysis	1992 Impact	Government/ Political	Distribution/ Retailing
Business Newspapers																	
Foreign Papers																	
Trade/Business Journals																	
Newsletters																	
Electronic Info Vendors																	
Electronic Info Producers																	
Specialist Services																	

Figure 8.3 Segmentation of the Information Industry by Content and Source. R.O.W. = rest of world

Table 8.2

Sector	Service
Food	Leatherhead Food Research Association
Packaging	PIRA
Automotive	Society of Motor Manufacturers and Traders. PRS

Table 8.3   Criteria applied by information users

Reliability
Timeliness
Sources
   UK
   Foreign
   Industrial

Content
   Financial
   Economic/political
   Industrial
   Flexibility

Languages
Tailoring
Availability of full text
Cost
Reputation/awareness
Delivery format
   Paper
   Electronic
   Combined
   Storage

Having refined the table and our relative competitive advantage, the swing factors indicating why clients use Infomat were identified as:

- Foreign source coverage
- Timeliness
- Reliability
- Languages
- Combined electronic and paper delivery
- Electronic storage capacity.

In subsequent conversations with information industry pundits we found that the combination of electronic delivery and storage appeared to be

	Foreign sources	Timeliness	Reliability	Languages	Cost	Paper	Electronic PCs	EIS	Combined	Storage
							Delivery Format			
INFOMAT	60 dailies	Yes	Yes	12	Good Value !	Yes	Yes	Yes	Yes	Yes
PRESS CUTTINGS	?	Average	Yes	1	Low	Yes	No	No	No	No
IN HOUSE ABSTRACTING	?	Average		2–3 ?	Very High	Yes	No	No	No	No

Figure 8.4   Why Clients Use Infomat

unique — regardless of the other advantages! (This uniqueness has subsequently been eroded.) (Figure 8.4.)

Actions taken

Based on this initiative we took the following actions.

1. Developed a clearer understanding of our product/services.
2. Adopted a new mission statement, clearly communicating our thinking to staff and clients.
3. Re-wrote our sales presentations with a very much sharper focus.
4. Upgraded our customer services activities as a prime source of client value added.

POSTSCRIPT

This work was very much the beginning. It took around eight man-days of senior executive time, working with a minimum of interruptions. The task was not complete and probably never will be, since we lack a great deal of numeric data to fill all of the gaps. We did, however, achieve a remarkable amount by thinking and re-assessing existing material.

During the subsequent three years we have maintained a growth pattern, although the impact of the recession has slowed the growth somewhat. Increasingly our clients are moving towards the creation of in-house databases with electronic delivery of their information, so that they can maintain facilities for tracking their own competitors, which they see as a key source of strategic advantage.

The latest emergent trend has been the ever-increasing focus on quality and quality systems, combined with customer service. In 1990, we launched our own Total Quality Management programme and this, combined with the earlier competitor analysis work has contributed to our further expansion.

9

THE COMPANY AS A COGNITIVE SYSTEM OF CORE COMPETENCES AND STRATEGIC BUSINESS UNITS

Hans H. Hinterhuber, Stephan A. Friedrich, Gernot Handlbauer and Ulrich Stuhec

University of Innsbruck

- All enterprises face the question of how to increase international competitiveness.
- Strategies should create value for all stakeholders.
- The successful enterprise invents its opportunities, rather than just hoping to find them.
- The authors describe a concept which shows that the organization is a cognitive system of core competences and strategic business units.
- Practical advice is given on determining core competences.
- They show why the customer is not always right.
- The context is the learning organization.

STRATEGIES TO INCREASE INTERNATIONAL COMPETITIVENESS OF THE COMPANY

The question of how to increase international competitiveness has become vital and indispensable to all enterprises. Today, all enterprises are faced with this

The Strategic Decision Challenge, Edited by D. E. Hussey
© 1998 John Wiley & Sons Ltd

question. Raising the competitive level depends on old and new competitors' abilities to develop and implement strategies that shorten innovation and cycle time, improve the quality of offered services and reduce costs. Strategies have to be aimed at creating values for all stakeholders, namely, customers, employees, shareholders, the "financial community", society, suppliers and for strategic network partners. Figure 9.1 (Hinterhuber and Popp, 1994) illustrates the evolutionary process of international competitiveness of an enterprise based on the further development of core competences.

The efficient development, effective exploitation and committed preservation of core competences distinguish a successful enterprise from an ordinary one. The aforementioned aspects determine whether an enterprise is experiencing an evolutionary or an involutional development. One has to alter past perception, orientation, management and organizational structure of the company to actually increase the value of an enterprise.

The authors present a concept that describes the enterprise as a cognitive system of core competences and strategic business units. They reveal that the customer is not always right. They also show that linking core competences with market orientation might result in lasting competitive advantages.

THE ENTERPRISE AS A COGNITIVE SYSTEM

The Customer is Not Always Right

The enterprise is a system with cognitive structures that enable the development of an idea of its environment. The concept of the enterprise as a cognitive system is based on the epistomological approach of constructivism. According to the latter, one will never really grasp reality (von Foerster, 1994). We do not "find" reality, we "invent" it. Hence, the representatives of constructivism argue that it is impossible to realize absolute truth. The enterprise is perceived as a "living system" characterized by autopoiesis, self-reference, a respective structure, structurally connected to and interacting with other units. The enterprise is a cognitive system that generates values via a multitude of relations with internal and external customers. Internal and external customers are buyers, employees, shareholders, financial community, society in the broadest sense of the term, suppliers and affiliated companies.

The enterprise obtains competitive advantages by being faster and better than competitors. By acquiring, developing and using core competences it creates values for all "stakeholders".

Core competences are both the starting point and the result of collective learning processes. It is the management's task to ensure that processes bring about an increase in value for all stakeholders. According to the modern conception of company, the process of creating values is not a sequential one.

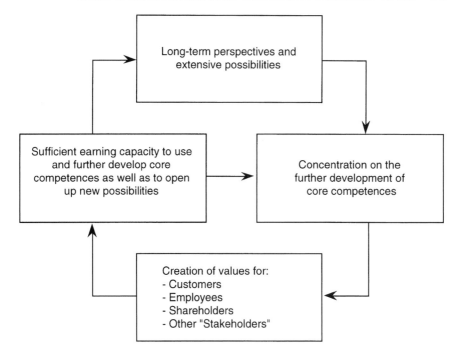

Figure 9.1 The Evolutionary Process of International Competitiveness of an Enterprise (Modified from DeWoot, 1990)

It does not start with raw materials and semifinished products. It does not end with the supply of products nor with the offering of services. The configuration of the increase in value process is like a network. During all its phases, complex interaction with a number of stakeholders takes place. Thus, the increase in value process of the company comprises the following complex activities.

• The managers responsible for core competences must endeavour to continuously produce new knowledge within the company or gain it from outside. This knowledge has to be grouped together and translated into core competences.
• The managers of the strategic business units have to satisfy all of their stakeholders and to "trace" new markets.

Unlike its competitors, the enterprise as a cognitive system secures competitive advantages by acquiring core competences differentially. It develops them further and uses them for its business units. Here, the construction of a basic organizational knowledge accessible to all company members is vital.

With employees and managers gaining more access to core competences, the freedom to discover new business fields and to question old ones grows. Whenever managers and employees become aware of their environment, they themselves invent it and offer new solutions to satisfy stakeholders. The mere imagination of increase in value, if sufficiently cherished by corporate culture, engenders increase in value: imagination produces reality.

Constructivists claim that the customer is king. He plays a central role among stakeholders. Frequently, he even becomes coproducer of products and services. On the other hand, the customer is not "king", he is not always right. It is, of course, important to know what the customer thinks. Particularly, in case one tries to tailor products or services to customers' wishes.

According to empirical studies (Martin, 1995), 90% of so-called new products are mere "line extensions". Their contribution to the appreciation of the company is very low. In contrast, the extent to which the 10% of really new products increase the value of the enterprise is out of proportion to the aforementioned 90%.

The danger of market research lies in companies becoming almost slaves of statistics. They confine their scope. What matters is only to meet the articulated needs. What happens is a confusion of quality and quantity. Quality stays the same, only quantity changes: less gasoline consumption, more PC performance, faster service, etc. In a world of fast changes, incremental thinking does not produce really new ideas.

Companies can only recognize qualitative change and benefit from it if they focus on core competences. Furthermore, they have to be open and increase the number of businesses "operated" by core competences. Chrysler's Minivan, Sony's Walkman, Compaq's Network-PC and Motorola's Handy are examples of companies that found new solutions to problems by trusting their core competences. They overcame buyers' bias. They increased their value by satisfying customers faster and/or better than customers expected that they would.

Summarizing, the customer is not "the measure of all things". Neither is he the one and only arbitrator in competition. It was constructivism that discovered the observer who does not only see the customer and other stakeholders. From a helicopter perspective he also sees himself, competitors and other reference firms. The taken perspective allows him to see how they all — himself included — are related to each other.

On the level of a "second order" observation — the observation of observation — we become aware that offered problem-solutions can work only for one observer. The observer does not realize that he does not see what he is not able to see. One can recognize and meet customers' needs more efficiently if managers and employees observe themselves by observing their relationship to customers and other stakeholders than by focusing too much on customers. If one wants to 'sense' a new content, one has to love its subject:

'Res tantum cognoscitur, quantum diligitur' (Augustine). In other words, one has to concentrate on what one excels in and on what is useful to others.

The Competence–Orientation of the Enterprise

Seen against the background of ever shorter product life-cycles, emphasizing products and markets is too short sighted. Products are only the "visible" surface of technologies, skills, processes and abilities. The listed things might contribute to the development of a whole range of products. Sony's miniaturization ability that manifests itself in ever new products such as the Walkman, the portable CD player, mini-TV, mini-disk and mini-hi-fi-sets is a case in point. A fundamental change is to be seen: future competition will be one of outstanding abilities which implies the competing for competence (Friedrich, 1995a).

As a consequence, strategic management has to put more emphasis on the company itself, on its own potential to serve the generation of outstanding competences. Such strategies should show the unique character of the company, determined by a specific potential, to its best advantage. The objective is no longer to adapt to new markets but to create and invent appropriate environments (Friedrich, 1995b).

The resource-based view constitutes the theoretical basis for the demanded competence–orientation. After years of neglecting it, more and more attention is paid to the potential aspect of the company (Wernerfelt, 1984; 1995; Lado et al., 1992; Rühli, 1994).

The following consideration is of central importance: companies increase their value by achieving competitive advantages. These advantages ensue from the unique resource endowment and distinctive competences that a company calls its own. In this sense, companies are considered bundles of resources. Idiosyncrasy, indivisibility and invisibility of potential prevent performance profiles to become alike and ensure lasting advantages (Barney, 1991). Here, intangible factors are of utter importance. What counts is what a company can rather than what a company has. The mastering of procedures, processes, special abilities and their translation into core competences of strategic networks belong to the "can" side of a company.

THE IDENTIFICATION OF CORE COMPETENCES

What are Core Competences?

Prahalad and Hamel (1990) define core competences as systematically clustered combinations of individual technologies and production skills underlying the variety of product lines of a company. Honda's core competence concerning engines and driving strands serves as an example.

Stalk et al. (1992) provide a broader definition of core competence. Their definition includes the entire value chain. Honda's management of traders and production development serves as an example. The attempt to synthesize both definitions engenders the following definition: core competences are integrated totalities of technologies, know-how and processes. They are coordinated through organizational learning processes that:

- customers perceive as valuable;
- are unique compared with those of competitors;
- difficult to imitate, and
- provide potential access to many markets.

SWATCH's core competence lies in "emotional goods". It is a combination of automation technologies, design and marketing. Swarovski's core competences comprise abrasive technology, design and marketing. Core competences are those integrated activities and functions where the enterprise is "best in world, not best in region or town" (Quinn, 1992). Core competences decisively influence the increase in value of a company. They "make the economic engine of a firm tick" (Hamel, cited in Randall, 1995).

In other words, core competences are the concentrated abilities, technologies and processes that maintain the "value-increase-mechanism" of a company. They are responsible for the strategic business units of a company being the leading competitors of their market segments.

The very origin of competitive advantages is the ability to translate technologies, know-how and production skills into core competences on the level of the whole company. By doing so they will hold leading competitive positions covering several business units.

Yet mastering technologies and other skills are not the most essential aspects. What is more crucial is the unique coordination and combination of resources with organizational learning processes. When being exploited on the market, customers perceive the latter as an additional benefit. In this way, learning processes have a vital impact on strategic success.

Core competences are not tangible or visible elements of the surface structure of a company (Rühli, 1994). Rather, they are part of the deep structure of the organizational world. The corporate culture mirrors them (Handlbauer, 1995). They can only be acquired through time-consuming learning by doing. In a "tacit knowledge" sense, core competences are often implicit elements of decision-making routine. Thus, it is enormously difficult for competitors to imitate them.

On the one hand, concentration on core competences generates growth processes if one opens up new markets. On the other hand, core competences cause shrinkage if the enterprise leaves business units behind that are not related to core competences. These processes of value-adding are more

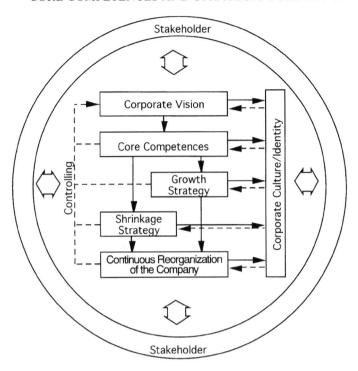

Figure 9.2   Core competences generate growth and disinvestment strategies

efficiently managed by thirds (Figure 9.2) (Friedrich and Hinterhuber, 1994; Hinterhuber, 1995c, 1996).

Summarizing, core competences are as follows:

1. Specific abilities within individual functional areas, for example, marketing, production, research and development, etc. Montedison, an Italian group of chemical companies, has lived on the inventions of one employee for many years. It was the Nobel prize winner Giulio Natta.
2. Specific abilities that cover several functional areas, for example, within fields of technology, information technology, logistics, etc.
3. Overlapping business processes aimed at satisfying customers as well as other stakeholders. Benetton's core competences on the process level provide an example. Benetton masters cutting, colouring, marketing and sales information in a way that revolutionized the market for leisure, sports and children's clothing.

Permanent competition renders core competences perfect. They represent the cumulative experiences of managers and employees. They constitute the very essence of the company, its uniqueness. They determine market performance and the ability of the company to co-ordinate it. They condition the way in which the company differs from its competitors.

The Analysis of Existing Competences

The analysis of existing competences is the first step of the management of core competences. The management has to find out about the current abilities and skills present in the company. The goal is to define the number, kind and significance of present competences. It is important to abstract from products and to focus on the knowledge underlying them. Such a procedure requires training and the ability to assess competences in the right way. This very activity might constitute a part of the core competence (Withney, 1995).

The analysis of value-adding concerning the employed skills and abilities is significant. First, it is necessary to find out which competences relate to part of a product or a product group. Also the knowledge made available by suppliers and affiliated companies has to be considered. It is important to recognize that relationships within strategic networks should suit the goals of the strategic business units.

The exclusive analysis of existing products and current production processes would be nothing more than an internal revision. Other approaches have to be applied as well, in order to track down competences that are not yet visible parts of the range of performance although they already exist. Such information can be obtained from discussions with internal and external key-persons, customers and knowledgeable observers of an industry.

Also the organizational structure often makes points of main emphasis of competence development transparent. Are there certain tasks, for example, logistics, that are concentrated in specific departments? If so, is this a clue to a more detailed analysis of the competences embodied by the respective department? In this way one can identify sectors that do not contribute to the increase in value of a company.

The normative outline conditions of the production of goods and services have to be part of a comprehensive analysis of current competences. Corporate culture and value system constitute a significant "storage" of organizational knowledge. Difficulties and inaccuracy should not deter managers from dealing with these "soft facts". Otherwise they would refuse to consciously influence an essential dimension of the company.

The analysis of existing competences does not concern only their content. It also includes considerations as regards the way in which competences are embedded in the organizational structure of a company.

The analysis is furthermore targeted at getting a general idea of where competences lie. It is important to know the departments and persons that represent competences. This is necessary for two reasons. First, in order to be able to construct specific protection mechanisms. Second, in order to be capable of planning implementation measures within competence development.

From all the competences available those of strategic relevance constitute the competitive advantage. Relevance seen from a competitive policy point of view. The chosen competences should also contain company internal development potential.

The Identification of the Relative Strength of Core Competences

The identification and accurate assessment of core competences are among the biggest challenges that face a company. The use of a portfolio in matrix-form with two mutually independent dimensions seems suitable to find out which competences are more important than others (see Hinterhuber and Stuhec, 1995).

Following the core competences concept means to link the resource-based perspective with the market and customer perspective. In order to do so, one has to recognize company-related as well as environment- and market-related success factors. In accordance with the aforementioned definition of core competences and their characteristics the subsequent matrix is generated: the relative competence strengths, compared with that of competitors, as abscissa and the present and future customer value of competences as ordinate. The chosen abscissa of "relative competence strength" contains the aspect "difficult to imitate". The latter is a must characteristic of core competences. The ordinate "customer value" considers further characteristics of the aforementioned definition.

One has to compare corporate competences with suppliers and competitors in order to determine the relative strength of competences. Benchmarking is a useful method of comparison (Mertins et al., 1995). Yet a comparison with only direct competitors and suppliers does not suffice. The comparison has to include all companies that are potential "best performers" concerning a respective performance. The comparison should not be limited to an analysis of rival products in the sense of "reverse product engineering". It should also cover processes and structures.

With a strengths–weaknesses profile the results can be illustrated. The performance profile of one's own company can be evaluated in relation to its competitors along a "low–high" continuum. The relative competence strength that determines the position of the respective competence within the portfolio derives from all the factors taken into consideration.

The Identification of the Customer Value of Core Competences

In order to identify the second dimension of the portfolio, the customer value of competences, one has to define the present and future critical success factors. Analyses on three levels are necessary: environment, sector and customer.

The environment analysis tries to find out about trends concerning the economy, technology, ecology and the social, political and legal fields. Most of the time the company cannot influence such tendencies. A sector analysis of competitors and suppliers enables the company to learn about two things. First, the "rules of the game" concerning competition. Second, to recognize the changing influences on the company that result from the industry structure. The same applies to an analysis of potential competitors and subsitution possibilities. However, most important is the customer analysis. In other words, the identification of articulated and if possible non-articulated customer wishes concerning product characteristics and product-related services. Such analyses make the crucial success factors of the company concerning customers clearly visible. The employment of a correlation chain has proven efficient for the actual assessment of the customer value of competences. As to its methodology, it resembles quality function deployment (QFD).

QFD means to deploy quality functions of a product in accordance with quality characteristics demanded by customers (Akao, 1992, p. 15). It is a product planning and development procedure oriented towards customers' wishes that consists of four phases. During these phases, one derives the product, its parts, its production and production process from customers' demands.

Yet the product-related QFD is too costly and too detailed to be applied for the identification of core competences on the level of corporate strategies. A two-phases' correlation chain appears to be more useful. It takes the success factors, crucial to competition, as a starting point. It defines the customer values of competences by looking at performance characteristics of products desired by customers. Again, the goal is to meet customer needs. Competences have to be deployed and further developed accordingly.

Thus, one can refer to this QFD pendant as competence deployment (CD). The latter consists of two "CD-matrices" and constitutes the competence portfolio. Figure 9.3 exemplifies an evaluated correlation chain. The used evaluation criterion is very general. It has therefore to be adapted to the company-specific situation.

The correlation chain ensures the transport of critical success factors concerning customers and competition via performance characteristics of products. The latter finally leads to the required competences of the company.

It is evident that individual performance characteristics depend on several competences and vice versa. The sum of the individual correlation provides the final results. The results indicate how important the individual competences are — or should be — with regard to the achievement of critical success factors concerning customers. The correlation chain allows for a rating of the current and potential customer value of competences. The concrete values provide the second dimension for the positioning of competences in the portfolio.

155

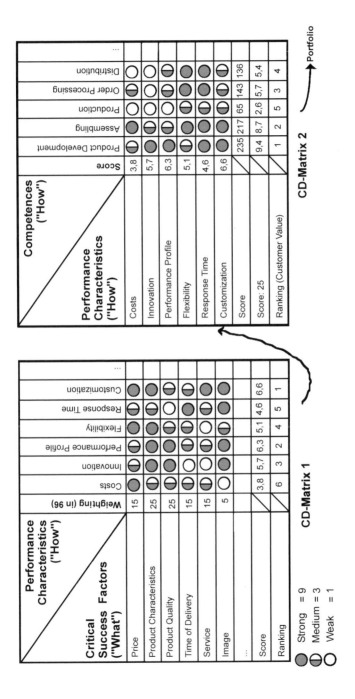

Figure 9.3 An Evaluated CD Correlation Chain.

The Portfolio of Competences

The portfolio method is a comprehensive and manageable instrument of analysis. It combines the results of individual analyses, reduces the information flow to its essentials and renders the results visible. Within the portfolio one can position the competences in four quadrants using the worked out relative competence strength and customer value (Figure 9.4).

Quadrant I: competence standards

In the portfolio, competences with low customer value and a relatively low competence strength are called competence standards. Customers do not consider them very important. Competitors are able to master them better or as good as we manage ours. The ability to keep normal business going is an example of the aforementioned competences. Such competences might also contribute to rendering the range of performance complete. Misdirects can also be part of the mentioned competences. Here, the company has not yet recognized the sign of the times. The listed competences do not generate competitive advantages.

Quadrant II: competence gaps

Customers attribute high significance to competences in this field. Yet the competence strength of the company is rather poor compared with that of its competitors. As a consequence, there are competence gaps between what the market demands (competence requirement) and what the enterprise is able to do (existing in-house competence). One frequently does not realize the situation. The reason for this lies in the fact that many companies do not examine their apparent knowledge of success factors on the market and with customers. Yet competences that belong to these fields are of strategic relevance. These fields require particular improvement.

Quadrant III: competence potential

Competences that the enterprise excels in — it is superior to others — yet which are not attributed high customer value are considered a potential. Many efforts to develop competences are wasted efforts for the following reasons. A number of enterprises do not really grasp customers' demand. They release products without carefully considering the problems of users. The *R&D syndrome* is a case in point. Here, one strives for *technology-loving* overperfection that the customer does not honour (*overengineering*). Competences of markets that have changed can also be part of this quadrant. Generally speaking, one has to try to relate existing potential (*strengths*) to market developments (*chances*).

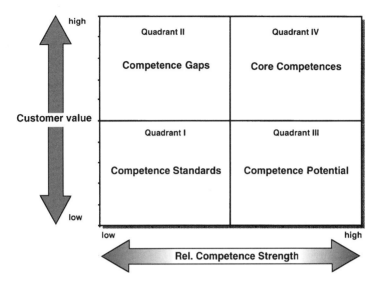

Figure 9.4   The Portfolio of Core Competences

Quandrant IV: core competences

Real competences that determine the corporate profile exist only in the following cases.

- If the competence strength of a company is high in relation to that of its competitors.
- If the competences can be attributed a high present and future customer value.

The strategic idea to focus on core competences is indispensably connected to the concentration of one's own strengths against competitors' weaknesses (Snyder and Ebeling, 1992). There are more or less comprehensive patterns of how to concentrate and coordinate competences within the enterprise. This makes it very difficult for rival companies to imitate competences. At the same time the aforementioned patterns allow for the building of relative competitive advantages.

THE MANAGEMENT OF CORE COMPETENCES

Competing on competence means to view the enterprise from a different perspective, to manage and organize it in a new way. It implies a profound change of organizational structures and requires managers and employees to unlearn old concepts.

Summarizing, there are four central points that determine the degree of strategic management competence (Friedrich, 1995a).

To Recognize Potential

Self-realization is a prerequisite of a competence-oriented management. One has to realize one's own potential by assessing and evaluating existing resources as to their strategic value. The separation of outstanding abilities from ordinary ones is no easy task. Core competences are not necessarily visible. They constitute highly complex, intangible and diffuse entities.

The wrong understanding of the essence and effects of competences might have fatal consequences for the company's future. Underestimation as well as overestimation can destroy values. Underestimation renders potential future business fields invisible to the company. The company overlooks them. Overestimation, on the other hand, makes the company incapable of competing.

Summarizing, the correct realization of competences is the basis for their optimal exploitation and further development. Existing competences are important indications as to the future development of the company.

To Exploit Potential

At this point the right use and optimal exploitation of the company's resources and competences are of central importance. Two things should be taken into consideration:

- the translation of relative different potentials into real advantages in the market place;
- the use of those options that competitors do not have.

The challenge one has to face is to maximize the *return on resources*. This statement might sound trivial. Yet it insinuates new performance targets for strategic orientation.

To Develop Potential

Exploitation implies a way of thinking that relates competences to markets. In contrast, the development of core competences demands an opposite move. On a long-term basis it is insufficient to exploit only existing resources and competences for they are subject to wear and tear. Thus, a dynamic management of potential is required. New competences have to be developed and achieved. The analysis of existing abilities is a precondition of the development of future abilities.

Here, one has to:

- find out faster than others about future business fields that offer challenges;
- inform oneself about the kind of competences necessary for the aforementioned endeavour;
- fixate standards concerning the way of development. In other words one has to establish an estimated competence profile;
- formulate procurement strategies for missing competences. They determine the extent to which knowledge can be developed inside or outside the company. One obtains knowledge from the outside through partnerships and acquisition. This knowledge has to be absorbed and internalized.

Timely possession of the right competences is decisive for lasting success. So the competence to develop competences is crucial. It is the ability that determines the competitiveness of the company on a long-term basis. It is crucial to the generation of new knowledge. Yet the following abilities are also highly significant: to coordinate and combine many factors, to manage integrated processes, and to develop routines in order to translate knowledge into concrete action and actual problem solutions. The question of the development of core competences thus leads to the question of organizational learning (Helleloid and Simonin, 1994). What it all comes down to, is the demand on the company to increase its willingness and its ability to learn.

To Keep Potential

Finally, competence-oriented management has to be targeted at preserving competences. One has to "cherish" competences. Resources have to be protected from fragmentation and atrophy within the company. At the same time, their unwanted and uncontrolled outflow or others' access to one's own competences has to be prevented.

STRATEGIC ARCHITECTURE—DESIGN FOR THE FUTURE

Process Organization

The company needs a design for the future in order to develop core competences and to link them with strategic business units (Stuhec, 1993). The development of a future-oriented architecture requires more than 'getting rid' of a few 'weak points' and the precise coordination of existing tasks and processes. One has to critically question what exists and what one has achieved in order to master change. A new orientation of the entire company is necessary.

Hamel and Prahalad (1990) use a tree metaphor to illustrate an appropriate strategic architecture: as a tree develops from its roots, the company develops from its core competences. They supply the nutrient for the trunk and the longer branches that form the core products. The twigs are the business units. Leaves, blossoms and fruits represent the final products. Individual employees and technologies, however, do not mirror the roots that nurture and sustain the tree. Above all it is organizational learning processes that constitute the roots. For example, the way unequal resources and abilities are coordinated as well as the way that technology streams are combined.

Sequential Taylorism and division of labour must be replaced by a continuously learning, departments-overlapping process organization. Such a structure has to be horizontally oriented towards satisfying customers and other stakeholders (Ostroff, 1992; Hinterhuber, 1994 and 1995b; Eversheim, 1995).

The image of permeable streams flowing through functional units and company departments symbolizes horizontal organizational structures. These streams consist of processes that combine resources of the company and involve—while transcending boundaries—suppliers and customers (Wildemann, 1993; Ostroff and Smith, 1992).

The entire processes contribute to the functioning of the company, but it is the core competences that decide about the success of the company. Here, the following principles apply:

- the concentration of resources and processes determine core competences. Core competences determine customer value and increase in value of the company. They might ensue from business processes and are produced by the interweaving of resources with abilities.

  Sony's ability to construct miniature radios, for example, is based not only on the theoretical knowledge of how to integrate a whole radio into a chip. It

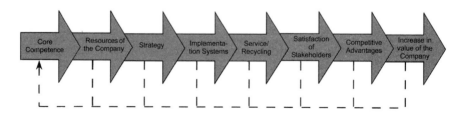

Figure 9.5   The competitive concept of a strategic business unit (example)

is the organizational learning process that combines R&D, production and marketing which engenders Sony's unique core competences in miniaturization. Competences that cannot be imitated.

- Core competences can be considered strategic business processes if they produce decisive value for the customer and other stakeholders (Zahn, 1993).

The Competitive Concept as a Connection of Strategic Business Units and Core Competences

Each strategic business unit develops a strategy that makes it a leading competitor in its market segments. The business unit utilizes corporate resources (managers, employees, material and financial resources, information technologies, R&D, and production, distribution and service potential) and resources of network members. The unit needs such resources to hold leading competitive positions.

The competitive advantages of a strategic business unit are usually based on one or a few core competences that the unit shares with other business units. Figure 9.5 portrays the competitive concept of a strategic business unit.

The objective is to satisfy stakeholders faster and/or better than competitors and benchmarking enterprises. This would increase the value of the company. The competitive concept links the strategic business unit with core competences (Figure 9.6).

The entire competitive advantages of strategic business units combined with the core competences of the strategic network constitute a global matrix structure. Such a structure implies radical changes concerning the personnel and organizational structure of the network company (Hinterhuber and Levin, 1994).

Coordination between each employee and a number of persons who belong to the strategic network is required. Such coordination follows the respective competitive concept for the interests of various functional or regional units and companies—each part of the network is simultaneously affected.

In companies, working on a global basis the exchange of managers and employees between the various countries is essential (Handlbauer, 1995). This allows employees and managers to familiarize themselves with a respective culture 'on the spot'. The ability of the company to learn is vital; it is the outcome of the ability of the company to produce new ideas and new competitive concepts. Furthermore, it is the ability of the company to make it the common property of all affected network members.

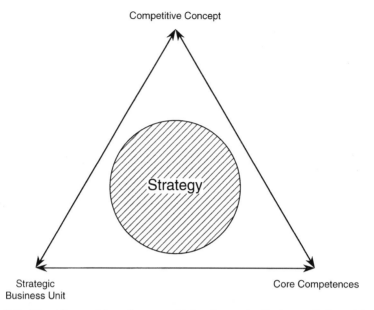

Figure 9.6 The Competitive Concept Links Strategic Business Units with Core Competences

THE LEARNING COMPANY AS THE IDEALLY COMMUNICATING GROUP

Like life, the company is in a state of "restless development". It does not know any kind of standstill. Successful enterprises are — as cognitive systems — always in motion. They create values for their stakeholders. They change and renew themselves. They adapt themselves, taking action, to continuously changing conditions for things turn out differently from what was expected. Each successful company is a permanent new beginning. A new beginning lead by the striving for increase in value that determines the essential continuity of the enterprise.

The enterprise as a cognitive system of core competences and strategic business units seems to evolve into a network company. Each member of this network concentrates on its core competences and constantly develops them further. Within the business units the different core competences create value for stakeholders.

This is the new vision of a network kind of company. One can realize this vision to the extent to which managers and employees fully develop their personal competences, assuming responsibility for internal and external customers. Responsibility that transcends their immediate working sector.

This vision is furthermore realized to the extent to which employees and managers are involved in decision-making processes. A last factor that influences the extent to which a vision can be realized is the availability of efficient communication systems. Systems that guarantee the communication between all members of a network (Dess et al., 1995).

Companies that learn faster and more efficiently than competitors are ahead of the latter in this new and altered world. This advantage concerns management systems and the combining of core competences with strategic business units. Yet it particularly concerns the change of employees' and managers' attitudes.

We are approaching a period in history that will be dominated by professional and social powers. By powers of the mind *and* the soul (Russel and Mahrabian, 1977). The latter can only operate coming from the inside. If powers of the mind and the soul determine future competition, ideas will be attributed more value than material and financial resources.

The network company needs managers and employees whose thinking transcends the working field for which they are responsible. They have to be able to put themselves into the internal and or external stakeholders' position. They have to offer values and benefits to stakeholders. This presupposes an ideally communicating group. It obliges to:

- consensus reached by discussion;
- the creation of working and communication conditions that allow for coming very close to this ideal.

These demands are based on the following realization: compromises enforced by hierarchical authority contain destructive potential; there is a danger of suppressing structural problems that need strategic solution. Employees might give up their personal commitment concerning the enterprise. The variety of the cognitive system might be lost and its dynamic paralysed. One also has to point out that consensus reached by discussion presupposes a heterogeneous interpretation of the latter. The aforementioned phrase does not stand for an ultimate state of balance. Consensus refers to a present stage of discussion and not to its *final goal* (Lyotard, 1984).

Here, we are talking of a dynamic balance that assumes an altered communication and discussion culture. This new quality of relation requires openness towards the limits of the manageability of cognitive systems. It calls for self-reliance, mutual trust, honesty and modesty. The confrontation with insecurity brought about by constant change and the admission of painful alteration are also part of the quality of relation.

Arduous work lies ahead for those who commit themselves to increasing the international competitiveness of the enterprise. Yet the following aspect will render the work more attractive and less difficult: the fortunate combination of what one considers desirable from a human perspective and of what is advantageous to the development of the (network) company as a system of core competences and strategic business units.

REFERENCES

Akao, Y. (1992). *QFD-Quality Function Deployment*, Landsberg/Lech, Verlag Moderne Industrie.

Barney, J. (1991). Firm resources and sustained competitive advantage, *Journal of Management*, **1**, 99–120.

Dess, G. G., Rasheed, A. M. A., McLaughlin, K. J. and Priem, R. L. (1995). The new corporate architecture, *The Academy of Management Executive*, **9**, No. 3, 7–20.

DeWoot, P. (1990). *High Technology Europe*, Oxford, Blackwell.

Eversheim, W. (1995). *Prozeßorientierte Unternehmungsorganisation*, Berlin–Heidelberg–New York, Springer.

Friedrich, St. A. (1995a). Ressourcen und Kompetenzen als Bezugspunkte strategischen Denkens und Handelns–zur Renaissance einer stärker potentialorientierten Führung, in: H. H. Hinterhuber (ed.): *Die Herausforderungen der Zukunft meistern*, 321–354, Lang-Verlag, Frankfurt.

Friedrich, St. A. (1995b). Mit Kernkompetenzen im Wettbewerb gewinnen. *IO Management Zeitschrift*, **64**, No. 4, 87–91.

Friedrich, St. A. and Hinterhuber, H. H. (1994): Strategischer Rückzug — Herausforderung für die Unternehmungsführung. *IO Management-Zeitschrift*, **63**, No. 7/8, 82–86.

Hamel, G. and Prahalad, C. K. (1994). *Competing for the Future*, HBS Press, Boston.

Handlbauer, G. (1995). Kernkompetenzen in internationalen Unternehmungen, in: Hinterhuber, H. H. (ed.): *Die Herausforderungen der Zukunft meistern*, Frankfurt, Lang-Verlag, 263–283.

Helleloid, D. and Simonin, B. (1994): Organizational Learning and a Firm's Core Competence, in: Hamel, G. and Heene, A. (eds.): *Competence-based Competition*, Chichester, Wiley, 213–239.

Hinterhuber, H. H. (1994). Paradigmenwechsel: Vom Denken in Funktionen zum Denken in Prozessen. *Journal für Betriebswirtschaft*, **44**, No. 2, 58–75.

Hinterhuber, H. H. (1995a). Die Strategie als System von Aushilfen, in: Siegwart, H., Malik F. and Mahari, J. (eds.): *Meilensteine im Management. Unternehmenspolitik und Unternehmensstrategie*, Zürich, 77–110.

Hinterhuber, H. H. (1995b). Business Process Management: The European Approach. *Business Change and Re-Engineering*, **2**, No. 4, 63–73.

Hinterhuber, H. H. (1995c). Management von Wachstums- und Schrumpfungsprozessen, in Corsten, H. and Reiß, M. (eds.): *Handbuch Unternehmungsführung. Konzepte-Instrumente-Schnittstellen*, Wiesbaden, 417–427.

Hinterhuber, H. H. (1996). *Strategische Unternehmungsführung*. Volume 1: Strategisches Denken, 6. Ed., Berlin–New York, De Gruyter.

Hinterhuber, H. H. and Friedrich, St. A. (1995). Gewinnen im Wettbewerb der Zukunft, *Gablers Magazin*, No. 3, 37–41.

Hinterhuber, H. H. and Levin, B. (1994): Strategic Networks: The Organization of the Future. *Long Range Planning*, **27**, No. 3, 43–53.

Hinterhuber, H. H. and Popp, W. (1994). Der Beitrag der strategischen Führung zu unternehmerischen Veränderungsprozessen, in: Gomez, P. *et al.* (eds.): *Unternehmerischer Wandel. Konzepte zur organisatorischen Erneuerung*, Wiesbaden, Gabler, 107–134.

Hinterhuber, H. H. and Stuhec, U. (1995). Kernkompetenzen und strategisches In-/ Outsourcing, in Cuomo, G. (ed.) *Scritti in ricordo di Carlo Fabrizi*. Padua, Cedam, 269–298.

Lado, A. A., Boyd, N. G. and Wright, P. (1992). A Competency-Based Model of Sustainable Competitive Advantage: Toward a Conceptual Integration. *Journal of Management*, No. 1, 77–91.

Lyotard, F. (1994). *The Postmodern Condition: A Report on Knowledge*, Manchester, Manchester UP.

Martin, J. (1995). Ignore your customer. *Fortune*, May 1, 83–86.

Mertins, K., Siebert, G. and Kempf, St. (eds.) (1995). *Benchmarking. Praxis in deutschen Unternehmen*. Heidelberg, Springer.

Ostroff, F. and Smith, D. (1992). The Horizontal Organization. *The McKinsey Quarterly*, No. 1, 148–167.

Prahalad, C. K. and Hamel, G. (1990). The Core Competence of the Corporation. *Harvard Business Review*, No. 3, 79–91.

Quinn, B. R. (1992). *The Intelligent Enterprise*, New York, Free Press.

Randall, R. M. (1995). How to Reshape Your Business to Fit the Future. Interview: Gary Hamel. *Planning Review*, **23**, No. 1, 6–11.

Rühli, E. (1994); Die Resource-based View of Strategy, in: Gomez, P. *et al.* (eds.), *Unternehmerischer Wandel. Konzepte zur organisatorischen Erneuerung*, Wiesbaden, Gabler, 31–58.

Russel, J. A. and Mahrabian, A. (1977). Evidence of a Three-Factor Theory of Emotions. *Journal on Research in Personality*, **2**, No. 3, 273–294.

Snyder, A. Y. and Ebeling, H. W. (1992). Targeting a Company's Real Core Competencies. *Journal of Business Strategy*, No. 6, 26–32.

Stalk, G., Evans, P. and Shulman, L. E. (1992). Competing on Capabilities: The New Rules of Corporate Strategy. *Harvard Business Review*, No. 2, 57–61.

von Foerster, H. (1994). *Wissen und Gewissen*. 2nd ed. Suhrkamp, Frankfurt am Main.

Wernerfelt, B. (1984). A Resource-Based View of the Firm. *Strategic Management Journal*, **5**, No. 5, 171–180.

Wernerfelt, B. (1995). The Resource-Based View of the Firm: Ten Years Later. *Strategic Management Journal*, **16**, No. 3, 171–174.

Wildemann, H. (1993). *Lean Management: Strategien Zur Erreichung wettbewerbsfähiger Unternehmen*, Frankfurt, Frankfurter Allgemeine Zeitung.

Withney, D. E. (1995). Is the make-buy decision a core competence? Working paper, MIT Center for Technology, Policy, and Industrial Development, May 11.

Zahn, E. (1993). Die strategische Renaissance des Unternehmens, in: Zahn, E. (ed.) *Fit werden für den Wettbewerb*, Stuttgart, Poeschel.

10

MANAGEMENT EFFICIENCY IMPROVEMENT STRATEGY AND ITS APPLICATIONS

Seiichiro Yahagi

President, Yahagi Consultants, Inc

MANAGEMENT EFFICIENCY

Efficiency and productivity are important in management control. However, it is seldom the case that these are discussed during the process of the formulation and evaluation of management strategy.

Suppose that there is a company that consists of five divisions:

Division A — efficient
Division B — very efficient
Division C — inefficient
Division D — efficient
Division E — very efficient.

If you are the president of this company, how can you decide what actions are necessary to create a more efficient business mix? It would be dangerous to rely only on your intuition to judge your business portfolio, so you must have rational, quantifiable criteria to judge your portfolio in total, and its efficiency in particular.

The Strategic Decision Challenge, Edited by D. E. Hussey
© 1998 John Wiley & Sons Ltd

Management efficiency is the ratio between management results (numerator) and management inputs (denominator). Therefore high management efficiency means that a relatively small amount of management resources is able to generate large management results. The role of management is to increase the overall efficiency of business, but, unfortunately, top management thinks about management efficiency intuitively, rather than utilizing a rational approach to management efficiency decisions.

MANAGEMENT EFFICIENCY STRATEGY

Management efficiency strategy was developed to establish a logical, objective method for performing rational decisions to increase the efficiency of business. It is one of four management strategy systems developed by Yahagi Consultants (Figure 10.1):

- corporate structure innovation strategy
- resource allocation strategy
- management efficiency strategy
- management resource input/output strategy.

The purpose of management efficiency strategy is to achieve a high level of output from a low level of input. Efficiency in this context is measured using six ratios, based on four items (see later).

CONCEPTS/CHARACTERISTICS OF MANAGEMENT EFFICIENCY STRATEGY

The concept of management efficiency strategy consists of the following factors.

1. Six-dimensional overall balancing strategic decision making.
2. All six ratios are calculated from four variables: sales, profits, investment and manpower.
3. A wide range of applications are possible in different industries and different management functions (research and development (R&D), sales, production, etc).
4. Multistage level of applications such as macro, semi-macro, and micro levels.
5. Complex analysis and conclusions conveyed at a glance through six-dimensional visual representations (EPM charts).

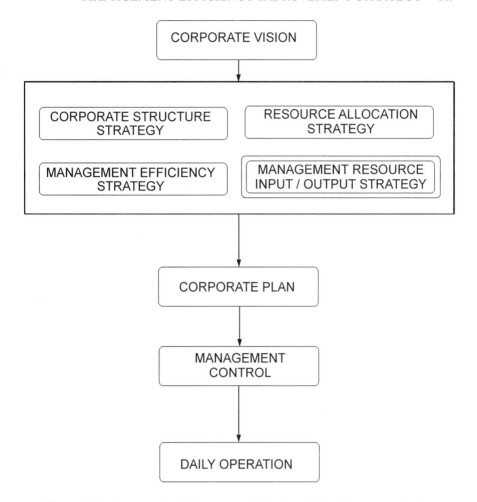

Figure 10.1   Framework of Management Strategy in the Management cycle

6.   Multifaceted computer simulation for powerful analysis of management efficiency improvement strategy.
7.   Follow-up by strategic control.
8.   Linkage to medium- and long-range planning.

TYPICAL APPLICATIONS IN INDUSTRY

Management efficiency improvement strategy is useful in a variety of industries, as well as all management functions. The following are examples of management functions.

- Corporate-level management efficiency strategy.
- Sales force efficiency strategy.
- R&D efficiency strategy.
- New business efficiency strategy.
- Competitive efficiency strategy.
- ROI strategy.
- Human resource efficiency strategy.

Yahagi Consultants have applied this strategy in various industries such as textiles, computers, chemical, distribution and wholesaling.

MANAGEMENT EFFICIENCY CHART—HOW TO MAKE AND HOW TO APPLY

Management efficiency chart is a useful tool to formulate corporate strategy or divisional business strategy. The management efficiency strategy chart consists of a series of concentric circle sets the positions and sizes of which encapsulate certain performance ratios of the individual products or businesses within the company. Six ratios are used for each product/business, according to the chart's special design (Figure 10.2):

1. left axis: profit per dollar invested
2. right axis: profit per dollar sales
3. top axis: sales per employee
4. bottom axis: profits per employee
5. size of dotted circle: investment per employee
6. size of solid circle: sales per dollar invested.

Each set of concentric circles is positioned according to the balance between the four axial ratios. This balance is found by the following technique. Using the same plotting technique used in constructing an "IS-LM curve" macroeconomic model, the position of each product/business circle set is determined as follows. The specific values for the four axial ratios are summarized by connecting the values of the two horizontal axes with a straight line and connecting the values of the two vertical axes with a straight line; at the intersection of these two lines, position the two ratio circles for that product or business unit. Repeat the process for each product/business.

The management efficiency strategy chart is divided into four quadrants. Each of these reveals characteristics that by definition, are common to all circle sets in that quadrant. To facilitate remembering the characteristics particular to each quadrant, names have been given to each one (Figure 10.3, Table 10.1).

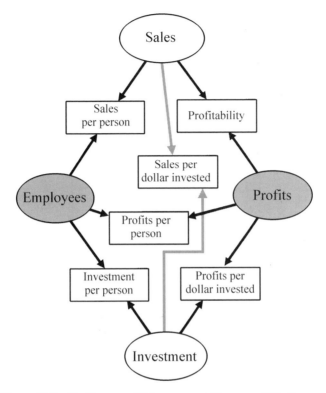

Figure 10.2   Six Factors of Management Resource Effectiveness

When you utilize this chart to examine management efficiency by product or division, good management efficiency is a large solid circle surrounding a small dotted circle, located in the upper right corner; and bad management efficiency is a large dotted circle surrounding a small solid circle, located in the lower left corner. The chart allows you to see immediately the effects that adjusting one of the factors—sales, profits, investment, or manpower—will have on management efficiency because the position and size of the chart circles will be modified accordingly. The combination of computer graphics and computer simulation allows multidimensional and quick analyses of alternative management efficiency scenarios.

STRATEGIC DECISION MAKING OF
NEW BUSINESS: THE CASE OF COMPANY A

The top management of a Japanese supermarket requested the services of Yahagi Consultants for a new business strategic decision-making project. This

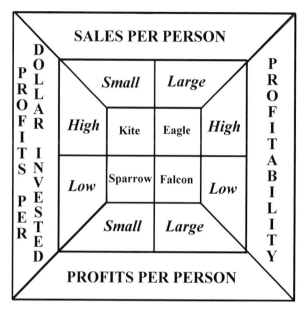

Circle 1: INVESTMENT PER PERSON
Circle 2: SALES PER DOLLAR INVESTED

Figure 10.3 Management Efficiency Strategy

Table 1

Name	Characteristic	Quadrant
Eagle	High sales/employee, high profitability (high profit/ employee) (high profit/investment)	Upper right
Kite	Low sales/employee, high profit/investment (low profit/employee) (high profitability)	Upper left
Falcon	High profits/employee, low profitability (high sales/ employee) (low profit/investment)	Lower right
Sparrow	Low profit/employee, low profit/investment (low sales/employee) (low profitability)	Lower left

supermarket had started five new businesses in the past few years and, at that time, the executive vice-president was evaluating the second stage of the company's new business development programme, including the allocation of management resources among the five new businesses. Regarding resource allocation, he did not have confidence in the proposed budgets for personnel and investment, but had no method for judging the necessity of the resource numbers requested.

By first discussing with the executive vice-president, the consultant was able to ascertain rough figures and tolerances for personnel and investment efficiency in business situations similar to the company's five new business units. Using the management efficiency chart to visualize manpower and investment needs *versus* sales and profit projections over the next five years, the consultant was able to show the executive vice-president which business units were overallocated.

Subsequently, additional information was collected to verify the reliability of the forecasts for the growth and prosperity of those five businesses. These refined numbers were then fed into computer simulations (e.g. sensitivity analyses) to get exact projections for investment/manpower needs and an optimal resource allocation scenario considering the company's limited management resources.

Showing the results of these detailed simulations on the management efficiency strategy chart (Figure 10.4) again allowed the executive vice-president to commence with confidence the implementation of the second stage of his new business growth strategy.

IMPROVEMENT OF UNBALANCED EFFICIENCY: THE CASE OF COMPANY B

An aggressive Japanese manufacturer had implemented a diversification strategy 10 years earlier. The top management of this company wanted to evaluate the results of this diversification strategy to formulate a new diversification strategy for the next 10 years.

Yahagi Consultants provided consulting services including management strategy evaluation. In this company's case (Figure 10.5), there were too many small, diversified businesses which were situated in separate and isolated business fields. The recommendations from the consultant were summarized by a comprehensive diversification strategy based on the comparison and contrast of alternative business portfolios, using management efficiency strategy simulation techniques such as sensitivity analysis, target feasibility studies, and "attainability *versus* importance" prioritization evaluations. Qualitative judgment for the growth possibilities of each business were also presented, based on strategic decision rules for determining the key factors of strong competitiveness against rival companies.

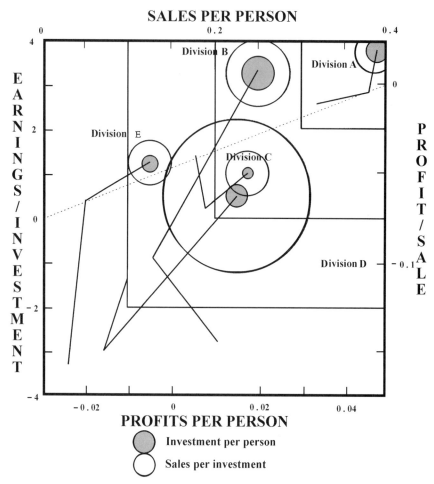

Figure 10.4 Portfolio Analysis Using Efficiency Improvement Management of Company A

APPLICATION OF THE MANAGEMENT EFFICIENCY STRATEGY FOR EVALUATION OF STRENGTHS AND WEAKNESSES IN INDUSTRY

In the process of conducting over 500 projects over the past 13 years, extensive intelligence has been gathered on the strengths and weaknesses of companies in various industries. This information is continually fed into a massive database used to evaluate the performance of Japanese corporations, including their growth rate, market share, profitability, etc.

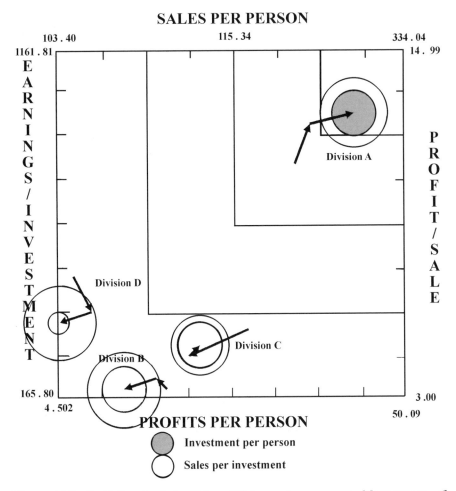

Figure 10.5 Portfolio Analysis Using Efficiency Improvement Management of Company B

The information in this database is fed into our management efficiency software. As such, we have evaluated the strengths and weaknesses of industries such as machinery, chemicals, computers, supermarkets, construction, and automobiles (Figure 10.6). The differences in efficiency among the key players in an industry are examined to illuminate strengths and weaknesses used within the industry and to forecast the balance of power in the future. Various alternatives are shown by altering the assumptions of management strategy in specific companies.

In this database are also quantifications of qualitative answers to an annual questionnaire given to over 200 Japanese companies each year. Analyses of

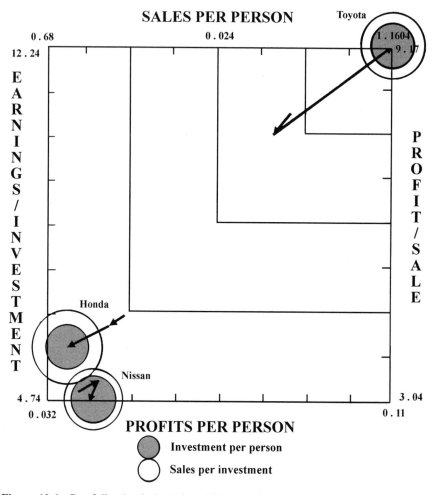

Figure 10.6   Portfolio Analysis Using Efficiency Improvement Management of the Japanese Automobile Industry

these responses were utilized to develop a "corporate climate" strategy to improve the working environment (culture, climate, atmosphere), and ultimately the efficiency of the workers and management. A new artificial intelligence management software has been developed integrating qualitative factors (knowledge base) and quantitative factors (database). The influences of these factors have been tested against various management hypotheses concerning competitiveness and management efficiency.

11

STRATEGIC GUIDELINES FOR OUTSOURCING DECISIONS

David Jennings

Nottingham Business School, Nottingham Trent University

This chapter:

- examines outsourcing as a potentially complex decision that has been associated with both the development of strategic advantage and the loss of strategic capability;
- discusses a range of perspectives that have been proposed for evaluating the outsourcing decision, including the role of competitive advantage and environmental change, cost, capability, the need to retain and develop essential relationships, choice of technology and the monitoring and revision of sourcing decisions;
- develops guidelines for the decision;
- makes reference to the experience of companies in a variety of industries.

INTRODUCTION

Developments in supply markets increasingly present organizations with the opportunity to outsource activities. The potential for using outside supply has moved on from those activities that are normally regarded as of peripheral concern to a business, such as cleaning, catering and security, to include critical areas of activity, such as design, manufacture, marketing, distribution and information systems. Almost the entire value chain is open to the use of outside supply.

The Strategic Decision Challenge, Edited by D. E. Hussey
© 1998 John Wiley & Sons Ltd

Outsourcing has become recognized as an area of strategic importance. Quinn et al. (1990) propose that developing the use of outsourcing has numerous advantages: access to economies of scale, flexibility, the ability to focus on the remaining specialized activities, increased leverage, reduction in overheads, and a flatter and more responsive organization. Similar support for the use of outside supply is provided by Venkatesan (1992) and Snow et al. (1992).

The extensive use of external supply has helped a number of companies to achieve outstanding performance. A notable example is provided by Benetton, where a high level of investment in internal activities has been complemented by the extensive development of external supply. Benetton has 7000 shops in 110 countries. In 1989 the company directly employed 1500 people, with a further 8500 working through outsourcing, agency and franchising arrangements. Benetton enjoys a considerable degree of flexibility, twice a year the company introduces a set of 2000 new items. At the same time Benetton has achieved high levels of productivity and has recently been able to increase sales through price cuts of up to 40% (Ketetlhohn, 1990; *Economist*, 1994).

The imaginative use of outside supply can help companies meet their particular strategic problems. Rolls–Royce are the world's third largest manufacturer of aero engines. General Electric and Pratt and Whitney each have aerospace sales of almost $6 billion, as against Rolls–Royce's sales of $3 billion (1994). In an industry that requires extensive funds for research and development, the company's size is a disadvantage. Aero engines require a range of fully advanced parts and technologies, consequently outside suppliers are essential for the provision of the final product. With certain suppliers Rolls–Royce are able to develop a relationship that helps offset the company's comparative lack of scale, this is through establishing Risk and Revenue Sharing Partners. These partners contribute cash towards the engine programme in anticipation of benefiting from the future sale of parts. The arrangement supplements Rolls–Royce's research funds and reduces its exposure to risk.

For other companies the use of outside supply has brought disadvantages. Harley Davidson is one of a number of companies that have reduced cost by reinstating in-house supply (Economist, 1991). More generally, Bettis et al. (1992) propose that the improper use of outsourcing has played an important role in the competitive decline of many Western firms.

Quinn et al. (1990) provide guidelines for the decision to use internal or external supply. The organization should define

each activity in the value-creation system as a service; carefully analyzing each such service activity to determine whether the company can become the best in the world at it; and eliminating, outsourcing, or joint venturing the activity to achieve 'best in the world' status when this is impossible internally (Quinn *et al.* 1990).

The statement is invitingly straightforward but it over simplifies the sourcing decision. Strategic outsourcing decisions must consider a wide range of factors (Figure 11.1).

DEVELOPING A SOURCING STRATEGY

Competitive Advantage and the Business Environment

The outsourcing of major activities has strategic consequences. As with any other strategic decision, such outsourcing decisions must be evaluated by their effects upon competitive advantage and the decision's consonance with changes in the organization's environment (Rumelt, 1980). Illustrations 1 and 2 describe the strategies of two companies in each of two industries, home games and packaging. The illustrations provide insight into the influence of business strategy and environmental change upon sourcing decisions.

The businesses that form an industry will, if they are to compete effectively, assume different competitive strategies (Porter, 1980). Those strategies may in turn require particular approaches to the sourcing of activities.

Illustration 1: The Home Games Industry

The home games industry provides an example of two companies each enjoying considerable success, although following very different approaches to the sourcing of activities.

The *Games Gang Ltd* is an American company that follows a strategy based upon the widespread use of outside supply. The company identifies games that are selling well in local markets and tests the games that appear to have potential. Suitable royalty arrangements are made with inventors, while outside suppliers manufacture the product. Marketing is to a large extent informal and based upon public relations programmes and a reliance upon word-of-mouth to spread awareness of products. The company has produced successful games such as Pictionary. The 25 employees generate annual sales in excess of $125 million (Deutsch, 1989).

The Games Gang's sourcing strategy achieves a high level of leverage for the company's financial, human and intellectual assets in the development, production and marketing of a series of new games. The strategy is also a response to the uncertainties of the market, the inability to predict demand for a new game and, once established, the game's life cycle.

Games Workshop follow a markedly different business and sourcing strategy. Games Workshop provide their customers, largely adolescent to young adults, with complex fantasy games. Each figure used in the games has a considerable amount of detail. The customer collects and paints the figures. The games and their ranges of figures, are continually being developed. The customers'

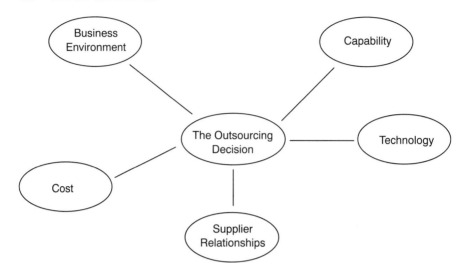

Figure 11.1   Evaluating the outsourcing decision

enthusiasm for the games is supported by a monthly magazine, introducing and discussing new developments in the company's games. The magazine features the games' designers and Games Workshop events.

Unlike the Games Gang, Games Workshop compete not by marketing a series of games but by providing a hobby, based upon the customers' enthusiasm for collecting and gaming. To support this strategy the company follows a largely in-house approach to sourcing. The design of games and figures requires the use of an in-house design team to sustain the distinctive 'Games Workshop' style and game themes. The availability of in-house design also supports other parts of the product including content for the magazine. The detail of each figure, established in design, is essential to the product's success. To ensure that this is realized in the final product, manufacture is also in-house. The company also operates its own shops in which facilities are available to paint figures, view game layouts and attend gaming events. The shop's staff add to the customers' experience, through their knowledge of existing and forthcoming games and by creating a lively and participative atmosphere.

Games Workshop competes through differentiation, the sustaining of product themes, the detail of its figures and the development of its customers' enthusiasm. This strategy requires a largely in-house approach to sourcing.

Within the home games industry (Illustration 1) the Games Gang and Games Workshop have each developed an effective, but very different, sourcing strategy to support their competitive strategy. For the Games Gang the extensive use of outside supply provides a means to rapid growth without requiring high investment. The company enjoys a high degree of leverage and in a market where each product introduction entails high risk, the low commitment of resources provides a way of avoiding loss, while outside supply can be increased to match the success of products.

The competitive strategy followed by Games Workshop requires a fundamentally different approach to sourcing. The company's highly differentiated product requires a design process that sustains a theme over all product development, together with high-quality production that captures the detail created by the designer. The company's distribution system provides further opportunities for differentiation.

Illustration 2: The Packaging Industry

Changes in customer behaviour can reduce the effectiveness of a business strategy and hence bring into question the sourcing strategy which supports it.

By the 1980s *Reed International* had developed a strategy for its packaging interests that involved a high degree of vertical integration. Reed's operations began with raw materials, the company collected and recycled waste paper. For the production of corrugated cases Reed manufactured its own board as well as "converting" board into box packaging. The company utilized its technical resources to innovate the product in terms of strength, the materials that could be contained (for example, oil and a variety of other fluids) and the colour printing of packaging.

During the 1980s the UK packaging market experienced a marked increase in the buying power of the supermarkets, not only in the negotiation of price but also in determining the characteristics of the product. The supermarkets required less packaging, preferring a cardboard pallet with plastic shrink wrapping in place of a complete cardboard container.

For an important part of Reed's market, not only did the volume of board required decline, the differentiating characteristics established by Reed lost their relevance. Small companies, using board purchased from the large manufacturers and often employing second-hand equipment, were able to meet the supermarkets, new, low-cost requirements (Jennings and Mullins, 1993).

Strategy is a way of responding to changes in the business environment. Illustration 2 provides an example of a company, Reed International, that despite having a leading share of the market and developing considerable in-house resources was unable to compete when a major group of customers developed a preference for low-cost products. The in-house investments that had guaranteed the supply of raw materials and board and had provided innovation became extra overhead in an increasingly price-sensitive industry.

Sourcing decisions must support business strategy and may have to be revised as competitive conditions change.

The level of environmental uncertainty may also affect sourcing decisions. High levels of uncertainty concerning demand and volatile competition can mitigate the advantages of in-house investment by presenting the risk of over-capacity (Harrigan, 1985). The cost of misjudging the uncertainties present in a market can be costly. Between 1986 and 1991 the Prudential Corporation spent £230 million building up a chain of 830 estate agencies. In 1991 the Woolwich Building Society acquired 190 of the agencies for £21 million. For the Woolwich the integration may be justified by the low cost of the assets, the necessity of increasing access to their core market (mortgage lending) and the development of customer loyalty through provision of a wide product range. However, for all organizations involved in the UK housing market, fundamental changes in the behaviour of that market had increased the riskiness of investing in in-house operations.

Competitive Advantage and the Business Environment

When deciding on a strategy the following points should be covered.

- Develop a clear understanding of the unit's business strategy.
- Consider potential environmental changes that may alter the competitive forces in the industry and hence require a change or development of the business strategy.
- Consider the implications of the sourcing strategy for the achievement of business strategy, including the effect upon cost, quality and flexibility.
- Question investment in in-house facilities when fluctuations in demand make the economics of their utilization uncertain.

Cost

Cost reduction has been the traditional motive for outsourcing. All businesses, including those that compete through differentiation, need to achieve the lowest level of cost consistent with their competitive strategy. Outsourcing allows the customer organization to benefit from the superior set of cost drivers, factors such as scale, learning and location (Porter, 1985), that are available to the supplier. As a consequence outsourcing can make a significant contribution towards reducing cost.

Cost considerations require a careful evaluation of service levels and the various components that make up cost. The costs of delivering a defined level of service are far ranging and include both explicit and implicit costs. For a decision considering the outsourcing of software development, the following would be relevant:

- man–day costs of employees
- environment costs
- machine use
- cost of non-computing support staff
- hardware and software costs
- staff training.

If the organization provides staff welfare benefits, such as a restaurant or membership of a health care scheme, those items should also be recognized as a part of each employee's cost. For certain resources there is also a need to consider opportunity cost. The decision to outsource software development can be instigated by excess demand upon internal software development resources. By outsourcing specific software projects the organization can release resources for alternative revenue generating projects, an opportunity cost that must be considered in the cost calculation.

Some costs that have been allocated to an activity, such as head office costs, will be incurred by the organization whether or not an activity is outsourced. These costs are unchanged by the decision and should not influence the outsourcing decision. Following a decision to outsource, those costs would still have to be met by the organization, and would constitute an increased burden upon the remaining in-house activities, thereby enhancing the case for further outsourcing (Bettis et al., 1992).

When considering outsourcing, the following points must be taken into account.

- Recognize the importance of cost and potential cost savings for the organization's competitive strategy and profitability.
- For any in-house service area that is being considered for outsourcing, fully define the service provided, including such aspects as "free" advice and flexibility.
- Costing exercises must include all costs, including the alternative net revenue available through releasing staff and facilities.
- Avoid developing cost penalties for those activities that remain in-house, through increasing cost allocations or loss of economies of scale.

Core and Peripheral Activities: Maintaining Relationships

While cost reduction is important, comparative cost is not a sufficient justification for outsourcing. Evaluating all activities only on the basis of cost fails to recognize the strategic significance of some activities and may lead to the loss of strategically important capabilities. This concern has been recognized for over a decade with the possible emergence of the 'hollow corporation', an organization that, through an incremental approach to outsourcing, has lost the distinctive capabilities that underpinned its competitiveness.

Outsourcing should reduce the scope of an organization's activities, allowing management to achieve increased focus upon the development and exploitation of core capabilities and their increased leverage (Quinn et al., 1990; Venkatesan, 1992). However, it is often difficult to differentiate between core and non-core activities. For businesses engaged in the supply of financial services, the core activities have been variously defined as those concerning the information system, the product development process and the distribution system. Each definition of the core opens up the possibility of very different outsourcing strategies.

The core activities of a business are essential parts of the business's capability, the set of business processes that consistently provide superior value to the customer (Stalk et al., 1992). Superior performance in an activity does not, of itself, necessarily indicate that the activity is part of the strategic core. That activity's performance must be considered as part of a value adding process. In the packaging case (Illustration 2), Reed's superiority in technological development was not recognized by a major customer group, the supermarkets, who required low cost packaging.

An organization's distinctive capability may be based upon innovation, reputation or the organization's architecture, the system of relationships within the firm and between firm, suppliers and customers (Kay, 1993). The relationships that provide architecture lead to competitive advantage through the acquisition of organizational knowledge, the establishment of organizational routines and the development of a co-operative ethic (Kay, 1993). Such capabilities require a seamless integration of activities, their operation and development. Consequently, when considering the outsourcing of near to core activities, great care must be taken to ensure that the essential relationships that underpin the creation of value will remain available and can be maintained and developed.

Such relationships can be successfully built across organizations (Lorenz, 1991; Miles and Snow, 1992; Lamming, 1993; Boyle, 1994). Canon's capabilities in producing technically innovative products and low-cost manufacturing are partly built upon trading and buying specific technologies from a variety of external partners. In manufacturing Canon undertakes backward integration only on parts with unique technologies. For other components there is a preference for developing long-term relationships with outside suppliers (Ghoshal and Ackenhusen, 1994).

Core Activities

- Great care must be taken to protect and develop core capabilities and the integration of the activities that provide capability.

- Outsourcing decisions are opportunities to improve the organization's focus upon its distinctive capabilities and to further the leverage of those capabilities.
- The creation of a competitor through leakage of knowledge concerning essential technologies or customer information should be avoided.

Supplier Relationships

The relationships that develop between an organization and its suppliers can provide the opportunity for improving performance and competitive advantage and may lead to far reaching change in the customer organization. However, supply relationships may also expose the organization to new dangers.

Use of outside supply requires a careful consideration of the potential power of suppliers (Stuckey and White, 1993). Should an outside supplier prove disappointing or attempt to impose price increases, the customer company may face switching costs including the cost of negotiation with new suppliers. In a market where there are few reliable sources, the replacement of a supplier may require the customer company to approach potential suppliers that have earlier been rejected. If a suitable replacement cannot be established the buying company may need to consider a return to in-house supply, however redeveloping the required expertise may prove both a difficult and an unattractive use of scarce resources.

To avoid early disappointment both parties to a supply arrangement need clear and shared expectations concerning service, with the buying organization fully aware of the hidden aspects of the existing in-house service, such as advice freely available when given in-house. For the customer company consideration must also be given to the strategic intent of potential suppliers, including the possibility of the outsourcing arrangement developing a potential future competitor (Bettis et al., 1992).

Assessing Supply Markets

The first steps to be taken when assessing supply markets are as follows.

- Identify the number of viable suppliers.
- Ensure that there is effective future competition in the supply market or that the power of suppliers can be countervailed.
- Evaluate the cost of having to switch supplier.
- Avoid helping to create a monopoly in supply.

Increasingly the long-term expectations of organizations concerning cost reduction, quality improvement, technical progress and product/service development are shaping supply arrangements. This development implies a collaborative relationship based upon mutual interest. Such relationships are intendedly long term, providing access to the benefits associated with outsourcing, enhanced by advantages that arise from adaptation between supplier and customer, whereby each organization in the supply network is able to develop its own expertise while adapting to the requirements of other members. Adaptation may take many forms. Logistic (by adjusting stock levels or delivery systems), administrative (planning and scheduling), financial (by the way in which payments are handled) or in terms of technical development (Johanson and Mattsson, 1991). The development of trust between network members supports shared learning and, by reducing the need to specify unforeseen circumstances, can reduce transaction costs (Jarillo, 1993). The leading firm may act to stabilize the network and invest in its development to ensure the future viability of suppliers (Snow et al., 1992).

Collaborative networks can be used to provide the final customer, wherever they may be, with an increasing level of value added service (Vandermerwe, 1994). Such networks, through improved flexibility and learning, improve the organization's ability for self-renewal, adaptation without loss of effectiveness (Miles and Snow, 1992).

Collaborative sourcing arrangements promise a considerable development in strategic capability and they have been proposed as an extension of the application of business process re-engineering (Short and Venkatraman, 1992, McHugh et al., 1995). However, there are difficulties in the creation and management of collaborative arrangements. Such close working relationships create significant levels of dependence and vulnerability for both parties while increasing the opportunity and incentive for opportunistic behaviour. They require the creation of a situation where each partner cannot easily obtain similar benefits outside the existing relationship, or the value of specific investments is lost if the relationship is terminated (Pilling and Zhang, 1992). Success in developing cooperative relationships has been associated with high levels of information exchange, the sharing of benefits and burdens, flexible problem solving behaviour, the monitoring of performance and expectations that the relationship will have continuity (Pilling and Zhang, 1992). The expectations of both parties may be formally explored and stated through a joint planning exercise. However, the scope for such planning is limited by uncertainties concerning the future potential of the partnership (Lorenz, 1991).

Benefits from long-term relationships can be achieved by all organizations irrespective of size. The Derbyshire, a medium-sized building society, has a regional focus. The society attempts to compete through differentiation, providing a service and image that reflects the society's complex understanding of its particular market. If the society can communicate that understanding to an advertising agency and the agent responds to that knowledge, then the society can benefit from both the wider expertise of the agency and the society's own understanding of the market. Such relationships may not require the sharing of a common culture but they do require an understanding of how each party operates, how decisions are made and the personalities involved. Shared understanding is facilitated by relationships being longer term and the Derbyshire has a preference for developing long-term supply arrangements.

Developing Supply Relationships

The following points are vital in developing good supply relationships.

- Careful selection of supplier, evaluation of the supplier's capability and culture and their complementarity to that of the customer organization.
- Explicitly state and agree expectations concerning service levels and their development.
- Create a situation that is seen as equitable.
- Ensure that key individuals and groups see the overall rationale for the relationship and support the relationship.
- Specify and communicate the performance that is expected from each partner and how that performance will be measured and compensated and how disputes will be settled.
- Aim for a simple contract so that attention and scope can be given to developing the relationship.
- Practise extensive monitoring of supplier performance.
- Avoid managing the partner's assets and accepting responsibility for their output.
- Restrain the use of power or relationships may not develop.
- Aim to develop trust and commitment.

Technology

For a business to develop and sustain competitive advantage requires access to one or more technologies and the ability to benefit from, or even lead, the development of technology. A typology of strategies for technology sourcing is provided by Granstrand et al. (1992). The development of technology can be expensive and may not ultimately bring strategic benefit. Consequently, the decision as to which technologies should be developed in-house must be made on a selective basis that ensures support for sustaining competitive advantage. Guidelines for evaluating the outsourcing of technologies are provided by Welch and Nayak (1992). For each technology consideration should be given to:

- the importance of the technology for competitive advantage
- the maturity of the process technology
- the company's relative technological performance versus that of competitors.

The first guideline recognizes the need for an organization to focus investment and management attention upon those technologies which provide its distinctive product and service characteristics. This in turn requires an understanding of how the business strategy may have to evolve. As demonstrated in the packaging case (Illustration 2) changes in the competitive environment may dramatically alter and even reduce the importance of a particular technology for competitive advantage.

The maturity of the technology should be determined by scanning other industries as well as that in which the business operates. There is a need to avoid recreating developments that have been achieved elsewhere and that may be available through purchase, licensing or other outside supply arrangements.

Finally, relative performance must be considered. If there is a wide gap between the company's technological performance, measured by cost, quality, flexibility or other suitable measures, it may not be possible for the company to close the gap through internal development. The technology may have to be accessed through an outside supply arrangement.

Welch and Nayak's guidelines can be illustrated through considering Benetton's commitment to design technology. A high level of performance in design is central to Benetton's competitive advantage. The company designs 2000 new garments for each of its half year fashion seasons. For each garment there is the need to achieve a good degree of style and colour. Design technology continues to change providing higher productivity in the use of designers, increased ability to use colour and to evaluate designs before producing a garment. The vital role of design technology is reflected in the resources Benetton has devoted to the activity. The company employs 200 designers and has established its own international design school. In addition, the design process is fully integrated into the company through being physically located at the centre of operations, adjacent to the area where buyers view the collections of garments.

The following points need to be borne in mind.

- Commitment to in-house technology is expensive and must be made on a selective basis.
- Selected technologies must support the distinctive aspects of the business strategy. It is highly desirable to anticipate changes in the business strategy that will alter the relevance of a technology.
- Investment in mature technologies is especially open to question. Maturity should be assessed by scanning the full range of industries. The scan may also identify potential suppliers.
- Where an organization lags in a technology it is unlikely that sufficient resources can be allocated to attain a progressive position, outsourcing may be required to regain performance.

Revising the Sourcing Decision: Organizational Learning

Although sourcing decisions are often long term in their implications they should be open to revision as the context of the decision changes. Such developments may be prompted by changes in the business environment and technology, they may also arise from organizational learning.

Elfring and Baven's (1994) study of the sourcing of knowledge-intensive services in the automobile industry, defines a four-stage pattern of evolution. The in-house development of services, often undertaken due to the lack of externally available sources of know how, leads to the in-house operation selling the service to outside customers. This may be followed by the unit developing a spin-off relationship to its parent company, possibly through a joint venture with another company. A fourth stage is development of the unit's capability to become a full-service organization offering integrated packages of services to customers. The developing sales to third parties provide leverage of the unit's knowledge resource. Outside clients, especially if they are demanding, offer opportunities for learning that develop functional and application capabilities.

Organizational learning may also lead to a contrasting pattern of development whereby an outside supply arrangement is replaced by in-house supply. This process may be assisted by changes in technology. An example is provided by the financial services industry's sourcing of network services. To provide a national network for Automatic Telling Machines, financial service organizations formed a consortium, Link, for the provision and management of the network and access authorization. Experience with the service has removed earlier uncertainty concerning the service features that are required by each organization's customers. In addition, technological change and learning have since occurred making it feasible for individual organizations to provide the service in-house, selling access to the network to other financial institutions.

Sourcing decisions need to be monitored, not only to ensure that the service provided is to an agreed and progressive standard but also to consider the possible need to revise the sourcing decision. To achieve effective monitoring and the ability to develop suppliers, the customer organization must retain the capability to assess the standard of provision and review the evolving market and technological considerations that may require a change of sourcing strategy.

When revising the sourcing decision the following points need to be borne in mind.

- Sourcing arrangements need to be reviewed and consequently developed or revised.
- Review requires a reconsideration of the potential cost and performance of service functions and the unit's evolving business strategy.

- The ability to review requires the organization to retain, directly or through a third party, a progressive understanding of each technology and an impartiality towards existing supply relationships.

CONCLUSION

The outsourcing decision, traditionally made on the basis of comparative cost, has become recognized as a decision that can provide a range of other strategic benefits — including improved quality, focus, flexibility and leverage. In seeking these benefits organizations must avoid adopting "me too" strategies. A strategy that appears to work for one organization may not be appropriate or practical for another, even in the same industry.

Strategic sourcing decisions need to consider a wide range of factors. The article has developed a series of guidelines with which to assess the outsourcing decision. Perhaps the most important of these concerns the protection, development and exploitation of core activities and the need to relate sourcing decisions to the organization's competitive advantage. These concerns are central to strategic development and competitive performance.

There is a need to consider the overall way in which an organization's outsourcing is intended to develop. Benefits can be achieved from outsourcing through an incremental approach, providing the opportunity for experimentation with the decision and consequent improvement in decision making. An incremental approach offers the opportunity to limit risk taking but may fail to realize the full potential of outsourcing for developing collaborative supply networks. Such a development not only affects performance it requires a transformation of the organization's scope, structure and managerial roles (Snow et al., 1992). As such it represents a quantum rather than an incremental change in strategy.

Even in the most extensively outsourced company there is a need to retain a progressive understanding of technologies. Nike, the athletic shoe and apparel company, is "basically a research, design, and marketing company" (Quinn, 1992). However, the company retains a small domestic manufacturing operation focused on leading-edge designs. This activity maintains Nike's ability to work with suppliers and helps to avoid costly design errors. The knowledge provided by such activities assists the monitoring of outsourcing decisions and, if necessary, their revision in order to introduce new suppliers or to reintroduce in-house supply.

REFERENCES

Bettis, R. A., Bradley, P. and Hamel, G. (1992). Outsourcing and industrial decline, *Academy of Management Executive*, **6**(1), pp.7–22.

Boyle, E. (1994). Managing organizational networks in Britain: the role of the caretaker, *Journal of Management*, **19**(4).

Deutsch, C. (1989). A toy company finds life after Pictionary, *The New York Times*, Business Section, 9 July.

Economist (1991). The ins and outs of outing, 31 August.

Economist (1994). Benetton: the next era, 23 April.

Elfring, T. and Baven, G. (1994). Outsourcing technical services: stages of development, *Long Range Planning*, **27**(5).

Ghoshal, S. and Ackenhusen, M. (1994). Canon: competing on capabilities, in B. De Wit and R. Meyer, *Strategy: Process, Content, Context*, West Publishing Company.

Granstrand, O., Bohlin, E., Oskarsson, C. and Sjoberg, N. (1992) External technology acquisition in large multi-technology corporations, *R and D Management*, **22**(2).

Harrigan, K. (1985). Vertical integration and corporate strategy, *Academy of Management Journal*, **28**(2).

Jarillo, J. C. (1993). *Strategic Networks: Creating the Borderless Organization*, Butterworth Heinemann.

Jennings, D. and Mullins, C. (1993). Reed International, European Case Clearing House, Cranfield, UK.

Johanson, J. and Mattsson, L. (1991). Interorganizational relations in industrial systems: a network approach compared with the transactions-cost approach, in G. Thompson, J. Frances, R. Levacic and J. Mitchell (eds), *Markets, Hierarchies and Networks: The Coordination of Social Life*, Sage Publications, London.

Kay, J. (1993). *Foundations of Corporate Success*, Oxford University Press, New York.

Ketetlhohn, W. (1990). Benetton, *European Case Clearing House*, Cranfield University, UK.

Lamming, R. (1993). *Beyond Partnership, Strategies for Innovation and Lean Supply*, Prentice Hall, International (UK).

Lorenz, E. H. (1991). Neither friends nor strangers: informal networks of subcontracting in French industry, in: G. Thompson, J. Frances, R. Levacic and J. Mitchell (eds), *Markets, Hierarchies and Networks: The Coordination of Social Life*, Sage Publications, London.

McHugh, P., Merli, G. and Wheeler W. A. (1995). *Beyond Business Process Reengineering: Topwards the Holonic Enterprise*, Wiley.

Miles, R. E. and Snow, C. C. (1992). *Causes of Failure in Network Organizations*, California Management Review, Summer, pp. 53–72.

Pilling, B. K. and Zhang, L. (1992). Cooperative exchange: rewards and risks, *International Journal of Purchasing and Materials Management*, Spring, 1992.

Porter, M. E. (1980). *Competitive Strategy: Techniques for Analyzing Industries and Competitors*, Free Press, New York.

Porter, M. E. (1985). *Competitive Advantage: Creating and Sustaining Superior Performance*, Free Press, New York.

Quinn, J. B. (1992). *Intelligent Enterprise: A Knowledge and Service Based Paradigm for Industry*, Free Press.

Quinn, J. B., Doorley, T. L. and Paquette, P. C. (1990). Technology in services: rethinking strategic focus, *Sloan Management Review*, Winter, 1990.

Rumelt, R. (1980). The evaluation of business strategy, in: Glueck, W. F. (ed.), *Business Policy and Strategic Management*, McGraw Hill, New York.

Short, J. E. and Venkatraman, N. (1992). Beyond business process redesign: redefining Baxter's business network, *Sloan Management Review*, **34**(1), pp. 7–21.

Snow, C. C., Miles, R. E. and Coleman, H. H. (1992). Managing 21st century network organizations, *Organizational Dynamics*, Winter (20/3), 1992.

Stalk, G., Evans, P. and Shulman, L. (1992). *Competing on Capabilities*, Harvard Business Review, March/April, (70/2).

Stuckey, J. and White, D. (1993). When and when not to vertically integrate, *Sloan Management Review*, Spring, 1993.

Vandermerwe, S. (1994). Building seamless service structures: some whys, whats, hows, *European Management Journal*, **12**(3), pp. 280–286.

Venkatesan, R. (1992). Strategic sourcing: to make or not to make, *Harvard Business Review*, November–December, 1992.

Welch, J.A., and Nayak, P.R. (1992). Strategic sourcing: a progressive approach to the make-or-buy decision, *Academy of Management Executive*, **6**(1).

12

STRATEGIC ALLIANCES IN
THE AIRLINE INDUSTRY

Wendy Hall

Department of Corporate Strategy and Planning, KLM Royal Dutch Airlines

D. Jan Eppink

Professor of Strategy and Environment, Faculty of Economic Sciences and Econometrics, Vrije Universiteit, Amsterdam

INTRODUCTION

"Everyone is talking to everyone" is a saying that can often be heard in the airline industry. Airlines all over the world are talking to many other airlines in order to explore the possibilities of entering into co-operation of one kind or another.

Many different reasons provide the motivation for alliance talks. The dynamics of the airline industry environment will rapidly change in the next 10 years. One factor primarily affecting European airlines is the move towards a liberalized airline market within the European community. Instead of being limited to a base in one's own country of 15 million to 55 million inhabitants, airlines will gradually be free to serve a market of 350 million inhabitants.

The dynamics of the European free market system do not affect European carriers alone. Japanese airlines, American airlines and other major carriers will want increased access to the Common Market. In order to create a fair playing field, countries (or groups of countries) must offer reciprocally free airspace to European carriers in their own countries. Instead of negotiating

The Strategic Decision Challenge, Edited by D. E. Hussey
© 1998 John Wiley & Sons Ltd

with each individual country on a bilateral basis, the European community may eventually negotiate as a body representing all European community airlines. Analysts insist that only with "open skies" within Europe, the United States of America (USA) and Japan can the world's major airlines compete on a fair basis.

The second major factor influencing the use of alliances between airlines is that of globalization, which is occurring with the growth of the triadic market. Airline customers are international passengers, international freight forwarders and internationally operating companies. As customers concentrate their investments abroad within the Japanese, the American and European markets, airlines are forced to develop a presence in each of the three key markets.

Each of the world's major airlines has a natural base in one leg of the triad, but no key internal position within the other two legs of the triad. Airlines competing as major carriers must serve their customers who are located within Europe, the USA and Japan and who fly between Europe, the USA and Japan.

The industry is in turbulence, literally and metaphorically. To meet the needs of the triadic customers, airline companies must reconsider their strategic positioning options.

In this chapter, we will first describe the various kinds of strategic choices that can be distinguished for an airline in the 1990s. Next, we will present the reasons behind the strategic alliances in this industry. We will also discuss some earlier forms of strategic alliances between airlines to compare and contrast them with current forms. Finally, some practical issues in the formation of alliances between airlines are addressed.

STRATEGIC CHOICES

All companies, irrespective of the industry, have to make choices regarding the three dimensions of strategy.

The first dimension is that of position in the market. Two well-known concepts in this respect have been developed by Porter. He suggests that a company can gain competitive advantage through either following a lowest price strategy or differentiation. In the latter case, the company delivers a product or service with one or more unique characteristics.

The second dimension is that of the scope of its activities. The first aspect of scope is product scope. A company has to decide whether it wants to be active in one single product group, or in several ones. In the last case, it still has to decide whether or not these different product groups have to be related by research and development, production or marketing. In the first case, one can speak of a strategy of a related product strategy. In the latter case, one speaks of a strategy of diversification or conglomeration.

The second aspect of scope is that of geography. Some companies work only on a local basis, whereas others are active on a national level. Many companies have followed a multinational strategy, where each national market is managed independently of the other national markets. In case of a global strategy, the company plays a sophisticated game of co-ordinating the activities in the various national markets to produce additional synergy.

The last aspect of scope is that of vertical integration. A firm can choose to perform only a limited number of steps in the chain of activities from raw material to final product, or it may want to perform many steps in order to gain more control over critical ones in the chain.

The choices that a company makes in the field of positioning and scope can be summarized under the term market strategy.

The third dimension of strategy relates to the way in which the company wants to gain the position it has chosen. There are several ways in which the desired position can be reached. First, the company can try to reach the position through its own strength. This has the distinct advantage that the company does not become dependent on other companies. Do-it-yourself positioning can have disadvantages in terms of speed, costs and risks. In view of the hectic talks between airlines, it is clear that many of them do not think that this is a valid option for surviving in the turbulent industry of the 1990s.

A second possibility is to acquire another company that may help to reach the desired position earlier or with less costs or risks. This is not always a feasible path. Other companies may not want to be taken over, or legislation may prevent such a move. In the airline industry, many countries view their airline companies as strategic assets and an extension of the national image as flag carriers. Therefore, legislation in the airline industry prohibits cross-border takeovers. The acquisition option, while attractive, remains an impossibility.

A third option is to merge with another firm. Within country borders this is feasible, but history has shown that cross-border mergers are difficult for several reasons. In the airline industry, the Scandinavian Airline System (SAS) is an exception. The respective governments of Norway, Sweden and Denmark shaped the merger out of geographical and economic necessity.

A fourth way to reach a desired strategic position is to establish a joint venture. As by definition joint ventures are a form of combining forces to start up new activities, these are seldom found in the airline industry.

The last possibility to gain the position that the company desires is by way of a strategic alliance. This is a form of co-operation where two or more companies decide to work together on the basis of a long-term agreement. Alliances are unique in that each party retains the option to withdraw from the agreement if it is not working to their satisfaction. In some cases, these co-operations are cemented by minority equity participation. In this category, we will also include those forms of co-operation that do not fit into any of the four categories mentioned earlier.

WHY STRATEGIC ALLIANCES ARE FORMED
IN THE AIRLINE INDUSTRY

Airline alliances are being formed in all of the three dimensions of strategy. Alliances can help airlines to reduce their cost structures, in order to position themselves in the market. Although prices have historically been regulated, lower cost airlines gain better margins, allowing them to reinvest in newer and better aircraft.

Gaining access to markets in the airline industry is determined by governmental bilateral negotiations. Most airlines bargain with reciprocity rights. When airlines do not have enough bargaining power by offering their own home market, alliances have been formed to gain market access through other means. Some airlines form an alliance to provide know-how or technical services in exchange for landing rights. These co-operative agreements provide a win–win solution to an otherwise problematic market access.

Alliances in the airline industry have been formed to share risks, as well as to split the costs of investment. When the large-widebody jet aircraft first arrived, airlines hesitated at undertaking the enormous investments necessary to maintain them. Technical alliance agreements were formed to share the maintenance investment costs and responsibilities. KSSU, the technical alliance between KLM Royal Dutch Airlines, SAS, Swissair and UTA (now a daughter company of Air France) provided benefits for all parties for many years. Each airline has its share of the work and its share of the benefits. By specializing in certain types of jet aircraft, and handling higher volumes, the four airlines saved the costs of investing in the skills, equipment and know-how to maintain all of them.

Alliances are also formed when timing becomes critical and the airline alone cannot match the speed of its competitors. A clear example is the development of frequent flyer programmes. Given enough time, each airline could develop its own programme. But the first movers (the American carriers) created such an advantage that other airlines needed to catch up quickly. British Airways did increase its pace enough to introduce the first European frequent flyer programme. Other airlines, however, formed co-operative agreements with carriers who had existing mileage programmes. CRS, distribution system technology, provides a second example whereby airlines formed alliances in order to keep pace with the speed of developments.

Airlines combine power through alliance agreements to optimize the utilization of available capacity. Instead of both carriers flying between two points on Monday, Wednesday and Friday, carriers can agree to spread the coverage through the week to target a broader customer base. Similarly, where traffic streams between two points are too thin to warrant two carrier services, airlines co-operate to offer one carrier service, but split the sales of the seats. This form of alliance is known as a blocked-space agreement and differs from the old-fashioned pool agreement, as carriers remain competitors in selling the seats. KLM and Northwest airlines have a blocked-space agreement on the Amsterdam–Minneapolis route. Alitalia and Iberia have several blocked-space agreements on the Madrid–Rome–Bangkok and Rome–Madrid–Mexico City routes.

Increased market coverage is provided through code-sharing alliance agreements. British Airways and United Airlines pioneered this type of alliance by introducing the concept of seamless transfer. Flights between London and Denver were listed under one shared code. British Airways flew the London–Chicago link, while United Airlines flew the Chicago–Denver link. Code sharing has generated discussion, as customers may perceive the route to be non-stop. Market research is also investigating the customers' reaction to being transferred to a different carrier during one journey.

Another alliance trend in the industry is demonstrated by Japan Airlines, one of the largest airlines in the world. Japan Airlines and Lufthansa initially formed a co-operation together with DHL in the air-cargo business. Recently, Japan Airlines and Lufthansa announced that they would also pursue extensive co-operation in the passenger air-travel business.

Eastern European carriers are being carefully investigated as potential alliance partners by several European, Far Eastern and American carriers. As the Eastern European governments introduce privatization efforts, they have expressed a preference for investment in their airlines to be made by another airline. Equity participation by a fellow airline yields not only financial rewards, but also airline management expertise, which is necessary for development and growth.

A worldwide trend for privatization of airline companies is yielding an ever-increasing potential for partnerships. Iberia Airlines bought a partner through their investment in Viasa Airlines, a product of the Venezuelan government privatization efforts.

CHARACTERISTICS OF PAST ALLIANCES

Given the global situation and the long-term positioning strategies of the major airlines, the alliance tool remains in the limelight. The press, industry analysts, investors and airline trade magazines are full of descriptions of the latest linkups or partnership discussions.

Alliances have always been an important tool in the airline industry, although their character has changed over time. In the pioneering phase, it was political and technical aspects that led to alliances in the industry. This type of alliance was characterized by underlying subcontracting and co-ordination, rather than actually sharing activities.

Past alliance synergies were sought on key parts of the airline-value chain. Consequently, the stakes of the alliance agreements were relatively low. Little investment was required, risks were limited to certain activities and payback was relatively short term. When problems arose, management time and effort were applied to resolve the issues at the expert level. As partnerships tended to focus specifically on visible objectives in order to save costs, or to add routes, the benefits of the agreement were able to be estimated, and the deal revised where necessary.

Partnerships tended to be fragmented across a number of different airlines in different markets. If problems in the alliance became insurmountable, the difficulty affected only part of the airline activities. Alternative partnership options could be evaluated or the do-it-yourself option could be resumed.

CHARACTERISTICS OF PRESENT ALLIANCES

Instead of being driven only by efficiency and internal motives, alliances are increasingly being driven by external, market or competitive conditions.

The global airline system will follow the trends in the world economy in constructing its network together with partners. With more than 20 major airlines positioning themselves for a slot in a global carrier network, the importance of alliances has taken on tremendous proportions.

Carriers now rely on alliance synergies for survival in their core business. Partners are not only chosen for synergies in one part of the airline-value chain. Instead the strategic decision makers consider the value chain as a whole, demanding, "which partner provides the most synergies within the total framework?"

With the link between privatization initiatives and airline alliance partnerships, much investment is involved. The equity participation in a carrier signifies a long-term versus a short-term alliance agreement. Still, as a financial investment an airline itself provides a marginal return, is susceptible to economic downturns and can provide a multiplier effect in the airline industry cycles.

Problems in an alliance agreement can have far-reaching strategic consequences. As the alliance objectives are difficult to quantify, the net benefit to either partner at any one point in the agreement remains a question of interpretation. Which partner gains the most advantage might become visual only in hindsight; and with the given dynamics in the industry, revising or correcting the direction of the agreement must be based on a shared vision of expected future developments. In addition, the airlines' visions may provide conflicting conclusions for the alliance's further development.

In an airline alliance, no partner has exclusive managerial control. The advantages of the combined objectives must be weighed against the economic self-interest of the partners. Alliances eventually require some degree of mutual dependency in order to reach long-term goals. Managers implementing the alliance must overcome the natural urge to protect the territory initially brought into the agreement.

Insurmountable problems in today's alliance agreements require careful decisions in order to proceed, withdraw from the agreement or to set a deadline for alliance synergy payback. By definition of an alliance agreement, either partner can withdraw, leaving the other partner vulnerable. The most ideal partners are quickly paired off. Your airline may deem the alliance to be a success and wish to continue with it, while your partner airline steps out. The constant trade-off between self-interest and creating a win–win situation for your partner requires a particular sort of management skill. Managing the same trade-off to remain loyal to multiple partners is almost impossible.

Alliances require special attention to deal with unforeseeable critical issues on a timely basis. Management should not make the mistake of managing alliance investments in the same way that they manage subsidiaries or other operational partnership agreements. Strange as it may sound, alliance management skills can be learnt from contingency management (Nakamura, pp. 45–57).

In today's alliances, the choice of partners is fewer, the mutual goals are greyer, the consequences are more risky, but the need for alliance success are higher than ever.

PRACTICAL ISSUES IN STRATEGIC ALLIANCES BETWEEN AIRLINES

Many practical issues have been brought to light as the number of airline alliances increase.

Cross-border alliances face challenges by national government air political authorities. On the one hand, it is the market restrictions imposed by the air political authorities that have led to the need for alliances, but on the other hand, the same restrictions limit the possibilities for completing an alliance agreement.

Alliances also face challenges by concentration authorities, which consider whether or not competition is being limited by the scope of the co-operative agreement. The KLM–British Airways–Sabena alliance agreement to establish a Euro-Hub in Brussels was investigated not only by European Community officials, but also by the Monopolies and Mergers Commission in the United Kingdom.

Airlines that form an alliance geared at introducing a new brand identity face marketing difficulties. Swiss Air, Singapore Airlines and Delta Airlines originally planned to introduce one new brand with global appeal, but have not yet succeeded. The European Quality Alliance brand remains less well known than the component names, Swiss Air, SAS and Austria Air. The national image in most cases remains indelibly intertwined with the image of their respective carriers. "Think global but act local" works in other industry alliances but is difficult to implement in an airline alliance.

Practical management problems of alliance implementation are compounded by the increase in complexity. While several airlines have formed few tight-knit partnerships, many airlines have formed up to ten different partnerships. Each partnership is with airlines that have their own respective partnerships, whose partners also have partners, etc. Even a basic competitor analysis exercise to estimate market shares becomes a spider web. Iberia Airline's market share in South America may be small in itself, but they have more than four alliance agreements with equity in South American airlines. What is Iberia's real market share in South America, and does it represent excessive concentration?

Finally, the dynamics of the airline industry environment are turbulent and are predicted to become gale force. Alliance agreements that are in the best interests of both carriers today, may no longer be valid tomorrow. The extensive closure of partnership agreements limits a carrier's remaining alliance options. But a quick decision could mean a short-term alliance success followed with long-term regret. Competitors' partnering policies can create new threats or new opportunities. The next ten years especially will demonstrate the extensiveness and effectiveness of airline alliance decisions.

Once a firm decision has been made, the strategic objectives should guide the way to successful implementation. From the airline industry example, one can draw some general alliance management principles. Never separate strategic alliances from the guardians of strategic planning. Strategic plans should monitor alliances by continually evaluating the following four points.

1. Is the alliance tool being applied towards the strategic objective for which it was intended?

   It is tempting for managers to implement alliances to provide a short-term visible gain rather than to work toward a longer term, less-structured objective.

2. Is the alliance tool making progress toward the objective?

   Both complete success or the lack of success in reaching strategic objectives can signal the end of the alliance's usefulness.

3. Is the objective for which the alliance tool is being used still part of the overall strategic plan?

Objectives change over time because of changes in the competitive environment. Objectives that were important when the alliance was negotiated become irrelevant, making the alliance outdated.

4. Is the alliance tool still the best choice for meeting the objective?

Sometimes an alliance is the only way to reach an objective given the political barriers or financial constraints. As your company's situation changes over time, managers have the option to move from dependence on an alliance partner to a less risky merger or acquisition strategic tool.

As the dynamics continue to impact the driving forces of the industry, airline executives must consider and reconsider their strategic choices of positioning in the market, product scope, geographical scope and the degree of vertical integration. Executives must also develop systematic processes for evaluating and ranking their options: do-it-yourself, acquire a company, merge with another company or establish a joint venture or other alliance agreement.

REFERENCE

Nakamura, Gen-Ichi. Turning external and internal surprises into opportunities and strengths: Japanese experiences, *The Turnabout*, Felix and Company, Amsterdam.

13

MANAGERIAL PREFERENCES IN INTERNATIONAL MERGER AND ACQUISITION PARTNERS

Sue Cartwright, Cary L. Cooper and Joseph Jordan

Manchester School of Management, University of Manchester Institute of Science and Technology

- Merger and acquisition (M&A) activity is predominantly driven by a rational-economic model.
- A growing body of evidence suggests that M&A outcomes also depend on sociocultural dynamics, especially perceived cultural compatibility.
- The issue of perceived cultural compatibility, and the emergence and acceptance of a new organizational culture and integrated managerial style are particularly critical to long-term success.
- When the M&A is performed at an international level, then the dynamics are complicated by differences in national cultures and associated managerial styles.
- This chapter reports on a study to establish whether different national managerial groups ($n = 480$) have similar/dissimilar attitudinal preferences towards strategic alliances with foreign partners. These preferences are then considered in the context of current patterns of actual activity.

INTRODUCTION

The continuous cycle of merger and acquisition (M&A) activity and other forms of strategic alliance indicates the importance of these organizational

The Strategic Decision Challenge, Edited by D. E. Hussey
© 1998 John Wiley & Sons Ltd

changes in the business arena. M&As are initiated by a diverse range of motives and needs. They provide a means of expanding corporate size, power and economic health, quickly entering or controlling markets, acquiring a product or technology, or protecting profits from taxation. They can also act as a defence against the threat of a hostile takeover or to fulfil the personal, often avaricious needs of an individual or groups of individuals within a company (Cartwright and Cooper, 1992; Cartwright, 1994).

M&A gains are notoriously difficult to assess. However, evidence, based on a range of performance indicators, both financial and behavioural, consistently demonstrates that M&A activity has an adverse impact on shareholder wealth (Hunt, 1988; Porter, 1987) and employee performance and wellbeing (Cartwright and Cooper, 1993). The UK Monopolies and Mergers Commission (1978) following an examination of the economic effects of post merger performance concluded that

> mergers are often found to be unprofitable by those carrying them out and little in the way of efficiency gains seems to be realised.

A more recent examination suggests that between 50 and 80% are acknowledged as failures (Marks, 1988). Despite the high risks attached, the rate of M&A activity and interorganizational collaboration continues to grow internationally. The global value of M&As has risen rapidly from £60 billion in 1984 to £355 billion in 1990. Some 37% of the 1990 figure relates to cross-border international M&As. In Europe alone, the number of cross-border M&As has increased almost ninefold in a period of 5 years (Cartwright and Cooper, 1993).

Traditionally, M&A failure has been attributed to financial miscalculations and/or incompetence. These aspects range from an inadequate valuation model to incorrect assumptions regarding inflation, exchange rates or inability to achieve the desired economies of scale. However, in recent years, the role of human factors, particularly the cultural compatibility of the corporate partners, has become the source of considerable speculation and research attention. This has served to emphasize the importance of partner or target selection, based on additional and different criteria from traditional practice.

The issue of cultural compatibility and its implications for subsequent integration is important in the context of any interorganizational combination or collaboration. Cultural differences and the concept of cultural distance can inhibit and positively obstruct management attempts to integrate and create a cohesive and coherent organizational entity. Such problems are unlikely to be confined to domestic M&A activity. Certainly, combinations between two organizations within the same country are likely to result in a greater degree of physical and procedural integration of their membership than cross-border M&As. However, in order to be successful, international M&As will also, at least minimally, require certain groups of key individuals to work together and to establish a shared or joint understanding of common objectives and strategy.

CULTURE IN THE CONTEXT OF INTERNATIONAL M&As

Culture is considered to be a collective phenomenon, because it is, at least, partly shared with people who live or work within the same environment, where it is learnt. The core of culture is *values*. Values are broad tendencies to prefer certain states of affairs over others and act to influence behaviour. Morgan (1986) focuses on the metaphor of culture as a shared sense of reality. Those who do not possess a culture which is compatible, do not share the same reality, and as such, cannot therefore enact reality with each other.

Culture as it relates to business activity can be considered to operate at two levels: national and organizational. In the same way that different nations develop different cultures, it is also meaningful to consider different organizations or occupational groups as having different types of cultures and preferred values and ways of doing things. The national culture in which an organization operates will to some extent influence the type of culture and style of work organization that companies will adopt.

National or societal culture is a pervasive influence on the behaviour of societal members. National ideologies are reflected in the relationship between business and government, the shape and orientation of the economy, financial institutions and trade union influence. However, within the same national economy, research has demonstrated the potential diversity and plurality of corporate cultures which operate across different business sectors and industries (Harrison, 1972; Deal and Kennedy, 1982; Peters and Waterman, 1982). It is suggested that this potential plurality of organizational cultures is more likely to be appreciated in the context of domestic rather than international M&A activity. Whereas in domestic M&As the compatibility of *organizational* cultures will be the most salient issue in partner selection; in international combinations, the attention of those involved is more likely to focus on the perceived compatibility of *national* cultures.

Researchers in this area (Altendorf, 1986; Cartwright and Cooper, 1992) have found that the first thing organizational members do in a merger situation is to make assessments and draw conclusions about the "other culture". Comparisons of similarities and differences can be based on direct experience, rumour, secondhand reporting and implicit theories, and involve inference. When the partnering organization is also foreign, assessment of the 'other culture' is likely to involve reference to national cultural stereotypes and ideologies.

Olie (1990) has noted that the perceived threat of concentration and nationalism is a barrier to international M&A. One of the characteristics of culture is that it creates a form of ethnocentrism in which one tends to regard activities that do not conform to one's own view of doing business as abnormal and deviant.

This chapter reports on recent research conducted amongst senior/middle managers ($n = 480$) to establish whether different national managerial groups have similar/dissimilar attitudinal preferences toward foreign M&A partners. It is suggested that preferences amongst a managerial population will reflect both a stereotypical judgement and an assessment of direct experience with other business cultures. The population that was targeted in this study could be classed as the 'international manager', well travelled, with a knowledge, comprehensive or not, of foreign business cultures, and representing organizations that had been and expect to continue to be engaged in M&A activity. These expressed preferences are then considered in the context of current patterns of actual M&A activity within Europe, and its implications for future cross-border alliances.

METHODOLOGY

The questionnaire which formed the basis of this study was developed following the content analysis of a series of face to face and postal interviews with a small sample of international managers ($n = 19$). A pilot questionnaire was then produced which was further refined and developed with a group ($n = 18$) of full-time MBA students. This group represented a variety of nationalities drawn from four different continents, i.e. Europe, America, Africa and Asia. An important consideration in the design of the questionnaire, which was administered in English, was that it had to be simple, short and concise. Therefore, a major part of the development work was concerned with designing a questionnaire which was option driven and required respondents to select from a series of presented alternatives. While open-ended questions were included to accommodate alternative responses, the intention was that these should be minimally used by respondents; in order to avoid the generation and analysis of a substantial amount of qualitative data which might create bias through culture-bound interpretation. The final questionnaire consisted of three parts.

(i)   *Biographical/organizational information:* items relating to nationality, function, organizational size and experience of M&A.

(ii)   *Attitudinal preference:* this section invited respondents to place in rank order (1–3) their preferred/least preferred choice of foreign merger partner or acquirer, and indicate the rationale for their choice(s).

(iii)   *Compatibility and admiration:* in this section, respondents were asked to indicate which foreign country they considered was most/least compatible with their own in terms of managerial style, and which country they most admired in terms of the way in which it conducts its business. Data were also collected on managerial expectations concerning their organizations' future involvement in M&A activity over the next three years.

Following negotiation with airport authorities at a major international UK airport, access was granted to the European, international and domestic executive lounges for a two-week period during summer 1994. During this period, questionnaires were distributed and collected from business passengers awaiting flights. A total of 496 questionnaires were collected. The total number of usable questionnaires which were included in the analysis (using SPSS for Windows) was 480.

RESULTS

Biographical/Organizational Information

Completed questionnaires were returned by managers representing 17 different nationalities. The majority of respondents were Northern European. Not surprisingly, given that the data were collected at a UK airport, 54.6% of the sample ($n = 262$) were British. In terms of function, the sample was split 50/50 between strategists and operational/non-strategists.

Over half (54.4%) of the sample worked for organizations with over 1000 employees. As Table 13.1 illustrates, the respondents were representative of organizations that were highly active in M&As and were particularly acquisitive. Furthermore, 50% of respondents indicated that it was likely/extremely likely that they would make further acquisitions within the next three years. In the same period, 40% indicated that they expected to become involved in joint ventures/strategic alliances, while 10% expected to merge.

Attitudinal Preferences

Table 13.2 shows the highest ranking 'preference dimension' choices for each of the analysed nationalities. This analysis was restricted to national groups which contained at least 10 respondents.

Whilst both the French and German managers chose themselves, this was actually found to be legitimate in terms of the question asked, in that the

Table 13.1   Type of Activity in which Organizations Had Been Involved During the Last Five years (1989–1994)

	No.	%
Merged	84	17.5
Made an acquisition	249	51.9
Taken over	45	9.4
Target of an unsuccessful bid	39	8.1
Party to a joint venture	148	30.8
Party to a strategic alliance	144	30.0

Table 13.2   Most Preferred Merger Partner or Acquirer

Nationality	No. of cases	1st preference	Rationale
British	262	American	Positive attitude
French	34	French	Know where you stand
German	58	German	Market access
American	19	British	Professional approach
Dutch	17	German/American	Professional approach/market access
Swedish	34	American	Professional approach
Danish	18	British	Positive attitude

managers sampled all worked for organizations of different national parentage to their own.

Table 13.3 shows the least preferred choice of merger partner or acquirer analysed by subject.

Compatibility/Admiration

In response to the question "in terms of managerial style, which foreign country would you consider to be most compatible with your own", the data (Table 13.4) tended to mirror the stated preferences of the sample.

All of the subsets analysed considered that the Japanese managerial style was the least compatible with their own. Four reasons were given for this: "desire to dominate", "protectionist", "arrogant" and "bureaucratic". However, it is interesting that 23% ($n = 112$) of the total managerial population stated that Japan was the country that they most admired in terms of the way in which it conducts its business activities. This was only 3% lower than the most admired country, namely Germany, chosen by 26% of the sample ($n = 123$), with America ranking second most admired by 25% ($n = 118$).

Table 13.3 Least Preferred Merger Partner or Acquirer

Nationality	No. of cases	Least preferred	Rationale
British	262	Japanese	Incompatible language
French	34	Japanese	Incompatible understanding
German	58	Japanese	Incompatible understanding
American	19	Japanese	Incompatible language
Dutch	17	Spanish	Incompatible understanding
Swedish	34	Italian	Never know where you stand
Danish	18	Italian	Incompatible language

Table 13.4 Most Compatible Managerial Style

Nationality	Most compatible	Rationale
British	American	"Makes it happen" style
French	American	Clear style, decision makers
German	American	"Makes it happen" style
American	British	Can do business
Dutch	German	Clear decision makers
Swedish	German	Clear decision makers
Danish	British	Compatible language

DISCUSSION

The results show that the mainly Northern European sample showed stronger preferences for merging with other North European and American organizations. Furthermore, their preference for a merger partner correlated highly with their perception of compatibility of management styles. The nationalities that were ranked as the least preferred partner were the Southern European organizations of Italy and Spain. It is interesting that previous cross-cultural research (Hofstede, 1990) has similarly identified that Northern European countries and the USA tend to cluster in terms of their orientation towards 'individualism' as opposed to 'collectivism', which is highly characteristic of both Japan and Spain.

On the basis of the available evidence, managerial preferences expressed in this study are in part reflected in the current patterns of actual M&A activity (Table 13.5). Traditionally, the USA has been a major player in the international M&As arena, with a highly concentrated level of activity within the UK. In 1993 alone, the USA acquired 135 UK companies. There is a certain reciprocity between these two countries as the UK remains the largest foreign investor in US businesses. It is also interesting to note that the preferences and perceptions of compatibility expressed by the French, German, Dutch and Danish managers appear to be borne out by the 1993 figures.

Table 13.5   Number of Deals

Acquirer	UK	France	Spain	Germany	Italy
USA	135	47	14	56	24
UK	—	34	8	32	10
France	13	—	5	17	5
Germany	14	11	3	—	4
Sweden	4	4	2	7	4
Netherlands	13	12	3	16	0
Denmark	9	2	1	0	1

Source: *Mergers and Acquisitions International*, January 1994, p. 8.

CONCLUSION

The globalization of trade has often been used as evidence of a trend towards a "global village". Advances in technology, transport and communication, and the creation of triadic trading blocks, may appear to make "the nation" less important, by subsuming its importance in favour of the larger enterprise; and cultural variation may appear to be subsumed along with it.

As a result, there is some debate as to whether doing business in other countries is a function of cultural compatibility or determined by economic and structural elements. However, the findings of this study suggest that managers prefer international partnerships with countries whom they perceive to be the most compatible in terms of their management style. On the basis of the evidence available, these preferences may be influential in determining activity patterns. This suggests that the concept of compatibility and cultural distance is an important issue in partner selection. In the context of international combinations these selection decisions are likely to involve stereotypical judgements to some degree. Unfortunately, there is a marked lack of empirical research in this area to establish whether these managerial perceptions of cultural distance are "real" or "imagined".

Furthermore, it could be speculated that Japanese organizations invoke the admiration of their Northern European competitors for the very reasons that make them the least attractive merger or joint venture partner. Traditionally, the Anglo-American model of M&As tends to require the other merger partner or acquired organization to assimilate and adopt the culture of the dominant partner or acquirer. "The desire to dominate" which is perceived to be characteristic of the Japanese managerial style suggests an inherent cultural resistance to accept the type of cultural imposition usual in such organizational combinations. This perhaps might partially explain why the Japanese regard M&A as a potentially "dishonourable" activity and a strategy of last resort. Indeed, the Japanese word for acquisition, "notori" also means hijacking.

REFERENCES

Altendorf, D. M. (1986). *When cultures collide: a case study of the Texaco takeover of Getty Oil and the impact of acculturation on the acquired firm.* Dissertation for Faculty Graduate School: University of Southern California.

Cartwright, S. (1994). Compatibility in the organizational marriage: a matter of choice or certainty? *Journal of Association for Global Strategic Information*, **3**(2), pp. 78–84.

Cartwright, S. and Cooper, C. L. (1992). *Mergers and Acquisitions: The Human Factor*, Butterworth-Heinemann, Oxford.

Cartwright, S. and Cooper, C. L. (1993). The role of culture compatibility in successful organizational marriage, *Academy of Management Executive*, **7**(2), pp. 57–70.

Deal, T. and Kennedy, A. (1982). *Corporate Culture: The Rites and Rituals of Corporation Life*, Penguin Business, London.

Harrison, R. (1972). How to describe your organization's culture, *Harvard Business Review*, May/June, **5**(1), pp. 119–128.

Hofstede, G. (1991). *Cultures and Organizations*, McGraw Hill, London.

Hunt, J. (1988). Managing the successful acquisition: a people question, *London Business School Journal*, Summer, pp. 2–15.

Marks, M. L. (1988). The merger syndrome: the human side of corporate combinations, *Journal of Buyouts and Acquisitions*, Jan/Feb., pp. 18–23.

Morgan, C. (1986). *Images of Organizations*, Sage, London.

Olie, R. (1990). Culture and integration problems in international mergers and acquisitions, *European Management Journal*, **8**(2), pp. 206–215.

Peters, T. J. and Waterman, R. (1982). *In Search of Excellence*, Harper Row, New York.

Porter, N. (1987). From competitive advantage to corporate strategy, *Harvard Business Review*, May/June, pp. 43–59.

14

GLOSSARY OF TECHNIQUES FOR STRATEGIC ANALYSIS

D. E. Hussey

David Hussey and Associates

- This chapter provides a glossary of analytical techniques.
- A brief description is followed by a list of references where more detailed information can be found.
- Techniques are cross-referenced where relevant.

INTRODUCTION

Anyone who sets out to offer a glossary is taking a great risk, and may well be accused of many sins of omission and commission (Table 14.1). There are almost certainly techniques which I have overlooked, and it may be that some people would quarrel with some of the descriptions. I feel less concerned about the second possibility because the main purpose of this glossary is to show sources where more detailed descriptions can be obtained. Thus the glossary is not trying to fulfil the role of a handbook, but instead gives a brief description of the major techniques, and leads the reader to more information. I make no claim that the references given are exhaustive in that there may be many other books and articles which describe the techniques at least as effectively. I have not tried to track down the earliest references to each technique: my task has been to provide adequate references, where possible quoting those which I find helpful and which are still readily obtainable. There is no need to try to provide a complete bibliography under each heading when the purpose of the glossary

The Implementation Challenge, Edited by D. E. Hussey
© 1996 John Wiley & Sons Ltd

Table 14.1   Techniques Listed in the Glossary

Techniques listed	Classification
Benchmarking	Methodology
Breakeven analysis	Financial analysis
Business definition	Information manipulation
Business process re-engineering	Methodology
Competitor analysis	Information manipulation
Competitor profiling	Information manipulation
Core competencies	Information manipulation
Corporate modelling	Mathematical relationships
Critical skills analysis	Information manipulation
Critical success factors	Information manipulation
Decision trees	Quantitative relationships
Delphi technique	Forecasting method
Discounted cash flow	Financial analysis
Discount rate of return	Financial analysis
Diversification matrix	Financial analysis
Du Pont chart	Financial analysis
Econometric model	Mathematical relationships
Environmental assessment: facing up to change	Information manipulation
Environmental assessment: Neubauer and Solomon	Information manipulation
Environmental turbulence matrices	Information manipulation
Equilibrium analysis	Information manipulation
Experience curve	Mathematical relationships
Gap analysis	Financial analysis
Generic strategy matrix	Information manipulation
Global strategy	Information manipulation
Group competitive intensity map	Information manipulation
Historical analogy	Forecasting method
Industry analysis	Information manipulation
Industry mapping	Information manipulation
Key success factors	Information manipulation
Learning curves	Financial analysis
Life cycle concepts	Information manipulation
MCC decision matrix	Information manipulation
Net present value	Financial analysis
PIMS	Empirical relationships
Portfolio analysis	Information manipulation
Product/market matrix	Information manipulation
Profits graph	Financial analysis
Risk analysis	Financial analysis
Risk matrix	Information manipulation
Risk-return matrix	Financial analysis
ROI chart	Financial analysis
Scenario planning	Information manipulation
Segmentation: strategic	Information manipulation
Sensitivity analysis	Financial analysis

Continued

Table 14.1   *(continued)*

Techniques listed	Classification
SOFT	Information manipulation
Strategic group mapping	Information manipulation
Strategy cube	Information manipulation
SWOT	Information manipulation
Synergy matrix	Information manipulation
Technology-based resource allocation	Information manipulation
Technology grid	Information manipulation
Trends projection	Forecasting method
Value-based strategy	Financial analysis
Value chains	Information manipulation
V matrix	Financial analysis

is only to point the way. A few of the entries might be more accurately described as aids to thinking rather than "techniques". They are usually approaches which I have found useful and are included for this reason.

This chapter appeared originally in *International Review of Strategic Management*, volume 3, edited by Hussey (1992). Approaches to strategic thinking move on, and this new version both updates some of the references and adds a number of new entries. I was tempted to include approaches to change and strategy implementation, but felt that few of these could be described as techniques. Most are processes, supported by step-by-step models. A glossary of these might serve a useful purpose, but would deserve a separate chapter.

There is no doubt that the glossary of techniques is capable of expansion in the future, both because new approaches will be developed, and because I will continue to learn about older techniques that I have missed. I should welcome hearing from any reader who has suggestions for expanding the glossary.

Techniques do not make strategy: this is the role of managers. However, they serve a useful purpose in presenting information in different ways so that new insight can be gained. There is no one right technique for all occasions, and the analyst's first task is to select approaches that are relevant and potentially helpful. My experience is that it is usually better to use two or three different techniques to let the information fall in different patterns, rather than to rely on only one. The analogy I like to use is that of a child's kaleidoscope. It is a number of pieces of coloured material in a glass-sided box, but each time the user moves the toy the pieces shift and a new pattern can be revealed. In analysis, the situation is not changed by the techniques, but the shaking up of the information brings out different pictures. And as every analyst knows, the application of a technique often reveals a need for information that has hitherto not been used in the organization.

Techniques may also aid the presentation of complex issues, and may be seen as valuable communication devices, on top of the role of analysis. It often becomes possible to reduce many pages of narrative plan to one or two of the diagrams which result from the use of some of the techniques listed in this glossary. The ability to compress information, thus making it easier to reach a shared understanding on complicated situations is to my mind one of the most important justifications for using many of the approaches listed.

It is also worth stressing what most readers will already know: techniques do not implement strategy, and we should not think that the job is done when elegant analysis leads to strategic decisions. We still have to make those decisions work.

There is no restriction on the development of new techniques. Matrix displays can give great insight, and I frequently find that using one approach sets me on the road to developing another that is original to the situation. The analyst should be willing to experiment. I also recommend using more than one technique when formulating strategy, because of the increased insight that this can give.

It would be wrong to move on to the glossary without drawing attention to three more detailed 'encyclopaedias', although the older of these may no longer be in print. Each of the books fulfils a different objective and all make a useful addition to the strategist's reference library.

BENCHMARKING

I hesitated over whether to include benchmarking, as like business process re-engineering, it is a process and method of approach rather than a technique. In the end I decided to err on the side of usefulness rather than purity of definition. Benchmarking is a primarily externally oriented activity, which compares processes between your organization and relevant others, which are not necessarily competitors, with the aim of using the findings to become equal or better than the best. To undertake benchmarking, the organization first needs to select the process that will benefit from comparison, and select and reach agreement with appropriate benchmarking partners. An essential next step is to fully understand your own process before studying that of another firm, as without this it may be possible to see that improvement is needed, but not why the other organization is better.

It is possible sometimes to benchmark against direct competitors, but is usually easier to reach agreement with organizations in the same industry where there is no competition (such as a power distribution company in the UK benchmarking against a similar company in the USA), or with an organization in a different industry which has a similar process to one of your own (such as a manufacturing company studying the customer service operation of an airline). The prime aim is continuous improvement, and it is an essential tool for aiding the drive to achieve world-class performance, and a useful tool as a precursor to business process re-engineering. It has some value in competitor analysis, mainly in aiding the recognition of competitive strengths and weaknesses, but ethical considerations, which are important for all types of benchmarking, are even more important here. Codes of conduct have been drafted and published, but the key to successful benchmarking is trust between the organizations involved.

Benchmarking is not just a comparison of performance ratios, although this may be helpful in the first stages of finding areas of weakness. It is a detailed comparison of processes.

Internal benchmarking has a value when comparing performance across companies in a group, or between branches. This may help to lift performance, but will be unlikely to lead to world-class performance unless one of the internal units is already a leader in the process.

See also: business process re-engineering.

BREAKEVEN ANALYSIS

Breakeven analysis is a very simple, very useful approach based on fixed and variable cost analysis which enables the impact of price and volume decisions on profit to be charted as a *profit graph*. In its basic form it enables the user to determine either the volume that has to be sold at a given price in order to breakeven, or the price at which a given volume must be sold to achieve the same effect. It is also possible to use the same concept to examine price/volume relationships at various target levels of profit.

The approach is very useful for a simple business, or at simple levels in a complex business. A breakeven analysis for the consolidated operations of a global company would have little value. A breakeven analysis for a new product launch in one trading unit, or for the operation of a focused business within a particular country, would be a very useful approach. The technique facilitates the exploration of sensitivities, and hence the understanding of the business.

It is also known as a profits graph (although graphical presentation is not needed as calculation can be made by formula). Some prefer this alternative title on the basis that businesses aim to make profits not to breakeven.

BUSINESS DEFINITION

Business definition is a form of three-dimensional *strategic segmentation analysis*, using the axes customer function, customer group and alternative technologies. This enables the organization to plot its own business definition, compared with that of competitors, both to understand the current business and plan future strategic moves. In essence, the concept is very little different from other multi-dimensional approaches to segmentation. Abell, (1980) argues that

> ...even portfolio strategy cannot be discussed until very basic decisions are made about the definition of the activity and the competitive arena(s) in which strategy will be implemented. This issue has been lurking in the background in the academic literature up to now. It has, however been of considerable concern to practitioners who have long recognised that contemporary planning methods can only be used once this more fundamental question of 'what business(es) are we in?' has been addressed.

See also: strategy cube.

BUSINESS PROCESS RE-ENGINEERING

Business process re-engineering (BPR) is more a method than a technique, although there are a number of aids to application (what is recommended tends to vary with the author). The approach is about rethinking the core business processes in the organization with a view to achieving fundamental changes to the way things are done.

Although frequently used for marginal improvements, the real purpose is to achieve a breakthrough which gives a leapfrog position of competitive advantage. Like many techniques it is often misunderstood, and many organizations which claim to be applying business process re-engineering, have merely renamed an existing function which is seeking cost improvement, but have not adopted the new methods. There are some behavioural pitfalls in that BPR usually requires teamwork from those in the processes under study, but frequently results in job losses.

More recent developments extend BPR across company borders to suppliers and customers so that processes in a value chain may be looked at in their entirety.

See also: benchmarking and core competencies

COMPETITOR ANALYSIS

Competitor analysis is not itself a technique, but a process, which is aided by a number of techniques. It is an approach to the systematic collection and analysis of information about competitors. The aims are to assess competitor strategies, their likely response to your strategy and to define approaches which build competitive advantage. In addition, good competitor analysis can aid the identification of alliance partners or acquisition candidates.

See also: benchmarking, business definition, portfolio analysis (note that competitor analysis is a subsidiary use of these techniques), competitor profiling, group competitive intensity map, industry analysis, industry mapping, strategic group mapping and, value chains.

COMPETITOR PROFILING

Competitor profiling is an approach that aids the analysis of competitors through the focusing of all data on to a one page profile for each competitor. This page is usually A3 size, and the identification of the key issues makes it easier to understand the competitor, to use the information that is available and to identify gaps in that information. The approach needs the support of an information system.

Boxes on the profile can be viewed as note pads to record historical performance, market share trends, key facts, strengths and weaknesses, strategy and critical success factor ratings.

The approach can also be used to profile other actors on an industry map, such as customers. From the combination of industry map and profiles a series of possible strategic actions can be identified, and the point in the chain where the action might be initiated.

Although competitor profiling can be used as a stand alone technique, it achieves its full potential when used in conjunction with industry mapping.

See also: group competitive intensity map, industry analysis, industry mapping, strategic group mapping and value chains.

CORE COMPETENCIES

The concept of core competencies has been suggested as a more useful way of looking at an organization than the strategic business unit concept. Competencies are the skills, knowledge and technologies that an organization possesses on which its success depends. Those that are core are the ones that should be nurtured. Instead of developing strategy based on thinking only of dominating markets, it may be more useful to think in terms of core competencies, which will segment the organization in a totally different way.

The references quoted at the end of this chapter do not offer a technique for analysing competencies, but it should be possible to move from the concepts to a form of portfolio analysis which positions activities by core competencies.

See also: MCC decision matrix and technology grid.

CORPORATE MODELLING

Computer-based simulations of the total company or of a business activity within the company are useful in assessing the expected results of strategies. Manual quantification of options can be tedious. Models speed this up, make it possible to consider more options and sensitivities, and reduce the risk of mathematical error. In the 1960s, when many of the earlier models were developed, modelling was a major investment of time and money and of course used mainframe computers making access difficult. With the availability of personal computers, modelling is now within the reach of all. Useful models can be built on spread-sheet programs, and can be highly sophisticated suites of models, or a relatively simple way of looking at changes in the pro forma final accounts.

CRITICAL SUCCESS FACTORS

(Also known as *critical skills analysis* or *key success factors*.)

This is an approach to strengths and weakness analysis which is also useful in competitor analysis and, if taken to lower levels of resolution, in the design of information systems. It seeks to identify the five to ten things that have to be done well in order to be successful in a specific business. Lever Brothers and McBrides (own label contractors) are both in the detergent business, but they do not have the same critical success factors. Among those critical to Lever Brothers are product innovation, market segmentation and promotional skills. None of these matter to McBrides, who among other things have to be able to formulate substitutes for branded goods quickly, produce to low cost and have flexible manufacturing capability.

Concentration on critical success factors is one way of honing the strengths and weakness analysis so that the important strategic issues are identified and dealt with. The approach also provides a standard against which it is possible to evaluate one's own business against those of competitors.

The approach is long established and predates the references given by many years.

See also: SWOT and equilibrium analysis.

DECISION TREES

A decision tree is a useful approach which sets out diagrammatically a chain of optional decisions and chance events. Each chance event has several possible consequences, and each consequence may require that different strategic options be considered. The technique allows a complex array of risks and decisions to be charted, and this alone can aid understanding and bring clarity of thinking.

The technique goes further by assessing financial consequences to each change event and calculating the outcomes of all the branches of the tree in financial terms. The combination of probabilities and outcomes along the various courses indicated by the decision allows an *expected monetary value* to be calculated for each possible final outcome. Quantification is usually in discounted cash flow terms, and the final figure aids the process of decision making. As with all techniques the worth of what comes out has considerable relation to the care with which the analysis is undertaken.

I have found this technique to be useful in brainstorming ideas, in communicating complex situations, as well as in analysis.

See also: discounted cash flow and risk analysis.

DELPHI TECHNIQUE

This is a technique which is used for developing scenarios of possible futures under conditions of discontinuity. A panel of experts is chosen and asked to complete a series of questionnaires about some future situation. In the second round they receive an analysis of others' views and are invited to defend or modify their own. It is a form of structured brainstorming of expert opinion. The technique, like all 'futures' techniques, was more popular in the late 1960s and early 1970s than it is now, possibly because emphasis has changed from forecast-dependent strategy to the management of strategy.

DISCOUNTED CASH FLOW

Discounted cash flow is a method of analysing capital expenditures which takes account of the time value of money by discounting future cash flows back to today's value. Hence it is also called *discounted cash flow* or *net present value*. The analysis is made on cash inflows and outflows, and provides a good basis for comparing options within a project. The time value of money is compared with the cost of money, usually a weighted figure that reflects the mix of debt and equity of the firm, the aim being to choose projects which offer a net gain over this figure.

The technique can be used in a way that takes account of inflation. It is also suitable for studying some elements of risk.

Although until recently used for project evaluation, the approach has for many years been advocated as a way of looking at all the strategies of the firm. Recently, this concept has flowered in the value-based strategy concept.

Discounted cash flow (DCF) demands a careful forward assessment of the project, and cannot be used unless a disciplined approach is taken. Results are affected by the conventions chosen, such as the treatment of residual value. Because of the discounting, this has more impact on the results if the project is evaluated over a short period, say five years, than it would if a long period were chosen, say 20 years. Against this, margins of error in the forecasts of costs and income are greater the longer the period chosen.

The technique measures the economic value of the project, and not its strategic desirability. It has been suggested that over reliance on DCF can lead to bad long-term decisions, for example, incremental changes to a factory to improve productivity give better returns than would the building of a state-of-the-art facility, yet in the end the gap in competitive performance that opens up over the years means that the firm is eventually unable to command the resources to take the big move that eventually becomes necessary. This caution does not invalidate the worth of the technique.

Among the measures that result from DCF are the following:

Discount rate of return, which is the rate which would leave a zero net present value at the end of the project. A 15% return would be better than 10%, but neither would be attractive if the cost of capital was 16%. This is sometimes known as the *internal rate of return*.

Net present value, which is the value *today* of the cumulative income/ expenditure stream at the end of the project, using a given discount rate.

Discounted payback is the number of years to pay back initial outlay using discounted figures.

See also: risk analysis and value based strategy.

DIVERSIFICATION MATRIX

A diversification matrix is one which seeks to stimulate new ideas and identify areas of synergy. One axis examines customers: same type, firm its own customer, similar type and new type. The other divides products into related and unrelated technology.

See also: product/market matrix.

ECONOMETRIC MODEL

An econometric model is a system of interdependent regression models describing some aspect of economic activity. It provides a basis for testing economic options and providing a quantified forecast. It is not a technique for amateurs, and specialist help is needed for effective model building.

ENVIRONMENTAL ASSESSMENT: FACING UP TO CHANGE

There are a number of similar approaches which use a structured checklist to help identify the trends in the environment, and study the likely impact of these on the strategies of the business. Many have in common a scoring approach which takes into account impact and probability, thus enabling the most critical trends to be separated from the rest, so that action can be taken. The most valuable element of these approaches is that the structured approach makes it less likely that things will be overlooked, while the scoring systems are of particular value in stimulating debate about the issues. In my view these approaches have more value in encouraging participative discussion than as a formal technique of analysis.

Some detailed approaches are proprietary to management consulting firms and have not been published. The references do not necessarily provide access to the most comprehensive of the approaches, but they are sufficient to illustrate the concepts.

See also: risk analysis and risk matrix.

ENVIRONMENTAL ASSESSMENT: NEUBAUER AND SOLOMON

There are several techniques for looking at the impact of the environment, and the Neubauer and Solomon approach has some characteristics of some of the methods described in the previous entry, in that it uses a concept of impact. Why it rates a separate listing is that it is a far more comprehensive approach, which hones down the vast array of influences from the environment to those with most impact, and relates these to corporate strategies and missions. The technique studies trends, and also the expectations of different groups, or constituents, in the environment. It is not a technique to be learned on one reading, and needs considerable practice to gain proficiency. The whole approach has the merit of being oriented to making the strategies compatible with the business environment.

The method goes through a number of steps, beginning with the identification of the current strategies and mission of the business. Trends and constituents are identified, and an impact matrix created to identify the threats and opportunities. The next step is to identify the effect of the issues identified on the strategies and mission of the business. In turn, this leads to a reassessment of strategies of mission and strategies.

See also: risk analysis and risk matrix.

ENVIRONMENTAL TURBULENCE MATRICES

This approach presents a novel and useful way of looking at all aspects of strategic management against a grid which shows the level of environmental turbulence to which the organization is subject. The levels are 1 repetitive, 2 expanding (slow incremental), 3 changing (fast incremental), 4 discontinuous (but predictable) and 5 surpriseful (unpredictable). The position on the scale, which for most organizations will vary over time, affects not only how the organization should plan strategy, but the types of strategic response and the type of manager who would cope best. In designing this approach Igor Ansoff (1990 and 1991) its originator, has provided a very useful diagnostic tool. It is not only of value to the analyst who is studying several businesses, but may also help the managers of single business entities think through the response needed as their businesses change position on the scale.

EQUILIBRIUM ANALYSIS

This is derived from the principles of force-field analysis, and is a very simple way of looking at strengths and weaknesses in relation to a particular issue, such as market share. A horizontal line represents the issue under scrutiny, and the diagram sets out to identify those factors which keep it as low as it is and those which keep it as high as it is. The technique attempts to weight the factors, and concentrates on designing responses to those factors which can be tackled and which are of most importance. It is an ideal technique to facilitate discussions, and an alternative to the rather long "shopping lists" of strengths and weaknesses that some planning activities seem to generate. It is action oriented.

See also: critical success factors and SWOT.

EXPERIENCE CURVE

This is a concept which is based on industrial *learning curve* theories extended from costs of production to the total costs of the whole firm. Empirically, it has been demonstrated that in most businesses the real costs per unit reduce every time cumulative output doubles. This is not the same as economies of scale (which relate to output over a given period), although this may play a part, and is related to the total cumulative experience of the organization.

If the experience curve is calculated it can be used to assess future costs based on volume increases. This leads to price and other related marketing strategies designed to gain volume to force costs down, often below the level at which most other firms can compete. In electronics, for example, the experience curve of larger companies has driven out many competitors who did not match their volume growth: calculators are a good example. The theory is less predictable in industries where there is frequent fundamental model change.

The experience curve is attributed to the Boston Consulting Group, although learning curve theory has been around since the 1940s.

GAP ANALYSIS

Gap analysis is a very simple technique with limited use. It measures the "gap" between company profit or growth targets, and what is likely to be achieved if no new strategic initiatives are taken. The aim is to use this information to measure the size of the strategic task and stimulate thoughts on new strategies.

The technique is mentioned in many books on strategic planning. It is so simple that the various authors can add little to the technique.

GENERIC STRATEGY MATRIX

This is a thought provoker rather than a complex method. It is a matrix based on the contention that all organizations have the choice of only three generic strategies: industry-wide differentiated, industry-wide cost leadership, or focus on a particular segment. The contention is not universally accepted.

GLOBAL STRATEGY MATRIX

More of an aid to thinking than a complex technique, this approach has been published in a number of variants. The two references given are thus not to identical matrices, although they are closely related. One variant has the need for globalization on one axis, moving from low to high. The other axis is need for local responsiveness, again moving from low to high. This matrix enables the globalization versus domestic requirements of various businesses to be compared. It may also be used to look at functions, or elements in the value chain, to establish the extent to which each of these should be integrated on a global basis. Questionnaires used in conjunction with the approach turn it into something a little stronger than an idea marshaller.

The alternative matrix studies the degree to which strategy is globalized against the globalization potential of the industry. In practice, there is not a great deal of difference between the two matrices.

GROUP COMPETITIVE INTENSITY MAP

Derived from research by McNamee and McHugh, (1990) this technique builds on the work of Porter. The map displays in quantitative terms, using ellipses on a matrix, the location of an industry's strategic groups, the competitive intensity they face and the relative risks to which they are subject. The approach aids the study of competitive behaviour in industries where there are many competitors, where studying each individually would be either impossible, or would yield results that cannot be interpreted.

See also: business definition, competitor analysis, competitor profiling, industry analysis, industry mapping, portfolio analysis, strategic group mapping and value chains.

HISTORICAL ANALOGY

Historical analogy is a form of forecast which analyses the history of something similar, or the same product in another market (for example, what happened when product X was launched in the USA — now what is likely to happen when we launch in the UK?). It is used in a minor way when the results of a test market are translated to the total market. Most applications are in-depth studies of a previous or analogous situation.

INDUSTRY ANALYSIS

Industry analysis is an approach to analysing the structure of an industry. The basic model examines the balance of power between suppliers, buyers and competitors in the industry. These are three of the "five forces". The remaining two are substitutes and entry barriers. The principles of this approach were drawn together by Porter (1980), although few of the components were new. Porter's contribution was offering a comprehensive basis for analysis out of a series of separate ideas. Industry analysis now underpins most modern thinking on strategic analysis.

See also: business definition, competitor analysis, competitor profiling, group competitive intensity map, industry analysis, industry mapping, portfolio analysis, strategic group mapping and value chains.

INDUSTRY MAPPING

This approach predated Porter's work, but was refined as a result of his structural analysis of industry concept. It expands the "five forces" diagram to model all the key groups of "actors" in the chain, from suppliers through to final buyers, in a block diagram, and adds a further dimension of those who influence a buying decision but do not themselves purchase: general practitioners who prescribe drugs, architects who specify a lift, consultants who recommend a computer system, for example.

Key factual data are entered on this diagram in summary form, so that all the strategic elements of the industry are portrayed on one piece of A3 paper. Some industries are too complex to fit on one sheet, but these are the exception rather than the rule.

The approach is often used in conjunction with competitor profiling. The two techniques in combination provide a series of headings that may be used in a database to store information.

See also: business definition, competitor analysis, competitor profiling, group competitive intensity map, industry analysis, portfolio analysis, strategic group mapping and value chains.

LIFE CYCLE CONCEPTS

The life cycle position of an industry or product has many implications for strategies and competitive behaviour. Empirically, it has been observed that products, for example, pass through a number of stages, each of which may be associated with a different volume of sales, and different levels of profits. One classification of stages is development growth, shake-out, maturity, saturation and decline. Not only do competitors tend to behave differently at each stage of the life cycle, but there are also many implications for management in the profits/cash needs of different positions, and in strategies to extend the life cycle. Marketing strategy is also likely to be different at each stage of the life cycle. Not surprisingly the concept also lies behind a number of approaches to portfolio analysis.

See also: portfolio analysis.

MCC DECISION MATRIX

Developed by John Nicholls (1995), this matrix looks at the use of resources and assesses the fit with the organization's mission and core competencies. It is offered in both a basic 2×2 matrix and a more complex 3×3 matrix. The matrix uses *Fit with the Mission* on the vertical axis, and *Fit with Core Competencies* on the horizontal axis. The 2×2 matrix has good and poor positions on each axis: the 3×3 version adds a mid-position. Products and projects are placed on the matrix, and the position on the matrix guides the appropriate action. Apart from its use in assessing overall strategies, this matrix has value in conjunction with discounted cash flow methods of capital evaluation.

PIMS

PIMS stands for Profit Impact of Market Strategy. It is an assessment of strategy and performance based on data provided by subscribers, which provides a sound empirical basis for deducing principles of strategy. It also provides a number of matrix analysis formats through which a firm might contrast its own businesses with the findings from the data bank. The data allow relationships to be established between return on investment (ROI) and such factors as market share, vertical integration, capital intensity and quality.

PORTFOLIO ANALYSIS

Portfolio analysis is a group of related methods of analysis of varying complexity which enables a variety of activities to be compared in strategic terms. The axes of the matrix may vary, but typically are some way of expressing market position compared with some way of expressing market prospects. There are some interesting variations, such as market prospects/corporate strengths. The approaches give a view of the relative strategic importance of a 'portfolio' of strategic business areas, strategic business units, or products, and can also be extended to consider the management skills needed to be successful in each position on the matrix. Too literal an acceptance of the findings has led many companies to take against portfolio analysis. However, careful usage can give considerable insight in complex situations, and can make it much easier to communicate the strategic shape of a multi-activity company. It makes sense to use the technique in conjunction with other analytical tools, and to be prepared to experiment with different types of portfolio analysis, including the devising of matrices which are useful in a particular situation. For example, the market share axis may be changed to contrast the technological position of the portfolio. Matrices may also be devised to study the portfolio on a geographical basis.

See also: risk matrix, risk-return matrix and technology grid.

PRODUCT/MARKET MATRIX

This is a simple but very useful way of thinking through strategic options. One axis looks at markets, existing and new. Another looks at products, existing and new. The matrix thus consists only of four cells. One value of the approach is that the patterns of risks are likely to be different in each. The matrix is sometimes represented as a product/mission matrix.

Variants of this matrix include the following.

- Changing the axes to suppliers and technology to analyse purchasing strategy.
- Changing the axes to sources of finance/uses of finance to study funding.
- A more complex variant which lists the four product market options on one axis, and on the other shows possible strategic actions, such as licensing, joint venture, and acquisition.

RISK ANALYSIS

Risk analysis is an approach using the Monte Carlo method to draw numerous possible values for all the factors in a capital project, with the chance of drawing any value being proportionate to its probability. This results in numerous combinations of factors, each of which is subjected to DCF analysis. The spread of outcomes gives an indication of the degree of risk to which the project is subject.

See also: discounted cash flow and sensitivity analysis.

RISK MATRIX

This approach was designed to be used in conjunction with a form of multi-factor portfolio analysis which had competitive position and market prospects as the two axes. The technique keeps the market prospects axis, and has degree of risk as the second axis. In concept this turns the portfolio chart into a 3D cube, although in practice it is easier to colour or shade the circles by which strategic business units (SBUs) are plotted to show different intensities of risk. The risk axis is reached through a worksheet which scores environmental factors for impact and probability.

The matrix allows three views to be taken.

- The degree of risk to which each area on the portfolio analysis is subject, relative to the other areas.

- The particular trends which have most impact on the activity (from the worksheet).
- The particular trends which have the most impact on the company as a whole.

See also: portfolio analysis and environmental analysis.

RISK-RETURN MATRIX

This approach is also known as the Cardozo-Wind risk return matrix, and is intended to help increase the productivity of SBU investments. The x axis shows risk, and the y axis shows return. The approach allows comparison of the various SBUs within an organization, and helps to set criteria for new SBUs. It is also useful in evaluating mergers and alliances.

See also: portfolio analysis, risk analysis and risk matrix.

ROI CHART

Sometimes called a *Du Pont chart*, this method allows presentation of income statement and balance sheet, in contribution analysis form, on one piece of paper. Complex information can be put into usable, easily communicated formats. The method concentrates on information that is important for strategic planning. It is a useful first step in strengths and weakness analysis, since it shows where contribution is coming from, and where financial resources are being used.

SCENARIO PLANNING

This approach to planning accepts that the future is uncertain. Instead of producing one plan, with sensitivities, a number of plans are drawn prepared according to the various scenarios developed at the start. The pitfall to avoid is an over-complex system driven by planners. The assumptions in the scenarios may drive the strategy without everyone understanding that this is happening.

SENSITIVITY ANALYSIS

This is a method for testing a plan for vulnerabilities. It may be applied to a strategic plan as a whole, or to an evaluation of capital expenditure. Essentially, it is an assessment of financial results to a series of "what if..." questions, and may lead to different strategic decisions if the risks look too high.

Typically, it deals with questions such as what if sales were to fall by 10%. Some care is necessary in definition, because sales value may fall because of a volume or a price drop, and the impact on profit and cash flow will not be the same in both situations. Sloppy descriptions of sensitivities can lead to misunderstandings.

Sensitivity analysis can be made more useful if it is accompanied by an analysis of the causal factors that contribute to success or failure (for example, what happens if the competitors react with a price cut, or where we would be if the government changed). A table of impacts should be prepared, such as costs, capital costs, prices, sales volumes, tax and the like, and the effect that these changes would have on results. In the end several factors may have identical end results, so the mathematical calculations may be fewer than the events examined. This approach may help the development of strategies that avoid risk, whereas the more common, more passive style of sensitivity analysis, ends at understanding where the project or plan is most sensitive.

See also: decision trees, discounted cash flow and risk analysis.

STRATEGIC GROUP MAPPING

Strategic group mapping is a method of matrix display which groups competitors in an industry by their strategic dimensions, such as price policy, cost position and specialization. Some 13 variables have been identified. For the matrix the analyst has to identify a few particularly important dimensions on which to construct the map. An example might be to use specialization (high to low) as one axis, and vertical integration (high to low) as the other. This concept, and there is no reason why two or three matrices using different axes should not be used, enables competitors to be grouped and positioned on the matrix by the common components of their strategy. This may be useful in any industry, but is particularly valuable in an industry with numerous competitors where little insight would be gained by studying each individually.

See also: group competitive intensity map and industry mapping.

STRATEGY CUBE

This approach to analysis has some similarities with the business definition concept. It argues that strategy can be looked at on three dimensions, technology, business and logistics. These are the three axes of the strategy cube. The position on each axis follows the subheadings familiar, partly familiar and unfamiliar.

SWOT OR SOFT

Strengths, weaknesses, opportunities and threats; a simple approach which appears under several names. 'WOTSUP', the common initials have the same meaning: UP stands for underlying planning, SOFT here fault is used instead of weakness, and TOWS same words, different order. If we wanted to be original I suppose we could call it TWOS analysis, which both stands for the same words, and indicates that they cover the two dimensions of internal and external issues!

The value of the approach is that it summarizes the key issues from a complex corporate appraisal, and can reduce these to one piece of paper. The pitfall is that for many it becomes a useless shopping list of weaknesses, few of which are strategic, accompanied by a few platitudes in place of real strengths. I am always suspicious when the only strengths listed are "a strong chief executive" and a "professional and loyal management team". This is not a fictional example!

SWOT works best when it is tackled with the mind-set of:

- strengths and weaknesses *relative to market needs*;
- and compared with the competition.

Simple techniques are often best for a situation, and SWOT can be recommended to those who are aware of the possible pitfalls.
See also: equilibrium analysis and critical success factors.

SYNERGY MATRIX

This is a matrix framework to facilitate the quantification of synergy in new strategic initiatives. The matrix analyses the effects on profit due to a pooling of competence, by functional areas. It is one of the first generation techniques of strategic analysis, but has some of the strands of thought that reappear in value chains, and in the debate on shareholder value.

TECHNOLOGY-BASED RESOURCE ALLOCATION

This is a matrix approach to deciding technology strategies. It is the third step in a methodology that consists of an audit, an understanding of the strategic implications of the technology portfolio, an implementation plan and a monitoring programme.

TECHNOLOGY GRID

This is a way of analysing the portfolio by technology. One method uses a matrix showing technology position on one axis, and relevance of the technology on the other. It was designed to give added insight to the positioning of SBUs on the more traditional competitive position/market attractiveness portfolio chart. A variant of this approach uses market growth and competitive strength as the two axes. In this case what would be plotted would be the key technologies. In common with portfolio analysis, positions would be indicated by circles drawn proportionately to their importance to the company.

See also: core competencies and portfolio analysis.

TREND PROJECTION

Most time series analyses and projections are poor for long-term forecasting, although useful in the short term. Trend projection is good for longer term forecasts. It designs and fits a mathematical equation to the data by, for example, measuring slope characteristics and using the results to project the curve.

See also: Delphi technique, econometric model and historical analogy.

VALUE-BASED STRATEGY

The debate about the need for strategic actions to add to shareholder value has led to the development of a mathematical technique that tries to ensure that all strategies are value adding, and that the business selects the options which add the most value. The method applies discounted flow analysis concepts to all the strategies of the entire organization.

The premises behind value-based planning are that the company's foremost obligation is to maximize returns to shareholders, and that the market value of shares is related to the expected cash-generating abilities of those shares.

There are several variations in the ways in which the concept may be applied, but all are based on forecast cash flow, discounted by the risk-adjusted cost of capital. Strategies are expected to deliver a discounted return in excess of the cost of capital.

If taken to its logical conclusion, the shareholder value approach moves from being a clutch of techniques to a philosophy and process for the strategic management of the organization.

See also: discounted cash flow.

VALUE CHAINS

This is a method for separating the activities the firm performs in order to identify the underlying areas of competitive advantage. All broad stages of the process from "inbound logistics" to after-sales service are identified. They are then broken down into more detailed chains of activity, so that the areas where the firm has advantages can be studied. Similar analysis is undertaken on competitors, leading to more effective competitive strategies, and a fuller understanding of how each competitor is achieving differentiation.

See also: competitor analysis, competitor profiling, group competitive intensity map, industry analysis, industry mapping and strategic group mapping.

V MATRIX

A graphical presentation which is based solely on financial data. Return on investment is plotted on one axis and weighted average cost of capital on the other. A diagonal line drawn from the zero points at the bottom left hand corner of the matrix to the opposite corner at the top right hand corner marks the position at which ROI and the cost of capital are equal. Anything positioned below this diagonal is likely to be inadequate: anything above it is adequate. A ROI of 4% would be adequate if the cost of capital was only 2%. However, a ROI of 14% would be inadequate if the cost of capital was 16%. The matrix allows the positions of all businesses in the portfolio to be plotted relative to each other.

ROI is defined as:

$$\frac{\text{Operating income } (1 - \text{the tax rate})}{\text{Assets}}$$

where K is the cost of capital and V is value.

$$V = \frac{\text{ROI}}{K}$$

Although the matrix uses an undiscounted return on investment, it would probably be possible to adapt it to a discounted rate of return. The main value of the matrix is that it focuses on more than ROI, which may be particularly in an organization with subsidiaries with local borrowing, or minority shareholders.

REFERENCES

Introduction

Argenti, J (1969). *Management Techniques*, Allen and Unwin, London.

Hussey, D. E. (ed.) (1992). *International Review of Strategic Management*, volume 3, Wiley, Chichester.

Karlöf, B (1989). *Business Strategy: A Guide to Concepts and Models*, MacMillan, London.

Kempner, T. (ed.) (1987). *The Penguin Management Handbook*, 4th edition, Penguin Books, London.

Benchmarking

Karlöf, B. and Östblom, S. (1993). *Benchmarking*, Wiley, Chichester.

Watson, G. H. (1993). *Strategic Benchmarking*, Wiley, New York.

Breakeven Analysis

Anthony, R. N. and Reece, J. S. (1983). *Accounting: Text and Cases*, 7th edition, chapter 16, Irwin, Homewood, Illinois.

Wilson, R. M. S. and McHugh, G. (1987). *Financial Analysis: A Managerial Introduction*, chapter 11, Cassell, London.

Business Definition

Abell, D. F. (1980). *Defining the Business: The Starting Point of Strategic Planning*, Prentice-Hall, Englewood Cliffs, New Jersey.

Business Process Re-engineering

Dale, M. W. (1994). The re-engineering route to business transformation, *Journal of Strategic Change*, **3**(1), 3–19.

Johansson, H. J., McHugh, P., Pendlebury, A. J. and Wheeler, W. A. (1993). *Business Process Reengineering*, Wiley, Chichester.

McHugh, P., Merli, G. and Wheeler, W. A. (1995). *Beyond Business Process Reengineering*, Wiley, Chichester.

Competitor Analysis

Fuld, L. M. (1987). *Competitor Intelligence*, John Wiley and Sons, New York.

Hussey, D. E. (1991). *Introducing Corporate Planning: Guide to Strategic Management*, 4th edition, chapter 5, Pergamon Press, Oxford.

Hussey, D. E. (1994). *Strategic Management: Theory and Practice*, 3rd edition, chapters 9 and 10, Pergamon Press, Oxford.

Porter, M. E. (1980). *Competitive Strategy*, Free Press, New York.

Porter, M. E. (1985). *Competitive Advantage*, Free Press, New York.

Stanat, R. (1990). *The Intelligent Corporation*, Amacom, New York. (Note that this book deals with information rather than analysis.)

Competitor Profiling

Hussey, D. E. (1991). *Introducing Corporate Planning: Guide to Strategic Management*, 4th edition, chapter 5, Pergamon Press, Oxford.

Hussey, D. E. (1994). *Strategic Management: Theory and Practice*, 3rd edition, chapters 9 and 10, Pergamon Press, Oxford.
Steiner, G. A. (1979). *Strategic Planning: What Every Manager Must Know*, p. 139, Free Press, New York.

Core Competencies

Hemel, G. and Heene, A. (eds.) (1994). *Competence-based Competition*, Wiley, Chichester.
Ohmae, K. (1983). *The Mind of the Strategist*, chapter 14, Penguin Books, London, (This book does not use the term core competencies, but offers some thoughts which are relevant to the concept.)
Prahalad, C. K. and Doz, Y. L. (1987). *The Multinational Mission*, pp. 62–3 and 240–2, Free Press, New York.
Prahalad, C. K. and Hamel, G. (1990). The core competence of the corporation, *Harvard Business Review*, May–June.

Corporate Modelling

Chandler, J. and Cockle, P. *Techniques of Scenario Planning*, McGraw Hill, London.
McNamee, P. B. (1985). *Tools and Techniques of Strategic Management*, Pergamon Press, Oxford.
McNamee, P. B. (1988). *Management Accounting: Strategic Planning and Marketing*, Heinemann Professional Publishing, Oxford.
McNamee, P. B. and McHugh, M. (1991). A hierarchical approach to modelling the strategic management process, in: D. E. Hussey (ed.), *International Review of Strategic Management*, **2.1**, Wiley, Chichester.

Critical Success Factors

Hussey, D. E. (1985). *Corporate Planning*, chapter 6, Gee and Co, London.
Hussey, D. E. (1991). *Introducing Coprorate Planning*, 4th edition, chapter 5, Pergamon Press, Oxford.
Leidecker, J. K. and Bruno, A. V. (1984). Identifying and using critical success factors, *Long Range Planning*, February **17**(1).

Decision Trees

Hussey, D. E. (1994). *Strategic Management: Theory and Practice*, 3rd edition, chapter 31, Pergamon Press, Oxford.
Mantell, L. H. and Sing, F. P. (1972). *Economics for Business Decisions*, chapter 16, McGraw-Hill Kogakusha, Tokyo.
Moore, P. G. (1968). *Basic Operational Research*, chapter 8, Pitman, London.
Pappas, J. L. and Brigham, E. F. (1979). *Managerial Economics*, 3rd edition, chapters 3 and 14, Holt-Saunders, Hillsdale, Illinois.

Delphi Technique

Chambers, J. C., Satinedes, K. M. and Smith, D. D. (1971). How to choose the right forecasting technique, *Harvard Business Review*, July–August.
Wills, G. *et al.* (1972). *Technological Forecasting*, chapter 2–4, Penguin Books, London.

Discounted Cash Flow

Anthony, R. N. (1983). *Accounting: Text and Cases*, 7th edition, chapter 22, Irwin, Homewood, Illinois.

Mantell, L. H. and Sing, F. P. (1972). *Economics for Business Decisions*, chapter 14, McGraw-Hill Kogakusha, Tokyo.

Pappas, J. L. and Brigham, E. F. (1979). *Managerial Economics*, 3rd edition, chapter 13, Holt-Saunders, Hillsdale, Illinois.

Van Horne, J. C. (1971). *Financial Management*, 3rd edition, chapter 12, Prentice-Hall, Englewood Cliffs, New Jersey.

Wilson, R. M. S. and McHugh, G. (1987). *Financial Analysis: A Managerial Introduction*, chapters 13 and 14, Cassell, London.

Diversification Matrix

Ansoff, H. I. (1965). *Corporate Strategy*, chapter 3, McGraw Hill, New York.

Econometric Model

Chambers, J. C., Satinedes, K. M. and Smith, D. D. (1971). How to choose the right forecasting technique, *Harvard Business Review*, July–August.

Environmental Assessment: Facing up to Change

Argenti, J. (1980). *Practical Corporate Planning*, chapter 6, Allen & Unwin, London.

Hargreaves, J. and Dauman, J. (1975). *Business Survival and Social Change*, Associated Business Programmes, London.

Hussey, D. E. (1994). *Strategic Management: Theory and Practice*, 3rd edition, chapter 7, Pergamon, Oxford.

McNamee, P. B. (1988). *Management Accounting: Strategic Planning and Marketing*, chapter 4, Heinemann Professional Publishing, Oxford.

Terry, P. T. (1977). Mechanisms for environmental scanning, *Long Range Planning*, June, **10**(3).

Environmental Assessment: Neubauer and Solomon

Neubauer, F-F. and Solomon, N. B. (1977). A managerial approach to environmental assessment, *Long Range Planning*, April, **10**(2).

Environmental Turbulence Matrices

Ansoff, H. I. (1991). Strategic management in a historical perspective, in: D. E. Hussey (ed.), *International Review of Strategic Management*, **2.1**, Wiley, Chichester.

Ansoff, H. I. and McDonnell, P. (1990). *Implanting Strategic Management*, Prentice Hall, London.

Equilibrium Analysis

Hussey, D. E. (1991). *Introducing Corporate Planning: Guide to Strategic Management*, 4th edition, chapter 4, Pergamon Press, Oxford.

Experience Curve

Hedley, B. (1990). Developing strategies for competitive advantage, in: P. N. McNamee (ed.), *Developing Strategies for Competitive Advantage*, Pergamon Press, Oxford (a selection from the journal *Long Range Planning*).

Hofer, C. W. and Schendel, D. (1978). *Strategy Formulation: Analytical Concepts*, pp. 132–135, West Publishing, St Paul, Minnesota.

McNamee, P. B. (1985). *Tools and Techniques for Strategic Management*, chapter 3, Pergamon Press, Oxford.

Gap Analysis

Hussey. D. E. (1991). *Introducing Corporate Planning: Guide to Strategic Management*, 4th edition, chapter 4, Pergamon Press, Oxford.

Kami, M. J. (1968). Gap analysis: key to super growth, *Long Range Planning*, June, 1(4).

Generic Strategy Matrix

Porter, M. E. (1980). *Competitive Strategy*, chapter 2, Free Press, New York.

Global Strategy Matrix

Hussey, D. E. (1994). *Strategic Management: Theory and Practice*, 3rd edition, chapter 18, Pergamon Press, Oxford.

Prahalad, C. K. and Doz, Y. L. (1987). *The Multinational Mission*, chapter 2, Free Press, New York.

Yip, G. S. (1989). Global strategy in a world of nations, *Sloan Management Review*, Fall.

Group Competitive Intensity Map

McNamee, P. and McHugh, M. (1990). The group competitive intensity map: a means of displaying competitive position, *International Review of Strategic Management*, **1**, Wiley, Chichester.

Historical Analogy

Chambers, J. C., Satinedes, K. M. and Smith, D. D. (1971). How to choose the right forecasting technique, *Harvard Business Review*, July–August.

Industry Analysis

Hofer, C. W. and Schendel, D. (1978). *Strategy Formulation: Analytical Concepts*, chapter 5, West Publishing, St Paul, Minnesota.

Hussey, D. E. (1991). *Introducing Corporate Planning: Guide to Strategic Management*, 4th edition, chapter 5, Pergamon Press, Oxford.

Hussey, D. E. (1994). *Strategic Management: Theory and Practice*, 3rd edition, Pergamon, Oxford.

McNamee, P. B. (1988). *Management Accounting: Strategic Planning and Marketing*, chapter 4, Heinemann Professional Publishing, Oxford.
Porter, M. E. (1980). *Competitive Strategy*, Free Press, New York.

Industry Mapping

Hussey, D. E. (1991). *Introducing Corporate Planning: Guide to Strategic Management*, 4th edition, chapter 5, Pergamon Press, Oxford.
Hussey, D. E. (1994). *Strategic Management: Theory and Practice*, 3rd edition, chapters 9 and 10, Pergamon, Oxford.

Life Cycle Concepts

Barksdale, H. C. and Harris, C. E. (1982). Portfolio analysis and the product life cycle, *Long Range Planning*, December, **15**(6).
Hofer, C. W. and Schendel, D. (1978). *Strategy Formulation: Analytical Concepts*, chapter 5, West Publishing, St Paul, Minnesota.
Hussey, D. E. (1994). *Strategic Management: Theory and Practice*, 3rd edition, Pergamon Press, Oxford.
Kotler, P. (1988). *Marketing Management: Analysis, Planning, Implementation and Control*, 6th edition, chapter 12, Prentice-Hall, Englewood Cliffs, New Jersey.
Yelle, L. E. (1983). Adding life cycles to learning curves, *Long Range Planning*, December, **16**(6).

MCC Decision Matrix

Nicholls, J. (1995). The MCC decision matrix: a tool for applying strategic logic to everyday activity, *Management Decision*, **33**(6), Summer.

PIMS

Buzzell, R. D. and Gale, B. T. (1987). *The PIMS Principles: Linking Strategy to Performance*, Free Press, New York.
Nebauer, F-F. (1990). *Portfolio Management*, chapter E, Kluwer, Holland.

Portfolio Analysis

Barksdale, H. C. and Harris, C. E. (1982). Portfolio analysis and the product life cycle, *Long Range Planning*, December, **15**(6).
Clarke, C. J. and Brennan, K. (1990). Building synergy in the diversified business, in: P. McNamee (ed.), *Developing Strategies for Competitive Advantage*, Pergamon, Oxford.
Hedley, B. (1990). Strategy and the business portfolio, in: P. McNamee (ed.), *Developing Strategies for Competitive Advantage*, Pergamon, Oxford.
Hofer, C. W. and Schendel, D. (1978). *Strategy Formulation: Analytical Concepts*, West Publishing, St Paul, Minnesota.
Hussey, D. E. (1982). Portfolio analysis: practical experience with the directional policy matrix, in: D. E. Hussey and B. Taylor (eds), *The Realities of Planning*, Pergamon Press, Oxford.

Hussey, D. E. (1991). *Introducing Corporate Planning: Guide to Strategic Management*, 4th edition, chapter 9, Pergamon Press, Oxford.

McNamee, P. B. (1985). *Tools and Techniques for Strategic Management*, chapter 3, Pergamon Press, Oxford.

Neubauer, F-F. (1990). *Portfolio Management*, Kluwer, Holland.

Ohmae, K. (1983). *The Mind of the Strategist*, chapter 12, Penguin Books, London.

Robinson, J., Hitchens, R. E. and Wade, D. P. (1982). The directional policy matrix: tool for strategic planning, in: D. E. Hussey and B. Taylor (eds), *The Realities of Planning*, Pergamon Press, Oxford.

Segev, E. (1995). *Corporate Strategy: Portfolio Models*, International Thomsom Publishing/Boyd and Fraser, London.

Segev, E. (1995). *Navigating by COMPASS: Corporate Matrix Portfolio Analysis Support System*, International Thomsom Publishing/Boyd and Fraser, London. (Includes computer disk to facilitate use of the various methods described.)

Product/Market Matrix

Ansoff, H. I. (1965). *Corporate Strategy*, chapter 7, McGraw-Hill, New York.

Hussey, D. E. (1976). *Inflation and Business Policy*, chapter 5, Longman, London.

Hussey, D. E. (1991). *Introducing Corporate Planning: Guide to Strategic Management*, 4th edition, chapter 7, Pergamon Press, Oxford.

Taylor, B. (1975). The crisis in supply markets: developing a strategy for resources, in: D. H. Farmer and B. Taylor (eds), *Corporate Planning and Procurement*, Heinemann, London.

Risk Analysis

Pappas, J. L. and Brigham, E. F. (1979). *Managerial Economics*, 3rd edition, chapter 13, Holt-Saunders, Hillsdale, Illinois.,

Van Horne, J. C. (1971). *Financial Management*, 3rd edition, chapter 12, Prentice-Hall, Englewood Cliffs, New Jersey.

Risk Matrix

Hussey, D. E. (1991). *Introducing Corporate Planning: Guide to Strategic Management*, 4th edition, chapter 9, Pergamon Press, Oxford.

Segev, E. (1995). *Corporate Strategy: Portfolio Models*, International Thomsom Publishing/Boyd and Fraser, London.

Segev, E. (1995). *Navigating by COMPASS: Corporate Matrix Portfolio Analysis Support System*, International Thomsom Publishing/Boyd and Fraser, London. (Includes computer disk to facilitate use of the various methods described.)

Risk-Return Matrix

Cardozo, R. N. and Wind, J. (1985). Risk return approach to product portfolio strategy, *Long Range Planning*, **18**, 2.

Segev, E. (1995). *Corporate Strategy: Portfolio Models*, International Thomsom Publishing/Boyd and Fraser, London.

Segev, E. (1995). *Navigating by COMPASS: Corporate Matrix Portfolio Analysis Support System*, International Thomsom Publishing/Boyd and Fraser, London. (Includes computer disk to facilitate use of the various methods described.)

ROI Chart

Anthony, R. N. and Reece, J. S. (1983). *Accounting: Text and Cases*, 7th edition, chapter 13, Irwin, Homewood, Illinois.

Hussey, D. E. (1991). *Introducing Corporate Planning: Guide to Strategic Management*, 4th edition, chapter 4, Pergamon Press, Oxford.

Scenario Planning

Chandler, J. and Cockle, P. (1982). *Techniques of Scenario Planning*, McGraw-Hill, London.

McNamee, P. (1985). *Tools and Techniques for Strategic Management*, chapter 7, Pergamon Press, Oxford.

McNamee, P. (1988). *Management Accounting: Strategic Planning and Marketing*, pp. 91–93, Heinemann, London.

Schoemaker, P. J. H. and van der Heijden, C. A. J. M. (1993). Strategic Planning at Royal Dutch/Shell, *Journal of Strategic Change*, **2**(3), pp. 157–171.

Sensitivity Analysis

Hussey, D. E. (1991). *Introducing Corporate Planning: Guide to Strategic Management*, 4th edition, chapter 14, Pergamon Press, Oxford.

Mantell, L. H. and Sing, F. P. (1972). *Economics for Business Decisions*, pp. 434–438, McGraw-Hill Kogakusha, Tokyo.

Strategic Group Mapping

McGee, J. and Thomas, H. (1992). Strategic groups and intra-industry competition, in: D. E. Hussey (ed.), *International Review of Strategic Management*, **3**, Wiley, Chichester.

Porter, M. E. (1980). *Competitive Strategy*, chapter 7, Free Press, New York.

Strategy Cube

Nakamura, G-I. (1990). New dimensions of strategic management in the global context of the 1990s. In: D. E. Hussey (ed.), *International Review of Strategic Management*, **1**, Wiley, Chichester.

SWOT or SOFT

Hussey, D. E. (1991). *Introducing Corporate Planning: Guide to Strategic Management*, 4th edition, chapter 4, Pergamon Press, Oxford.

Steiner, G. A. (1979). *Strategic Planning: What Every Manager Must Know*, chapter 8, Free Press, New York.

Synergy Matrix

Ansoff, H. I. (1965). *Corporate Strategy*, chapter 5, McGraw-Hill, New York.

Technology-Based Resource Allocation

Henry, J. P. (1990). Making the technology-strategy connection, *International Review of Strategic Management*, **1**, Wiley, Chichester.

Technology Grid

Clarke, C. J. and Brennan, K. (1990). Building synergy in the diversified business, in: P. McNamee (ed.), *Developing Strategies for Competitive Advantage*, Pergamon, Oxford.
Neubauer, F-F. (1990). *Portfolio Management*, chapter D5, Kluwer, Holland.

Trend Projection

Chambers, J. C., Satinedes, K. N. and Smith, D. D. (1971). How to choose the right forecasting technique, *Harvard Business Review*, July–August.

Value-Based Strategy

Day, G. and Fahey, L. (1991). Finding value in strategies, in: D. E. Hussey (ed.), *International Review of Strategic Management*, **2**.1, Wiley, Chichester.
Reimann, B. C. (1987). *Managing for Value*, Planning Forum, Oxford, Ohio.
Reimann, B. C. (1990). Creating value to keep the raiders at bay. In: P. McNamee (ed.), *Developing Strategies for Competitive Advantage*, Pergamon Press, Oxford.
Stewart, G. B. (1991). *The Quest for Value*, Harper Business, New York.

Value Chains

Porter, M. E. (1985). *Competitive Advantage*, Free Press, New York.

V Matrix

McNamee, P. B. (1985). *Tools and Techniques for Strategic Management*, chapter 5, Pergamon Press, Oxford.

ADDRESSES OF CONTRIBUTORS

Some of the authors have changed their affiliations since the articles were first published. The following list provides one contact address for each chapter in this book. This list was correct at the time the book was prepared for publication.

Dr Emily Boyle   *University of Ulster, Shore Road, Newtownabbey, Co Antrim, Northern Ireland*

Dr Sue Cartwright   *Manchester School of Management, UMIST, PO Box 88, Manchester M60 1QD*

Mr Sebastian Crawshaw   *Managing Director, Oats Ltd, 701 Delta Business Park, Great Western Way, Swindon, Wiltshire, OXN5 7XN*

Professor Gordon Greenley   *Professor of Marketing, Aston Business School, Aston University, Aston Triangle, Birmingham B4 7ET*

Dr Wendy Hall   *Postbus 239, 3620 AE Breukelen, Netherlands*

Ms Sylvia Handler   *63 Crofters Mead, Addington, Surrey, CRO 9HT*

Professor Hans H. Hinterhuber   *University of Innsbruck, Department of Management, A-6020 Innsbruck, Austria*

Professor David Hussey   *Editor,* Strategic Change, *44 Forestfield, Horsham, Sussex, RH13 6DZ*

Dr David Jennings   *Strategic Management and Marketing, Nottingham Business School, Burton Street, Nottingham, NG1 4BU*

Professor Per Jenster   *CIMD SA, Carl Feilbergsvej 9, DK-2000 Frederiksberg, Denmark*

The Strategic Decision Challenge, Edited by D. E. Hussey
© 1998 John Wiley & Sons Ltd

Mr Seiichiro Yahagi   *President, Yahagi Management Institute Inc, 434 Maya Shinanomachi 3-bankan, 18 Shinanomachi-ku, Tokyo 160, Japan*

Dr Frank L Winfrey   *The Clark and Mary Perkins Barton Associate Professor of Management, Division of Business and Economics, Lyon College, PO Box 2317, Batesville, Arkansas 72503-2317, USA*

Index